COWARD'S CUSTARD

Leta Jones

MINERVA PRESS

LONDON
ATLANTA MONTREUX SYDNEY

ISBN 0 75410 279 3

First Published 1998 by
MINERVA PRESS
195 Knightsbridge
London SW7 1RE

Printed in Great Britain for Minerva Press

COWARD'S CUSTARD

Preface

Drowning, we are told, brings reeling memories as death closes in. In late life, death approaches, often slowly, and we review our lives in a leisurely, cud-chewing process. I look back in surprise. I started life full of foreboding, hobgoblins and insecurity. I found the world a very undesirable place, full of things to be feared. At ten years, I told my mother she had no right to give birth to me since I had had no say in the matter. I decided against marriage and children who could say that to me.

My mother's simple magazine, Home Chat, pointed out that if one was not to marry, one's energies (sex!) should be sublimated by satisfying work. Social work caught me by chance. It was absorbing and exhausting; every post demanded unpaid overtime and annual leave varied from five to fifteen days per annum. I never danced or dined or attended concerts and theatres, except on holiday, until I retired. Retirement brought me better health and a delirious enjoyment of the friends, holidays abroad and hobbies which I had had to forego. It brought also the urge to write about a way of tackling one's life at more than survival level and of turning cowardice into some sort of courage through the alchemy of Christ. As an octogenarian, I found my wisps of memory interested others so I wrote snippets for the desperate editors of club newsletters. I began to enjoy writing. These haphazard notes are distilled from pure memory: I kept no diaries. As they do not purport to be anything more than recollections, I plead to be excused my inaccuracies and the chores of research; time is too short for me now. What I remember is not of grave importance, the little grey cells are choked with the things that amused or surprised me. I wrote to spring-clean my own mind.

I was the only child of good, gentle and self-effacing parents; I was shy and lonely. I wheedled my way to a kindergarten when I was three and a half and boarding school when I was thirteen. Unfortunately the kindergarten mob showed me the contempt in which my people, the Welsh, were held by the English. This triggered my awareness of foreigners and a glimmer of understanding of their position in pre-war Britain. But the scorn of things Welsh shrivelled my patriotism and I lost my heritage of language, music, poetry and wit. I grew wary.

'Little girls may be seen but not heard' was the dictum of those days, so I remained shy. I was also imaginative, afraid of confronting anything new. I hid my cowardice well as I manipulated my friends into doing my errands. Cheltenham Ladies' College was the successful remedy my parents chose for my spineless dependency. Liverpool University continued the training and my student days of social work in the appalling pre-war slums cured me of introspection and self-pity, but asked me many questions, especially about the reality of God.

As a solitary child, I had never hesitated to involve God in my small fears. Even adolescent know-allism had not quite severed my over-familiar attitude, and the imminence of war urged an exploration of Christ's teaching in order to discover the source of the inner strength I had found in others.

It appears to me that the development of faith has been the important thread through my life. The search added a dimension to my experiences and I found, when I reached a sufficient state of humility, that acknowledgement of Christ lifted a troublesome guilt complex and forgave my inadequacies; I began to find joy in life. The antidote for cowardice and shyness was to forget one's self and as a Jewish boy from Dachau concentration camp told me, 'Aide-toi et Dieu t'aidera.' I have never been let down if my conscience prompted intervention in some problem, and I have learned to pass the work to others better qualified than I in the freedom of not having to be the one who succeeds.

Even this book would not have materialised except for an unexpected friendship with a very patient and encouraging teacher who came to unravel my computer for me. I owe my finished pages to Dr Keith Bell. I owe my courage, faith and peace to David Edwards.

Part One

A Puddle of Nightmares, Kindergartens and Linguistic Muddle

It is still a good clear memory. Pinky-red tiles, as I later recognised them, came quickly up and hit me on the face as I leaned out from my high perambulator. I was in our little clean yard on a sunny day in 1913 at our corner house in Liverpool. I learned nothing from this but retained my curiosity; in any case, as can be imagined, I don't know what happened next.

Some more parental oversight left me upstairs for a siesta by myself. I set out to fill another void in my experience. I was still being potty trained so I did not know everything about upstairs. There was a little room on the corner by the staircase where grown-ups disappeared, and its secrets needed serious attention. I opened the door easily and went in to be confronted by a stern sort of seat. I remember looking at it and waiting for something to happen. When nothing changed, I shut the door to no effect, but the push-button age was already there in 1914. I saw a thumb-latch and slid it home. An only child is used to silence and a spot of nothingness, so I was still wondering what else I could do to find out what the room was for when my parents discovered me. My father's optimistic and patient instructions to push the little latch back were useless as my thumb was too weak. They must have talked to me through the door for a long time, because a flat grey cap began to come up the narrow window followed by an old gentleman with a beard who scrambled into the little space and unlocked the door... and that was love at first sight!

Next time I saw my hero, he was in the hall talking to my mother, probably being paid for his window cleaning. I was at the top of the stairs. In my excitement I gave one leap and, as in a true romance, he caught me as I was landing on the bottom step. All this trivial detail interests me because for some time in my life I was totally unafraid; but from then on I remember nightmares and, I have been told, developed a grave and suspicious attitude towards people and dispensed my smiles with care.

Fear of the unknown supplanted rash curiosity. One nightmare was of Winnie, our maid. She had indigestion and complained to Mother that she had a pain in her breast. It was burning – 'llosgi' in Welsh, a good sound: a real crackle of fire. And my dream was of the open grate in the kitchen range burning furiously in miniature under the shoulder strap of her white apron on her brown linen dress. It worried me. The next dream started off with the long-handled squeeze box which was our then modern vacuum cleaner. It wheezed like a very old man and in my dreams, coinciding with the early morning cleaning, the noise got nearer and nearer until a tomato-coloured ape appeared over my shoulder. He came day after day until I told my father. Unversed in psychology he told me that most people were good, and that I should make friends with the ape next time I saw him. So, in the next dream, I remembered and turned, offering my hand in the proper style to the sad-faced, rusty-haired pursuer. He and his signature tune of 'Half a pound of tuppeny rice... the monkey's (money's) on the table' disappeared for ever. I had had my first lesson in confronting unpleasant things.

In the winter of 1915 my father was sent to Wrexham and found only one rentable house. It had been built as a small orphanage. We arrived and struggled in the cold through a narrow hall into a huge red-tiled kitchen. Here, Sarah, missing her cosy farm home in Llandegla, was leaning over a big black range and hanging on to a brass rail running along the mantel shelf. She was stirring hopelessly in a saucepan while tears chased down her unhappy rosy cheeks. Sarah was the new cook, also to be my warm-hearted nursemaid. Her sister was the housemaid. We all spoke Welsh.

Mother soon found she could help the war effort. I was introduced to the town from a perch on heaps of oily knitting wool being distributed to unknown chattering ladies who were to produce thick, oily socks for marching soldiers. Brighter flag days arrived when I sat surrounded by flat cardboard boxes of pink cotton roses, or best, little sprigs of forget-me-nots attached to blue velvet baby ribbon.

Later, I remember the shop as a stationer's with a little space behind paper-bead curtains where we ate ice cream with horn spoons. The paper-beads interested me, as all my aunts used to roll snips of coloured pictures coated with smelly glue around steel knitting needles to make the latest fashion in beads. I saw more of the town.

Near the little shop in the High Street was a long cavern of a store smelling wonderfully of clean oil and steel. A pleasant, grave man presided, always finding the right screws or scissors in the bank of square oak drawers filling the wall behind the counter. The next good smell was of new leather at a corner shop up some steps. We went here for dog collars, and when there was a rabies scare for the almost impossible muzzle for our black pug. With the big Wynnstay Hotel on our right, we could cross the road to Daddy's Bank, the old North and South Wales which I called by its new name 'the Lunnunsiddleandmiddleun', these days mercifully reduced to Midland, losing London City. I was learning English.

Father was only the assistant manager, appointed to bring a Welsh element into business, especially for the farming folk. At weekends, father might be asked to look at security etc. and we would go in to find Mr Yates, the bank porter, working on the mahogany counters, erasing the dents made by falling sovereigns. He used a hot iron and blotting paper, and the wood shone like new chestnuts. Poor man, he was my next heart-throb. I demanded many piggybacks. He was, happily, a considerable athlete and trained splendid young men in spotless white to stand in pyramids at garden fetes. Further up the High Street, at the corner of the market, was a little shop, presided over by a most benign, dark-bearded gentleman, Mr M.D. Jones, a real tea-taster. He was sitting in front of a big oak shield with little silver shields on it, most of which, I believe, referred to his triumphs of the past, the present ones amply proven by shiny silver cups. We went for most of our groceries further up the street to a big sombre shop of whirring noise and lovely thick coffee smells. High chairs were set at the polished counters, more dented than the bank's. Pretty tins were stacked around on supports for an overhead shelf, the whole creating some privacy in each compartment for the ladies with their important lists and their little tasselled pencils. There were high chairs, too, at the large drapery shop. Mr Pritchard, all smiles, would place a tall chair, perhaps by the glove counter or haberdashery with the command 'Forward, Miss Andrews' and a neat and politely pleasant assistant would try to please the customer and propitiate the sulky child... well, who wants their head patted? Further up the street was a shoe shop. There was a very modern 'X-ray' machine where one stood on a vertical peep show and saw one's bones inside one's skin inside the shoe. No longer was it possible to say the shoe pinched in order to move from the dull brown to the ever-so-fashionable Dandy Boot made of grey leather buttoned-over-the-ankle and sporting a glorious base of shiny patent leather. A draper's shop was known as 'C.D.'s', and my father said it was owned by Mr Christmas Day Jones, and, of course, his brother was the tea-taster, Michaelmas Day Jones. Two shops led us into tireless play.

One, the corn merchant, H. and T. Jones, we imitated at home by hauling small bags of make-believe corn from the ground floor to the second floor landing through the balustrades.

The other shop was C.D.'s. They had a wonderful wire web on which hung wooden cups on a screw base. They whizzed across the shop from the counter, ending at a high desk where an elegant and forbidding lady registered transactions with celerity. At the counter, bills and pay-ments were put into the unscrewed boxes, screwed on to the wire and, with a smart pull, sent flying over to the accounting desk, examined and noted; and the change and receipt flew back, noisily important to the customer's assistant. Most satisfactory! Next door, Piper's Penny Bazaar was all a child could afford. It seemed more like a lucky dip when one examined the rubbishy purchase at home; a marble, a sweet, or four bars of music in large print, all to be thrown away.

To me, the town consisted of one long street which changed its name at different angles and was full of pubs with funny pictures outside. As I grew older I could count fifty-four of them. My father was appalled. He said later that when he came from Liverpool, he found the town so full of drunks that a special cart was on hand to carry them away, like the pink-curtained buses I saw in London during the Second World War, reserved discreetly for the Yanks. It was better, anyhow, than the stone Round Houses, like the one in Ruabon where they were all thrown in together for the night. The stench must have been unmentionable. There were eleven breweries in the town and the air was often thick with the smell of hops. They had finally taken over the civic dignity, and converted the big Tudor Town Hall into vaults – and a pub of the same name. It was pulled down in the fifties to make room for the traffic, strangled by the pub while it maintained its position at the top of the

High Street. The Tudor plaster ceiling may have ended up in the open-air residential home for unwanted architecture at St Fagan's, Cardiff. Like the pensioners, it will have been thoroughly disorientated by movement and the town is poorer for its loss. Fortunately, the nearby magnificent church of St Giles was not entangled in roads. It still remains to give the town an ancient dignity.

Few people had cars in 1914. Lady Palmer of Cefn Park would drive to shop from her light carriage and the rest of us walked except for those young enough for pushchairs or, less lordly, in a leather and brass-belled harness with reins. From town to home was not a mile and in the summer it was a tunnel of greenish light through lovely overhanging beeches, chestnuts and sycamores. At the top of the hill, going northwards to Chester, stood the gates of Acton Hall in a semicircle of pillars and plinths. On the plinths sat four greyhounds with thin curled tails. We were assured the dogs would turn round at midnight. Despite resolutions we never found out. Acton Hall lay beyond the gate, occupying the land down the hill as far as our house, except for two fields, one used for wartime allotments, the other opposite our windows, for sheep. My father offered to buy this for a green space for the town when development threatened, but he was told – untruthfully – that it was legally to remain green. At that time Wrexham was green to the east, marred only by two houses opposite us, already carved out of the sheep field, and a row of four houses behind it. They were reached by a red 'colliery ash' road, right round three sides of the sheep field, suitable for dolls' prams pushed by three tiny girls who were quite safe from abduction, the only encounter hoped for being with a kind, silver-bearded gentleman with a box of chocolates at his front gate. I was lucky to find two friends of my own age.

Our house was big, built of stone, and had a large arched stone plaque on the front. Later, I learned that a Colonel

White, living in nearby Gresford, had had a daughter of a kindly but masculine nature. She did not marry and it was said she smoked cigars, wore knickerbockers in the days of crinolines, and would hitch a ride to Gresford with any farmer's cart. She sublimated her problems with the establishment of an orphanage, almost a blueprint for the 1948 Curtis Report on the provision for children in care. She hoped to imitate family life, and decided the group should be no larger than sixteen, of different ages and of both sexes. The narrow hall and stairs led up to a first floor where a big drawing room and two thinly separated bedrooms would have given two main dormitories. There were three other rooms, and, on the second floor, two more and two large attics. Those attics were wonderful for children, full of 'dressing-up' clothes and ample space. Eventually, they were used as 'club rooms' where for misdemeanours we punished each other by locking the offender up in the dark and talking reassuringly through the keyhole. To me, the attics were frightening with the collywobbles of indigestion that beset the water pipes. I had the conviction that there lived up there a Canadian woman in leather high boots and blue clothes carrying a rifle and tramping noisily around as the water gurgled. I was very afraid upstairs if I found myself alone. My fears grew.

When I was six my 'big' cousin came to stay as Mother was ill. She read untiringly to me. I was introduced to the child's version of the *Arabian Nights*, pictures and all, to keep me quiet while Mother was in bed. It was not long before the forty thieves invaded my dreams, escaped from their big jars and charged around my parents' room where I slept and, on bad nights, teetered on my cot trying to pull the long crimson bell-rope out of its socket, hoping for rescue by Sarah. More nightmares followed. I really yanked at that rope when a huge cat crept across my parent's bed to my cot. I dreaded being left alone. I didn't 'grow out of it'.

Some years later, I went to a private school, little more than a dame school. It consisted of about twenty-five pupils in four groups at eleven different levels taught by three sisters for dancing, music and 'academic' subjects. The eldest sister had been crippled by an accident which left her with a heavy boot and a limp, and even heavier marks of pain on her sallow face. Her piercing dark eyes, ugly teeth and thin awkward body also haunted my dark. I slept alone in a pretty rose and white room. I was too afraid to have the light out. I was not allowed to read, but to stop my thoughts I persuaded my mother to let me read a French/English dictionary which was removed later when I had fallen asleep. A few hours later I would have one of my nightmares in which a gypsy, a witch of a woman, would come to kill my parents, by knife, broken glass, poison or, peculiarly, by stabbing with cigarettes. I was terrified to face the dark in the passage. A little coward somehow reached a mother's arms. I would lie awake looking at grinning skulls staring down until I slept. It was then that I bargained to be excused the sweet cocoa and biscuits for supper and promised to sleep on anything else, even coffee and gorgonzola cheese. I won and I still start to doze after any cup of coffee. Unfortunately, no one thought of moving me from the wretched school. The teaching was poor. I was accused of letting my parents do my drawing homework. I was even asked to coach the 'top' form in arithmetic! When I left, the remaining pupils were told that they should avoid speaking to me as I had gone to a common grammar school. They should just cross the road when they saw me as my Welsh accent was bad for their speech. In the bottom form of the grammar school I learned how poorly I had been taught.

That was not my first school or my first encounter with racism. I was at another dame school of a much better type, mornings only, when I was about three and a half. I longed to meet other children whom I often saw at the school about three minutes' walk from our home. Sarah and I would trot along, me very important in a muslin tabard tied at the sides, and a tartan Alice band behind my straight fringe to hold back the four short, fat curls produced through nightly discomfort in tightly tied cotton strips. The school was held in a one-time artist's studio with one very big, glass-roofed room where a different class was held in each corner. The autumn leaves drifted into the rather open cloakroom. The pleasant headmistress shared her tiny sanctum with her sister and a frizzy-headed, fashionable 'Mademoiselle' whose French was, to me, quite incomprehensible. The teaching of Welsh was unheard of. I needed a lot of help. I was learning English but not fast enough and without any clear understanding of the difference between it and my first tongue. I mixed words and used Welsh words when they fitted. Inevitably, I was seen as an aberration by the group. They took action. Whenever I appeared they turned their backs and refused to speak to me I was in Coventry and I was also in tears by the time I got home. There was no pride, no courage. I capitulated and vowed to my father, 'I will never speak that language again.' When I went to the Welsh Sunday school it was another story; I was taken for the English child from Liverpool. I had learned my simple verse in Welsh, my *adnod*, 'Yr Iesu a wylodd' (Jesus wept), an easy one for a four year old. The elderly teacher spoke to each child in Welsh, asking if they had an *adnod*, then turned rather scornfully to the new pupil from England. 'Have you got a verse?' My *adnod* was evidently not wanted but luckily I knew what a verse was. I had just learned one in day school and a triumphant *The Queen of Hearts* rang out, never to be forgotten or forgiven for the rest of my dreaded Sundays.

The anti-Welsh feeling changed in time. A Welsh school opened; it was clean and small, and the only children turning up seemed to belong to professional families.

Before long, English-speaking parents were deciding that
Welsh was an advantage. The Welsh are now a proud
minority, lapsing occasionally from English into Welsh,
unthinkingly causing sudden, sad bursts of irritation in
those who cannot understand and cannot stomach the right
to speak one's own language in one's homeland. Welsh is
now spoken freely, promoted by the political movement
with hackle-raising methods, but also culturally through
eisteddfodau. It is a pity it is so hard to learn.

This lack of Welsh produced another setback when I
was twelve. I needed to understand enough Welsh to
become an adult member of our Calvinistic Methodist
chapel. Till now I had sat quietly in one of the front pews
occasionally listening to a preacher who gave English texts
or very simple phrases. More often, I was twisting a wire
hairpin from my mother into caricatures of some of the
elders slumped uncomfortably in the wooden armchairs of
the 'set fawr' (big seat), a raised and railed dais under the
pulpit. From there, they peered over glasses and beards at
the restless children. The confrontation grew as hymns
were sung, the elders turning to face the church, the master
of the singing leading off with an embarrassing show of
epiglottis and pink tongue. More fun occurred when an
eisteddfod gold medallist took over and insisted on proper
singing. He would bang down his hymn book in despair,
stop the organ, give his own truly superior performance and
start again. When things went well, we sang the last lines
twice over but when it was bad the congregation was kept
in for a full practice while the wives bewailed the spoiling
dinners. All this under a ceiling bedecked with huge
raspberries which must have been meant to represent the
unripe grapes of the Promised Land.

I was now sent to a headmaster's house for Welsh lessons. He was very bored and so was I. We came to a
delightful new word, 'nhw' (they). Mischief and laughter

born of boredom rose in me and I snorted the 'n' and 'h' through my nose like a giant sneeze. Very quickly I was going home with a letter saying I was unteachable. A good Hungarian linguist later said total immersion in near monoglot countryside was the only answer. He had found a Welsh dictionary useless because of the mutation of the first letter of so many nouns.

My parents, both born in West Wales and then protected by the close links of a minority status in London and Liverpool, were nevertheless used to the pinpricks. But these experiences from toddlerhood had made me think what it would be like to be foreign, lonely, and, even worse, coloured. I brooded over the Chinese laundry folk and the sham 'nigger minstrels' whom I loathed. My parents, used to the international nature of London and Liverpool, had certainly conveyed their liberal sympathies to me. Our reward was in being regarded by the town as the family which could and would host the foreign visitors. I was fascinated and probably stared at them in rude absorption.

When I was about five, towards the latter part of the war, I went for a splendid day out with my parents. We went off in a taxi with nice Mr Yates, the bank porter sitting in front with the driver. It was summer and I was in my best dress, feeling pretty. They put me on a wooden box opposite mother and father who were on the big seat. The box was rough and prickly so I had a cushion and was told to spread my frilly dress out over it. The box was just the right height and my dress looked nice. I looked through the glass screen at Mr Yates in his bowler hat. He was very serious and had a big pistol on his knee under the tartan rug. The ride was long but at the end the whole taxi went on board the Mersey Ferry. I had often been on the Ferry going to New Brighton, but *never* inside a taxi.

Father was now a bit snappy, telling me not to chatter too much and Mother agreed with him by a little nod at me. Then we were rolling off the boat in the taxi and up a little back lane right into Liverpool. Before we got anywhere at all, we stopped at a small door into the lane and Father talked to two or three polite men. They took my seat away and took it indoors while I was still wondering what it was all about.

Everybody seemed happy on the way home in the taxi; so much nicer than the underground train. Father and Mother began to chatter and told me that I had been sitting on a box of gold sovereigns, the very last to leave North Wales. The Lunnonsiddleanmiddleun Bank was the biggest and had had to collect from all the other banks and take the whole lot to Liverpool with Mr Yates to guard it. When I was older, Father used to say he was very nervous on the ferry in case someone noticed the box. They could not have gone far with it on the boat. No one thought I might get hit as well!

In the war years sovereigns had been a great anxiety as trains got more irregular and old railway staff were replaced with youngsters. Apparently the bank staff would meet the Paddington through-train at night and dump the sacks of money labelled 'potatoes' amongst the other freight. No sacks were ever lost. London bank staff met the train in Paddington and rescued the vegetables.

As children we played games in the house. We dressed up and we found that by playing in the street we could attract the youngsters from a nearby crowded district. They would come surging down the street in full cry after us. Once we retreated into our yard, slammed the door in the high wall and put a hosepipe over the top. The next day stones were thrown at our windows. My father was very angry, not at them, but at us. He tried to make me understand that I was one of the lucky ones and that life was very difficult for others. We had no right to drench children when they certainly had fewer clothes than we had. At that time the colliers, whom I loved to hear singing haunting Welsh hymns as they went to work in the bleak hours of the night, began to resent the comparative comfort of the houses they passed. They wrenched the gates off their hinges and destroyed garden flowers as a small gesture of defiance. My father explained that they had already walked from their own villages down to the town and had two more miles to reach the pithead, then walking and crouching in miserable conditions underground for two or three miles to the coalface and their work. In fact they were working almost under our house and we could hear the hammering, sometimes.

By now, the heady days at the end of the Great War had gone. Then miners were piling into charabancs to bowl away in song and clouds of dust along unmetalled roads. There were even stories of a musical village where everyone had bought a piano or two! Certainly there had been foolish spending but the good times were now gone and the gulf increased between those who had and those who had not. Soon carrying a tennis racket would invite stone-throwing.

School, of course, was a cross-section of children and would have been better if the poorer families had been provided with school uniforms. The lack of one could forfeit them their education. There were obvious differences between 'labouring' and 'middle classes' but there were also layers of snobbery in the middle class. Our opposite neighbour confirmed, many years later, my father's description of the town as he found it in 1914. He had gone to dances, and found that there was a rope across the ballroom. On one side 'Trade' danced and on the other the professional class! After the Second World War I still could not believe it and asked the neighbour if it really happened. 'Yes,' she said, and then reminded me of a very beautiful girl, a jeweller's daughter, who had posed as Peace in a tableau at the Armistice. I was six but remembered her clearly in white with a (stuffed) dove on her hand. After this my neighbour had thanked her grandly for all she had done in the war effort. The girl replied, 'Yes. Now I suppose I am to return to the position I held before, when trade and professions never mixed!' The old lady confessed, 'I had the grace to say I hoped it would not be like that.'

This same neighbour had previously come to terms with us, for in 1914 when we arrived in the big isolated stone house opposite to her, she was asked if she would be calling on us. 'Calling' was an art. One had little cards printed for the husband and the wife, the husband's the smaller. One called, leaving both on a silver salver brought to the door. The husband's card, I think, had a corner turned down to indicate that he had not accompanied his wife, who was visiting another married woman alone. There were other corners to turn down, possibly conveying that one had the plague and was too infected to cross the threshold. In our case, the lady said she would certainly not be calling. 'They are Welsh. Besides they are also "Chapel".' Some of this nonsense was altered by the war, but the comfortably-off still had no conception of the struggle for life on the impossibly low wages of the working classes. Their difficulties and misery were held to be 'of their own making'. It was a state of mind to which certain parliamentarians have recently returned. The church, with the honourable exception of the Roman Church, did not reach out. The poor were afraid without some 'Sunday Best', to risk the snubs of attending a service. The only help deemed necessary from the nonconformists came in temperance tracts. Russia had, however, already started its revolution. Wariness became part of class consciousness.

Part Two

A Pool of Freedom at Grammar School and Boarding School

Grove Park, a long honoured grammar school, began my transition to adolescence and a wider world, mind-stretching to a ten year old.

The entrance exam was a private affair, as the headmistress lived nearby and attended the same chapel. My parents would pay, though it was not much, for my education. I went to the headmistress's house. She was very small, compact and important. She was fighting the battle of the sexes but would have been disturbed to have it spelt out. She had started with a day and boarding school for girls; by 1922 it had no boarders but had grown to four hundred girls. It had been matched with a boys' school with two 'heads' and one main hall. Swing doors opened at each end, one to the boys', the other to the girls' school. Boys were always hopefully pushing their swing door in during the girls' gym lessons. Our modesty was unmolested as gymslips were retained and PT was decorous.

I failed the entrance exam completely. It was oral and in Miss Annie Jane Jones's home. She sternly asked me to name the coaling stations for the British navy around the Mediterranean sea. I was dumbfounded. Nevertheless, I was accepted and with a friend went to Grove Park that September. We were to be the two youngest in the school for two years, as they raised the age of entrance to eleven. The first morning was wonderful. We sat and listened to the lovely voice of an English teacher reading the story of the Flying Dutchman. Then we found two other friends, and as we were all from Dame Schools sans education, ended up in a special low form (2b) with eight others. Next year we were in the lowest class of the second year (3b). By this time, work was easy. We did our homework in class, listening to one subject while scribbling exercises about another. The staff mistakenly thought we were 'nice little girls'. We giggled at our standing and called ourselves, ungrammatically, 'Us Four'.

All the second year classes, 3A1, 3A2 and 3B, were housed in a war surplus hut, well away from the main building. We had ample warning of staff visits as we made whoopee! We invaded the A forms, taking our water pistols with us and, nastily, with mushed-up purple berries from the thick hedge on the drive. We brought to class pet mice for the desk. Harmless snakes were kept snug under our blazer sleeves by a bangle at the bottom until it was time to disturb the teacher who was aghast and powerless as our beady-eyed friend slid down our hands. We loved our lessons, especially Friday afternoons when the musically voiced English mistress said she was exhausted and could 'only' read poetry. The teaching was excellent and we were really learning as we continued to fool about. So as not to miss any chance of a giggle, we had a code of hand signals enabling us to identify the sleeping pupil, the teacher's sagging petticoat or precarious hairdo and the complete incomprehension on some unhappy face, sometimes each other's. We got bad marks; twenty points off our total earned by work, and I nearly forfeited my prize. We still laughed even when poor 'A.J.', now coming exhaustedly to the end of her career, begged us to behave and retired in tears. Children are cruel. Sometimes we relented and formed pacts to be nice to individuals who were being hurt too deeply.

In her last year, the headmistress and her staff had lost a certain amount of control. We knew it! In a maths lesson, as each girl borrowed from her neighbour, I collected every ruler. When I stood on the seat to brandish my booty the teacher turned round and back to the blackboard in a sort of despair.

A.J. drifted into retirement and was replaced by a strong and flamboyant woman whom the governors found hard to rein in. She was Spanish-handsome with blue–black hair and eyes ready to ignite. Augustus John found her a good subject. We had prepared for fun in the new term by asking my mother to bring the widest possible hair-ribbon from London. Everyone was provided with one and we each balanced a huge black bow on top of our heads – all within the regulations – so that we appeared as a class of bunny rabbits, impossible to teach. Even the dynamic new Head took four days before she arrived in the fourth form to ask us to remove the distracting bows, which we did with immediate grace. We were always wasting time. We discovered that the Latin mistress was rendered helpless with suppressed laughter, by my sitting in the front row, my rapt attention producing a glazed and imbecile expression over large protruding teeth. Thereafter, I sat dead centre front, assuming said expression, and we learned very little Latin. Us Four redeemed ourselves by good exam results and continual money raising for Barnardo's Homes. This explained why, when I went to say goodbye on leaving for boarding school, the Head flashed in temper and slammed the door in my face. On meeting me half a century later, she said, 'Oh! The girl who left school!'

The staff were obsessed with keeping the boys and girls of Grove Park apart. Never, never must we be seen speaking to a boy. We were learning about sex from our well-loved little housemaid, only a few years older than us. She was an orphan with a sad and sordid background. She knew four-letter words, vulgar stories and enough irregular sexual practices to see me through school where I never disclosed such knowledge, and through studies for a diploma in Social Science. Much more helpful was her disclosure of menstruation which my mother had shirked to explain to me. One day, I returned from church and to the young maid's shocked enquiries about my health which I thought to be as usual. She told me that my bedroom, strewn with clothes and bedding, looked more than usual like a battlefield. I was duly equipped and my mother informed. Then I remembered my father's friend had been invited to borrow whodunits from my room! He was keen to cuddle me and I wriggled out of his arms and ten years later out of an impending proposal of marriage. My parents did not understand my antipathy to their old friend.

I was shy. My mother's magazine, *Home Chat*, threw me a lifeline. In it a man wrote that his spaniel obeyed him, but if commands were quick, people also obeyed without thinking. I tried it out, with great success. I was still spaghetti-spined, minding what others thought of me. I, loathing parties and unable to meet the assumed suave superiority of shop assistants, felt a fool outside my little circle. I depended on my friends to take on the outside world and to do my shopping. My pleasure in the friendship of an attractive boy was crushed by teasing I could not face. My parents saw my timidity and the need for me to stand up for myself.

So my desire to go to boarding school, away from smothering, bore fruit. Disappointingly for all of us, mixed boarding schools showed poor exam results. We wanted no more of the missed opportunities my kindergarten years had provided. I was sent to Cheltenham Ladies' College. The entrance examination took place on the eve of the 1926 General Strike. We wrote a paper and were cross-examined by senior mistresses. I irritated my interrogator by truthfully stating that I would like to be a missionary or a dress designer. Neither were considered important and my hope of taking physics and chemistry was quashed; there was too little time to start learning before our Matric... now O levels.

The return journey, when the strike had been declared, meant a night in Hereford and an early start in a train with a white-haired, white-bearded retired train driver, in charge and a little apprehensive. He got us to Shrewsbury and I could have hugged our Santa Claus who had rescued us so gamely.

Eventually, I caught the train to school, travelling with a shy, though senior, Welsh girl who kindly steered me to St Austin's, my house. I had spent weeks acquiring the uniform: discreet dresses and thick black woollen stockings. These were important as my grandmother had carefully darned the inside of the knees, heels and toes. Although at the end of my three years they were a green–black, I never had to waste time darning them. The residential side of school was served by about fourteen houses for our choice. Two, the most expensive, appeared to be for mollycoddling. Two others, the cheapest, were houses in their own right but also served as temporary stops for places in other houses. St Austin's was one of these. It backed on to the college grounds and had a good garden. It was friendly and happy and the house mistress pussy-catted around like a tame Persian. The senior girls were down-to-earth, kind and helpful it was not difficult to conform even to 7 a.m. lacrosse practice in the frosty garden. I moved to Bunwell but at Christmas I met some of them again in the sanatorium where we were all isolated with chickenpox. I cried bitterly when my mother travelled down with the car and took me back to being an only child.

I arrived at Bunwell, a Georgian family house in a Georgian square. It housed thirty-two girls and four staff in dull surroundings and some discomfort. Each morning the college houses disgorged their young in crocodile formation, two by two, shepherded by a house matron to school.

The seniors at the front walked sedately and the little ones at the back scampered to keep up. I used to wonder if the road could stretch under pressure. The length of stride must have produced this phenomenon. We were not to be deformed by lugging our homework to and fro; ancient horse-drawn cabs, smelling of dank hay, were filled above their seats with the bursting school bags to be collected from the cloakrooms. Here, a hushed struggle continued as we doffed hats, galoshes etc. and then wrestled with at least two tiepins, tucked in blouses into calf-length navy skirts and our hair into slides, or when we were sixteen years old into untidy buns. This was all ratified as correct by the poor house-mother and we rushed down the stairs and up the Marble Corridor to our classrooms.

The school was mildly Gothic in style. The spine was a long marble corridor, with alternating white and black squares which encouraged a basic training in perspective. The corridor was edged with heating gratings on which one must not tread. The girls walked swiftly on rubber-soled shoes, on the left-hand side. There was a complete silence rule. School was quiet except for the bang when anyone trod in their haste on the marginal gratings. On one end of the Marble Corridor was a two-storey music wing with small rooms insulated by thick walls and double doors. The doors had glass panels, the inside one plain and the outer one in stained glass except in two where men were teaching; once there had been an elopement! Good sideshows were Saturday morning gramophone concerts to educate us for any concerts to be attended in the Town Hall. The school choir was a joy to hear... but my low growling voice was suited only to a frog pond.

Our main functions took place in the Great Hall. It was lofty, built of red pine, with a deep gallery along the sides. Over the stage was an arch painted with about nine females dressed as Muses whom no one could explain. College sat on moveable wooden chairs in rows from a central aisle. Standing up without moving a single chair was well-practised and led to strong thigh muscles. Twice a week our kindergarten, for the children of expats, used to appear. Little boys and girls came in twos, hand-in-hand, down the centre aisle to sit in the very front, looking incredibly good and charming. They must also have been bewildered and very lonely.

The excellent science wing was at the bottom of the corridor. In the middle, in a wide recess, was a large mosaic panel commemorating our founder, Miss Dorothea Beale, known to us through the ditty:

'Miss Buss and Miss Beale, Cupid's darts do not feel!
They're not made like us, Miss Beale and Miss Buss.'

Miss Buss had founded the Girls' Public Day School Trust and was, like her friend, a very eminent feminine educationalist.

The college had another inspiring headmistress after Miss Beale, Miss Faithful. Unfortunately, in my day, our principal was not of such calibre. The only uplifting remark in our valedictory service was that we should remember to pay our tradesmen, bills then being run up as our plastic cards are today. Prayers in the Great Hall were enlivened by a young lady hired to play the organ which she did with care and a display of Directoire knickers as she manoeuvred the organ pedals. The address, prayers and notices were as bland as the principal but our efficient head prefect gave us a sense of belonging. She intrigued us by applying lacrosse methods to the daily ritual glass of water, arriving at full speed, swinging the glass rapidly on its mat without spilling a drop. We called her, with great admiration, 'the Hippo'. She was dependable and unstoppable. I think she represented the school to us. I met her again as a member of a

London committee. Her hat was formidable. I didn't tell her I had been in school with her. A little while ago she was her own, kind self on television sharing her wisdom, telling the elderly to be unafraid of death. I remembered that school had by the end given me wisdom as armour for living. My form teacher had offered us two maxims. She said, 'Don't obey a rule without understanding it, but remember it applies to a crowd as well.' Secondly, if we saw a problem, we should not say, 'Why should I bother?' but, 'What can I do about this?' By the time I left I had developed a positive attitude and I owe this to Cheltenham.

Sport should be mentioned. Staff sometimes said smugly that we were the female Eton. Certainly the playing fields dominated our lives. We only had morning school, so the afternoons were spent on hockey in the autumn, lacrosse in the winter, cricket and tennis in the summer and netball in the mud and rain. During our precious mornings we had three gym lessons a week in a splendid gymnasium. Here, we could sink all the apparatus into the floor in two and a half minutes; why, I don't know! In the houses we practised lacrosse before breakfast and cricket after supper according to the season. On Saturdays we had to watch the matches though we could take art and music lessons in the mornings. The cricket tedium we tackled by telepathy, sitting together and willing batsmen to send up catches or to miss the ball. Then one day a new history mistress thought she would recruit a few enthusiasts to look at Cotswold architecture. She hung up a list and invited names. She got three hundred! Cricket was not popular and we enjoyed stained glass, campanology, heraldry and the history and results of various architectural movements. It was an interest for life.

Discipline was all-pervading though our rules were unspoken. No one discussed wealth or backgrounds. Taking more than the minimum pocket money of sixpence per week was thought ostentatious. We were discreet. There was, unlike the grammar school, no talk of boyfriends, sex, make-up or film stars. The girls did have 'crushes' on seniors and teachers which were open and not unhealthy, given our adolescent emotions. The school was, however, terrified of lesbianism, which had apparently taken an unfortunate turn in another girls' school. Friendships were easily discouraged by placing friends in parallel but different forms. They did not even share the morning break.

Break was fun. We filed past a breast-high Gothic opening from which poured buns of all sorts: Bath, Chelsea, cream and Swiss. Once a boy from the nearby college joined the queue for a bet. He got his bun and no one knew what to do with him. Similarly, an African princess, god-daughter of Queen Victoria, had got on the cool roof in her nightdress. It was a new error and no punishment existed. There was a pecking order which provided complete discipline. In the house, especially, and also in college, everyone was aware of their place in 'seniority'. When no staff were present, the most senior girl was automatically in charge, but when she left it fell on the next in line. One had one's eyes peeled, waiting to be the most senior and trying to escape before one was. The senior took the blame for all misdemeanours happening in her presence. It was not fair to cause trouble and, anyhow, it could be your turn in charge next. Everyone was too busy to have time for mischief.

There was no competition. There were no lists of achievements; prizes were for high aggregate marks, not form positions, which were never disclosed. Prizes were given in private after prayers. As in boys' schools, competition was based on the house. Each house of thirty or more girls had its own colours worn as ties and hatbands. As we walked down the Marble Corridor our deportment was watched by prefects, upright in every way, like caryatids at intervals along the walls. They looked at our ties and said crisply, 'Don't swing your arms, St Austin's', 'Don't tread on the gratings, Sydney Lodge.' Woe betide a Bunwell girl who received one of these deportment marks. The drill was to report to the head girl of the house on return. The house with least marks obtained the Deportment Cup for the year. We, in Bunwell, always won; it was the only thing we did well, a purely negative achievement. One tread on the gratings could lose the cup and humiliate the clumsy-footed one.

Four Scottish staff regimented us in Bunwell. They had no sense of humour, they were very judgmental and they attracted no love. Sad people, dowdy but genteel. Our house mistress, tall and gaunt, silver-haired in a black velvet gown and a heavy ivory necklace, looked superb as we filed past to supper. The effect was ruined by a vicious cairn terrier tucked under her arm, level with some noses. 'Bite 'em, Donald. Bite 'em!' was her great witticism, unappreciated by the flock.

We were also dull and dowdy. We wore navy blue jackets and skirts to the lower calf. Blouses were continually adrift and produced an obsessive tucking-in reflex. Our ties, in house colours, needed skewering with tiepins at neck and bust. Later, we wore a navy pinafore dress which obviated the need for the frenetic pushing of blouses into waistbands. Our hair was short or plaited and at sixteen, if long enough, 'up'. 'Up' meant precarious buns fastened with rubber bands and wobbly pins, or coiled plaits over the ears known as 'listening-in' as they resembled earphones. Some looked very attractive with 'Eton crops'. These boyish styles and our flat chests (see later), were a post-war effort to counteract the homosexuality resulting from Service experiences; a logical attempt by women to re-attract the male.

We always wore hats, grey felt with hatbands, and we wore gloves. We wore black stockings, replaced on summer Sundays by unspeakable fawn lisle, whose creases cut into the back of one's knees. Underneath, we wore navy knickers and drainpipes. These cylinders of pink, brocaded cotton, hook-and-eyed down one side, were a menace. The top was shapeless and it compressed burgeoning breasts without giving real support. Breasts were positively indecent for a time. Chillproof underwear failed its claim. The bedrooms were unheated and on alternate days, when we did not have a ten-minute hot bath, we had a jug and basin of cold water, occasionally iced.

As a senior I shared a study bedroom and gas fire with an incompatible chaser of foxes, hares and young men. We got on. One chooses which of our myriad facets of character will find a response in the other person. Poor lass, we teased her into trying brown shoe polish on her unwanted freckles. I was worse off with a chilblain on the tip of my nose, walking with all the pride I could muster down the Marble Corridor with said nose covered in black iodine paste! No one smiled; we all knew how to ignore the unpleasant. Our leisure on Sunday evenings was spent in the large chintzy drawing room. We were seated in less and less comfort according to seniority. We read our books until the harsh voice of the house mistress addressed one. Immediately, the addressee had to look up, bright with the honour, and with no backward glance at the enthralling page, join in general bland small talk. It took me two years to read George Eliot's *Romola*. Once a term we took tea in the same room, four of us at a time, balancing our cup and saucer and also a crumpet on a plate. Conversation was an extra hazard.

A friend, reared to independence on the llanos and pampas, and I offended by refusing to watch a Convocation of Bishops in their magnificent copes and mitres. The infuriated house mistress calmed down at last and listened. We were both incensed by the simultaneously patronising and grovelling rector. He suggested that privileged and pampered girls could not understand race, poverty and handicap. We asked to be free of the Anglican church and, miracle of miracles, were allowed to walk alone to the Scottish Presbyterian church. We were welcomed with discretion and bibles in French. A deaf old gentleman with two mother-of-pearl horns protruding forward from his ears sat before us. The sermons were realistic and we listened with satisfaction. We seemed to be free from the hypocrisy often engendered by good manners.

We both broke a serious rule that summer. As seniors, we were rambling in a group on the hills when Jane recognised a friend's house. It was strictly forbidden but she went in. I followed to remonstrate and the pleasant young man tried to solve the problem by whisking us through a porch into the garden beyond. We stayed a minute or so but by the time we reached Bunwell we had been reported. The disobedience was grave and expulsion threatened. I pointed out our dilemma. It would have been rude to pass. It was wrong to have gone in but we had found a compromise in the garden; we hadn't entered the house. I was asked why I had not left my companion and I replied that it could have led to greater impropriety. The matter was dropped.

There were things we enjoyed. On Ascension Day, always a sunny Thursday in May, the whole House went to Cranham Woods where the knowledgeable picked lilies-of-the-valley and the stupid picked garlic. There were plenty of both and we were not robbers. We each had a boiled egg for tea. I shall never forget the exhilaration of swinging down the escarpment through the beeches using their long branches for safety. The sun glittered through the mosaic of the green canopy and beeches became my trees of Heaven, including a magnificent copper beech outside our form window. On Founder's Day we honoured Miss Beale, our founder. It was fun forming a crocodile, four deep, then going by bus through the Cotswolds to short-suffering villages for refreshments, and appreciating the lovely warm stone houses. Each had a regulation vase of delphiniums in the window, so regular as to remind me of the ubiquitous aspidistras in city terrace windows. The villages clustered around their churches in a glory of honey-coloured stone, unspoilt by petrol deposits in those days. On a later University visit I was appalled at the vandalism wrought by car exhausts.

A minor excitement was the invitation from the nearby boys' college to our senior forms to visit them for a film show. It was a documentary on the publication of *The Times*, a very suitable Establishment subject. We filed in primly and sat properly, filling the floor of their main hall. The boys sat in four deep tiers around. No eyes were lifted and few glances, I think, could possibly have been exchanged. A few years later 'the Boys' were to receive invitations to dance in the Girls' College. It was decreed that there would be no more than two consecutive dances with the same partner. In our time, we danced with the staff or senior girls. With dangling mini-pencils we filled in programmes of pretty cardboard. We escorted our partners to the buffet and sat on the stairs. By the time I left school, the opposite sex was a complete, off-putting puzzle. I saw girls chatting with young men and wondered what they talked about. I envied them but decided that swotting up on sports news was not worth the encounters.

In the Higher Class, after matriculation, we were to prepare for the Higher Certificate, the equivalent of today's A levels, and for university entrance exams. It was a sensible school. With lessons limited to mornings we had been restricted to a maximum of six subjects for Matric. Now we were told that we could only start serious work in the second year of the senior form and must use the first year to browse and to enjoy learning. We each chose a subject and were taught to use reference and source books. I chose the development of dress and enjoyed illustrating mediaeval costume. Essays on our class subjects were on a three-weekly basis and were an exercise in self-discipline, research and style. This ensured that we found no difficulty in settling into university life. We sat at tables, not desks. Our form mistress was the vice-principal, quiet and austere. We were allowed, now, to talk in class and her discreet reprimand of, 'Ladies! Ladies!' brought instant hush.

The library was freely open to us. The sun bathed the light oak floors, tables and bookcases which divided the room into sections. A spiral staircase reached a gallery. Windows were to floor level. Low bookcases enabled us to sit on the polished floor, pulling out books of poetry or essays, sampling the contents in a luxury of peaceful discovery. I found a heavy book on ecology which gave me an understanding of the natural world. We ourselves were very isolated apart from concerts and rare visiting speakers. One such was a Mr Jacks who warned us memorably that our greatest problem would be the use of leisure. The scourge and degradation of unemployment was not mentioned that day. Work and the workers, ourselves or others, were never considered as a problem. The majority of the girls were Tory and pitied us Liberals, but were downright horrified by a very intelligent girl who declared she would vote for the Labour Party.

In the last weeks of my sojourn in Cheltenham, I was called to the principal's office, hidden away upstairs. I had never spoken to her before. I had, however, attended a strawberry party for the senior classes and received a perfunctory greeting. At the interview I was asked rhetorically what I would do after leaving school, it was suggested that it should be a career in music. Perhaps it was my best subject? I kept a straight face and a polite expression, a valuable side of Cheltenham training, and replied that I was tone-deaf and had not considered music as a possibility. I filled the ensuing silence – 'Will that be all? May I go?' – and I tripped away before any other careers were pulled out of the lucky dip for me. I received no other guidance.

In fact, a family friend, herself a Cambridge graduate, had decided to push me into a university, preferably hers. I was stupefied. My science was impossible, my inadequate Latin a disaster for an Arts entrance exam. One subject shone with potential; Geography required no extra support. Economics and Divinity were compulsory lectures for the seniors gathered in the Great Hall. Economics appeared in our final year. By contrast, Geography was neglected. Our teacher had once climbed Mont Blanc; she had bedecked herself with rocky mementoes as cuff links and, on a grander scale, a pendant. She found maps mysterious. I decided sensibly to leave school, find a private tutor, and also attend lectures at the nearby University of Liverpool. I left college without regrets or permanent friendships. We all scattered, separated by space and interests. Still shy, I had learned not to show my feelings. Thereafter, whenever I found difficulty, I knew that the disciplines of Cheltenham gave me backbone and I could face whatever came. I had been taught self-reliance and also respect for the strength of women, but men were still an enigma to be avoided.

At the end of the term, two of us spent a delightful week in Stratford. The old theatre had just been burned down and the new not started. The picnics on the Avon, reading the next play to each other before the performances, were the only times I was able to steep myself in culture until I retired. I celebrated then with a week of Bolshoi ballet. After Stratford, my holiday with my parents produced a shameful episode.

We were in Llandrindod Wells for the waters. This quiet Welsh Spa awoke annually to a flutter of innocents looking for husbands amongst the young Nonconformist ministers also strangely attracted to the sulphurous springs. My boredom was shattered when my one-time Brownie Commandant suddenly spotted my mother. She strode up, bending her big frame over Mother so that her bellow would not pass unheard. Was I there? I was to join her immediately to prepare for the carnival taking place that week in the little town. There would be floats, cars and even individuals willing to make a spectacle of themselves. Another visitor owned a toffee factory and he had already promised two smart lorries with pert little messenger boys in red, to throw toffees to the crowds. The Commandant would take her car and represent the *Daily Mail*, as a postman – a proudly given pun. She squeezed herself into a real postman's uniform of navy with red piping and a postman's hat, a sort of casque dipping fore and aft and hiding her hair. A Boy Scout would accompany her. I was to be a Russian, the target of disapproval of dumped Bolshie petrol and the embodiment of all the Reds under all the beds. To make me fearsome, Mother bought tow from the chemist and made me a bird's nest of a wig with beard to match. It was much too light so, with another of her bright ideas, it was soaked in a solution of liquorice. The sickly smell was strong. Our conveyance was a bull-nosed Morris in feeble health. It was covered with references to the popular press, Teddy Tail for the children, straw and plaster sheep for the farmers, clumps of heather for the apiarists and Scots. The Boy Scout with a Union Jack sat in front with the postman and I, wrapped in red cotton and tow, cowered on a precarious 'dicky seat', unfolded from the boot, and waved my red flag with little conviction. The car shuddered into temporary action after a vigorous wrench to the starting handle. We were behind

Toffee Rex, rather overwhelmed; the pace was slow, the little car could not cope and we spluttered to a standstill. 'My man! My man!' shouted the acting postman to an innocent bystander, 'Come and start us up. Just swing the handle.'

'Who does he think he is? The cheek!' said the man to his wife.

The perceptive sex whispered, 'It's a woman.'

'No, he's not. He's got whiskers!'

'Get on. Do it.'

At this first of several similar stops we chuntered into movement again. Before long steam was hissing out of the radiator and thin spurts of hot water were destroying the brave show of wild flowers and red, white and blue ribbons. At last, alone, we hiccuped on to a huge field. The postman was now at Red Alert. 'You there! Have the prizes been given out yet?' Startled carnival officials stopped folding trestle tables and held out empty hands. 'Ah! Here is a fiver. You can give it to us as a fourth prize.' It was duly presented back by the mesmerised committee and the Boy Scout looked pleased with the outcome. I scuttled off as soon as possible. No one could have penetrated that disguise; so very undignified for a young 'Lady'.

Part Three

A Bubbling Stream Bringing Experience of University Life and the Depression of the Thirties

Soon after I left college, my father escorted me to Liverpool University's School of Geography where I was to explore the possibility of learning sufficient for my Cambridge entrance examination. Such an escort, today, would mean loss of face but after the perpetual supervision of Cheltenham Ladies' College, I was pretty helpless.

On a cold, foggy autumnal day we reached a shabby Abercrombie Square, its architectural intimacy forever broken by two main roads and its central garden dishevelled. A year later, I found it was laid out carelessly when we were given an exercise with plane tables to plot its pattern. I got poor marks from our kind but gullible lady tutor who was impressed by the quick-fix symmetry turned in by everyone else who had only measured half and then reversed their first stint!

On that autumn day, we reached a terrace house overlooking the sooty green gloom and were guided up two flights of narrow stairs to another fog – this time of blue smoke. Out of this uncurled a tall man with a long welcoming arm, Professor Roxby. A year or so later he came laughing from the barber's and told the gathered students that while he was covered in lather the customer in the next chair described a lecture he had attended the previous night. The man had been astounded to see a sort of 'missing link', his face somewhat like an ape's, talking on the platform. The Prof. was certainly tall; heavy brow ridges and a nose broken playing rugby could explain all. He had a very determined though not obstinate chin, but his face readily expressed humour, compassion and concern.

Roxby and my father had concluded that I should be a general student at a cost of eight pounds per annum; cheap because I was not aiming for any qualifications. I was to attend any lectures I fancied. I had no inkling of Roxby's international standing as a Human Geographer, neither had I any sense of the ridiculous in using him to gain an entrance elsewhere. I found a banquet of ideas, a width of knowledge integrated with art, poetry, religion and history. It was enough to inspire the most gormless of students, in fact all of us. Our affection for him bordered on idolatry according to students from other faculties.

My next ordeal was to meet the student world. Co-cooned in Cheltenham and brotherless, I had had little contact with young men. I would be travelling daily by a train also used by a posse of noisy vets and medics. I knew some of them but avoided embarrassment. Father bought me a third class ticket, there being no second class. The inconvenience of intermediacy was replaced by 'Us' and 'Them'; liberalism was already endangered. Father, who had realised that I had become a snob, out of touch with my fellow women and certainly men, made me promise to speak to a stranger every day. It was then safe to do so. I began to enjoy the experiment and invented all sorts of episodes to talk about... my six children were unconvincing despite my matronly build. I was seventeen. From the station I walked past the squalid shops and depressed people of Brownlow Hill to the varsity, and took a modest seat in the 'Geog' school. I made a friend of a quiet girl whom I continued to address formally as Miss Owen. At lunchtime I escaped down the hill to a cosy Kardomah café. The air embraced one with the smell of freshly ground coffee; copper-covered counters glowed and so did my stomach as I swallowed a delicious hot pie. My first male companion was an Indian student who also felt unable to face the dining room in the Students' Union.

I did not enjoy this companionship. He read my not very complimentary thoughts but he still pressed for invitations to my home. I learned that many of these mature, foreign students were unsure of their welcome in the university and were very lonely. It reminded me of my experiences as an unwanted Welsh child at kindergarten, and of the kindly patronage in Cheltenham when they thought I was Chinese. There was a problem in Liverpool which needed a solution – something I didn't forget.

With additional tuition at home from a grammar school master I prepared for the Newnham entrance examination in February – or so I thought. When I eventually got to Newnham my Presbyterian soul was shocked to be interviewed at ten o'clock on a Sunday night. The totally deaf tutor insisted my name was not Jones and that I had kept her waiting for three hours. We crossed swords. I had never used the measuring instruments she spoke of as essential to Geography.

Next morning, I was given a load of rusty chains for survey work but my tight-lipped competitors would not tell me what to do with them. The written examination on aeroplane routes was another unexplored mystery. The principal must have known I was a complete flop when she interviewed me. She commented on my taste for unfashionable poets – such as Kipling. Despite a relaxed demeanour, body language was on full throttle as her hands, resting on her knees, flexed her claws. I was told I was too young and should try the entrance exam again next year. I now knew what I wanted; not the boredom of physical geography but the mind-widening lectures from geomorphology to politics available in Liverpool.

I went to see Roxby on my return and asked if I might try to join his school. He laughed kindly and said, 'It's one thing to try to get into Cambridge but you will find it harder to get into Liverpool.' Indeed I did. The following autumn, from thirty-six applicants, he selected seven whom he thought would attain an honours degree. I was not one of them. He told me quietly to cram a little less and make a better display of fewer facts. He always wanted the thought processes to show. I was one of two squeezed in during the second term. I was very happy.

On changing to a degree course, I decided the daily train journey was too exhausting and joined the Women's Hostel. There I found five other students bent on an Honours degree in Human Geography. My next-door neighbour presented a very youthful, Rossetti look which changed to consternation, bordering on fear, when she opened her door at my knock. My Welsh bonhomie was too invasive and, in her panic, she shut me out. On my second visit, I pointed out that the cards on our adjacent doors stated we were doing the same course and as we would inevitably walk down to the university at the same time we might as well be friends. The logic worked and she and each member of her family remained my friends for life. Quakers, they empathised with my Celtic enthusiasms but remained constantly aware of our differences.

The hostel was sparse. Food was proudly provided on tuppence ha'penny per head per day for dinner, roughly a penny in the pound today. Anyhow, we missed these culinary delights as the hostel was too far from the libraries where we needed to work. After swotting until the early hours, we were late getting up, so skipped the smelly breakfast and avoiding the shaky tram walked a mile or so downhill to the Geog school. Lunch was often missed as we chased from building to building for our lectures. We eventually cooperated in a cheap lunch we scrambled for ourselves. It consisted of a thin slice of brilliant, pink brawn, two lettuce leaves, bread, margarine and tea. For special occasions we had bananas mashed with condensed milk. This cost fourpence ha'penny each and over a whole term the kitty surplus provided six lead teaspoons. A clown twisted them into knots and strung them up like bunting. We were furious. We found his scarf and slotted it down through the rungs of the balcony over the door, sure of the outcome. The clown arrived and seized it with glee, swinging his considerable weight on it, stretching it to a string. He stopped with a huge grin. 'It's yours, Freddie!' we said.

We had no set books and had to read widely from travels, manuals and hordes of statistics to gather knowledge. After the last lecture we would troop downtown to the rotunda of the Picton library. The architecture enchanted us as we could sit at one side of the rotunda and whisper insults to a student exactly opposite who alone would hear it as a loud voice. At 9.30 p.m. students and tramps were pushed out into the cold. We started for our hostel, buying a huge newspaper bundle of chips for tuppence. Fish was for plutocrats; we existed on one pound per week, but there were two hundred and forty pence to the pound. In the hostel we picked up our supper ration of a large bread roll, butter and ample milk to partner the chips and jam from home. A sweet, sticky fluid, 'Camp' coffee, was a convenience before 'freeze-dried' was invented; the coffee, milk and water would be boiled on an open coal fire in one of our bedsits. We sat on cushions, enjoying the main meal of the day... and talked. The vice-chancellor, in his address to freshers, had stressed the value of student discussions as possibly being equal to that of lectures. Our midnight discourse was not so uplifting. We lived as a family group, sharing cheap 'jewellery' and borrowing clothes. It was a community insurance scheme as the matron and her staff were oblivious to our well-being; we looked after each other if anyone was senseless enough to be ill. If illness gave us cause for concern, my kind and untiring mother was the nearest haven and an excuse to board the Wrexham train.

Our warden was an other-worldly classics scholar. We liked her and she trusted us. As freshers we were asked to give her the name and address of our evening destination. We were given a latchkey which on our return at one or two o'clock we slipped on to her bedroom bookcase just inside her door. She slept with the light on and never stirred so no one knew if there was a check on us. We were trusted and, I think, remained trustworthy. All changed with a new and business-like warden who immediately employed a night porter. We came back early, roused the somnolent little man so that he would note our return in his register and... went out again via the fire escape, also to be our return route. To prove a point, some students would invite their boyfriends in for a late coffee and toast. It was harmless but demonstrated the difference between trust and suspicion. The most terrifying intruders also evaded the night porter. We had a posse of huge Manx cats, the well-fed branch of the establishment. They would crawl along the roofs and the parapets outside our top floor windows. To have one drop on to one's slumbering stomach in the early hours was unforgettable!

Our family was most supportive. We were seven with several friends in another group of six, the two giving further supports to each other when any member was alone. It was a strong block, and viewed with misgivings by authority. We were, however, deputed to meet the new French tutor at the railway station. We adopted her into the family *nem. con.* and I had found a friendship that would last sixty-two years. The warden, however, regretted the relegation of the charming tutor to us and invited her to transfer to the staffroom and High Table. She also suggested that she should distance herself from us and circulate so as to improve everyone's French. Arlette, a consul's daughter, gave diplomatic short shrift and said she was not a human gramophone.

Our interest in foreign students expanded. We decided to invite as many as possible to the only good happening in Hall, our carol party. It was delightful. The students sang mediaeval carols, and the open fires flickered on holly and discreet tinsel around the walls and pillars of the spacious common room. It was something worth sharing with the strangers at our gate. We found many freshers too shy to find the guest we were each permitted, so we asked them to join our group and used their invitations for overseas students. Between us we expected a group of about forty Indians, Egyptians, Chinese and Europeans. The warden now acidly referred to her official list of guests and ours. But she had her revenge. We had invited a charming American girl who asked if she could bring her father who happened to be visiting her. He was the President of Salt Lake City and a Mormon leader. The ladies from the great philanthropic Liverpool families ruled the Women's Hall committee and raised a hue and cry over plural marriages. In vain I pointed out that our Mohammedan students were acceptable, but it cut no ice. My Quaker friend and I found ourselves in the large house next door, the Mormon stronghold, as it happened. We waited for what seemed like hours in an upstairs room, each secretly apprehensive, until a most gracious white-bearded gentleman welcomed us. We blurted out our discomfiture at withdrawing the invitation so unreasonably. He was surprised but, aware of our distress, sent us away calmer and wrote a letter to absolve us from responsibility for the gauche rebuff. Over coffee, we confessed and laughed at our thoughts of abduction during the long wait.

We were an innocent lot; we never discussed sex. Years later, I discovered that some were even unaware there was anything to know. Mild flirtations developed but in our group the norm was hoydenish horseplay and a platonic fellowship. In addition, there was the stark reality of low funds. The invitation would be, 'I will take you out if you will pay for yourself.' Unromantic, but it made for feminine independence and, I thought, pre-empted any need for kisses to pay for hospitality. My father's friend had reappeared and, after the first and certainly the last dinner and theatre, a small tribute was exacted. An unwanted embrace is a real intrusion and I dealt severely with the super-optimistic letter. I fell in love every week and transferred my affections hurriedly to another handsome face to inoculate myself from the previous dangerous distraction. Our *Sphinx* magazine carried a well-veiled suggestion that lovemaking was worth trying, but the women, if they noticed the article, would have been far too concerned with possible results. The blackmail of 'You are the only one who doesn't' had not been invented, neither had the Pill; to the women prophylactics were mostly a mystery. A year or so later, I was supposed to give contraceptive advice in a clinic on a rehousing estate. The women from the docklands, fortunately, knew what the clumsy goods were for; I did not. We were all sure that the safety net of marriage was indispensable.

Some courtships did develop, slowly. There was time to enjoy each small romantic advance and spin out the joys of discovering each other's attributes. The two or three marriages which eventuated were happy and permanent. Again the economic climate delayed home-making but the long joint struggle to furnish and to afford a family seemed to bind rather than fray the marriage relationship.

From the time of the General Strike in 1926 the depression, already the normal background of the unemployed and casual dock labour, was spreading. Liverpool oozed poverty. Students came to the red brick universities not on scholarships and grants but on repayable and inadequate loans. The loans were to be repaid to local education authorities by the students the moment they began to earn, if they ever got a post. The average woman in hostel lived on a pound per week (twenty shillings or two hundred and forty pence). A quarter would be spent on meagre lunches and coffees; the rest covered books, undies and shoe repairs, lipstick and cigarettes. We could lean on a brass rail at the back of the gods in the Playhouse for a shilling or go to seats at the front in the cinema. When the lights went down for the film, a livelier action was silhouetted against the screen as students, bent double, in a column tried to reach better seats further back. Our dances were called 'hops' and were held in a cheap room with a radiogram and our own catering. Many students hankered after a radiogram and procured them on hire purchase with a deposit which they usually lost before half term by unpaid instalments.

Drinking was causing disquiet. A fellow student, the brightest of his year, had never tasted beer. He went to sell our charity money-raiser Panto Sphinx in a pub and was promised a sale of one magazine for every pint he could drink. His was an immediate conversion, to alcoholism. He gained a miserable degree when one needed a first-class honours degree for a post in a grammar school. At our hops, held to attract freshers to join the sports or cultural societies, 'pass-out' tickets were issued. These enabled the men to go round to the nearest pub, get tanked-up and return as somewhat or more than somewhat undesirable partners for ballroom dancing. The increasing number of women students made complaints and their concern became general. The Students' Union was self-governing and two years later the student representatives threw out the request for a bar in new Union buildings when the plans were being viewed. Despite a good portion of sportsmen, I remember the temperance vote was unanimous except for the proposer and seconder.

It was, however, the end of an era, an era of Liberal policies which were not liberal or laissez-faire. Hard times engendered serious thought about waste – of money and of lives. Religious allegiances were waning but there was still some influence from the Nonconformist revivals at the beginning of the century and the student body felt a responsibility to promote decent opportunities. We were lucky, we had not quite lost hope.

The weather was cold and wet. My new, expensive, doubly reinforced, rainproof Burberry leaked after three weeks of Liverpool downpour, laced with acid smuts. The firm would not honour their guarantee and claimed the garment had undergone undue wear and tear. The trams wheezed slowly up and down the hills, but we splashed on; it was cheaper and depressing.

We found fun in a rare night at the Playhouse, lounging on the brass rail in the gods for a shilling. Friends occasionally got a walk-on part and that was borrowed glamour for all of us! Cinemas were changing from silent to talkie films and cost about ninepence; another treat. We also appreciated real-life drama when the drum beats began to fill the air as Orangemen challenged their Catholic compatriots to a confrontation. We would fling our macs on and dash out in the drizzle and gloom to catch a glimpse of a possible battle. Once we got between the rival parties which were marching down parallel streets to the docks while an agile police force manned the cross sections so that the twain should never meet. Later, I found the tenements, occupied by the Irish loyalists, had huge gloomy frescoes of King William riding his charger. The Loyalists preserved the picture through all the squalor.

One other strand of colour we could enjoy was the free organ recital in the Anglican cathedral, on a Sunday night, preceding the international service. The organ music filled the huge arches and melded into the high generous dark above us, lifting us with it into a fulfilment. We often stayed for the service to ascertain that the clergy loved all men with no racial condescension. We did not approve of the churches' handling of Christianity. My French friend, Arlette, had studied philosophy and nudged me into a little reading. I dipped into Descartes, took a side glance at others, and loftily decided that a précis of religion was 'God is Love' together with the precept that one must love one's neighbour as oneself.

Around the cathedral's Lady Chapel was carved, 'For God so loved the world that he gave his only begotten Son, that whosoever believeth in Him should not perish, but have everlasting life.' I heard this sung by the cathedral choir. It was moving and memorable and the phrase stayed with me without my considering its meaning or indeed having any yen for the hereafter. I did not try to explore other faiths but I sampled Christian Science and Quakerism. I felt at home with the latter, the Friends, as I liked to sit and contemplate which, indeed, had been my custom in the Welsh chapel during the incomprehensible sermons. In the Meeting House the Spirit might move a shy, elderly woman to face her embarrassment and say words that would answer my own problem. In the university we found the Student Christian Movement (SCM) and the Evangelical Union (EU) too pious for our taste. We laughed unkindly when two members of the EU found their exam papers distressing and knelt to pray by their chairs, a bit of exhibitionism which was not rewarded in their results. Two years later I was invited to take a Christian Egyptian student to the pleasant home of one of the members of SCM. They entertained us with country dancing of the 'picking up pea sticks' variety and rashly asked their handsome guest to reciprocate. He caught my eye and stipulated I should dance too! To a little oriental humming, I gyrated around with my hands held horizontally as in a tomb fresco.

Similar fresco imitations came from him and it was obviously time to leave. I never learned. A year later, I was persuaded to imitate Mae West in a charade at a conference. My innocence and complete ignorance of the star led to a walk-out by the professors in the front row.

Like an iceberg, eight ninths of our work was submerged. We attended only eleven hours of lectures a week, but each day we went to the Picton library in town for about five hours and then home to work until midnight. Prof. Roxby took our main course on the environment's effect on man. From geology to soil, interacting with climate, we studied agriculture, trade routes and markets, town planning and architecture. We were taught the French concept of a 'pays', a natural entity moulded by man from local materials, so becoming distinct from others. In those days, areas had remained very much as they had been for centuries and the rash of lookalike estates and multinational companies had not diluted their character. Remembrance of past scenes are now a sadness.

In the second year, the main course revolved round the battle between environmentalists and determinists. As in the first year, our source books were in French and we had to attend French in the Arts faculty. The French tutor despised us almost as much as we thought poorly of him. Once, a stray kitten, hidden from him by his large paunch, purred between his feet and reduced the bored class to senseless laughter. His anger grew and he demanded a translation about birds taking a dip in a fountain. He shouted 'You English! I speak your language better than you do. The correct translation should be "the birds made their matutinal ablutions".' He was frothing with rage and sprayed the nearest students. In the late thirties, a friend told me she was ashamed to have teased her French teacher by wearing a mackintosh hat in class. It had been the same pedagogue.

In the third year, Professor Roxby's course was on China. He loved the people and the country and had served them well as an adviser on education. Chinese scholars visited him and we had to escort a delightful oldish man, in a blue brocade robe, who stayed at our hostel. He played Chinese folk tunes on a bamboo pipe as a bribe to his audience and then expounded his idea of a no man's land around each state so that none could start a war. We, too, were talking of 'Peace armies', to lie between the combatants; the idealists were hopelessly uninformed on weaponry.

Roxby was to be asked on his retirement to help China again. In the winter of 1945 I met him in London bubbling with enthusiasm. He had been invited to China by Mao Tse Dong to organise his new People's University. He could not have known of the real hardships of the University of the Red Army in the caves of Szechuan which he was being asked to endure nor of the disappearance of the mandarin class of scholars. Both the physical strain and the cultural shock could have accounted for his death a short time after he reached western China.

Other courses and seminars were undertaken by three tutors, able but uninspiring. An elderly lady of gentle disposition supervised our inaccurate survey of the gardens in the square. She had another problem. We were overrun with Liverpool mice, addicted to students' crumbs. Our kindly tutor hated traps and produced a dreadful alternative, a tray of green jelly. The wretched mice struggled all night in the thick mess and more desperately as students tramped by. Roxby grew angry waiting for his squeamish colleague to arrive with wads of cotton wool and chloroform so as to put the creatures out of their misery – we hoped – and in the bin.

Our workspace was crowded and we resorted to the map room leading into the garden. All was jolly as we drew contours and painted in topography. Then the paint water would dry up and, ignoring the nearby cloakroom tap, we would dash into the garden to replenish our pots from the antediluvian Merseyside weather centre. The rain gauge and a thermometer were in working order. Some sunny day, later, our consciences would blossom and one or more students would bethink themselves of that rain gauge and replenish it from the tap. Youth is generous. The upshot was a learned article by our lady tutor in the professional geographical magazine. The article was entitled 'The Peculiar Weather of 1932'.

Our 'outside' lectures were French, economics, history (of no bearing on our work) and geomorphology. For the last, we galloped a mile to the School of Geology, picking up bags of monkey nuts to stop our stomach rumblings as we invariably had no time for lunch after one of the Prof.'s protracted, but never to be missed, lectures. Nowadays, peanuts are naked; then, they had to be shelled making pale mustard coloured heaps under the desks to the very articulate wrath of the Geology caretaker. Our individual ordeals were the seminars when one lectured, each term, to one's peer group on a given subject. Legs jellied and knees knocked as one tried to remember one's script and let go the grasp on the reading desk to teeter to the wall maps in a desperate effort at communication.

Apart from work, Panto Day was the big spree of the year. We females dressed up in weatherproof clothes and gowns and mortarboards, very seemly! The men indulged their manhood with hours of scrums to achieve the possession of Sister Jane, a semblance of a rag doll. Perhaps there had once been a beautiful blonde on the Royal Hospital nursing staff who had started the feud between the engineers and the medics; she was now irrelevant. The rest rattled collecting tins, trespassing happily into offices, warehouses and shops amongst the good-natured Liverpudlians, until it was time to capture the Mayor of Wallasey. He would – surprise, surprise – be waiting, bedecked with his chain of office, for the arrival of some inappropriate form of transport. A large part of the funds we collected for Liverpool charities came from *Panto Sphinx*, the special edition of our student magazine. It had to banned by authority to make it sell. In 1934, we did not need the usual modicum of smut to achieve sales. We had published a splendid anti-war woodcut of schoolboys facing enemy guns. The City fathers could not contain their wrath; it was banned, and cursed as well. The students were genuinely concerned in Liverpool and all other universities that war was looming, unnoticed like the iceberg that sank the Titanic. We discussed pacifism as we thought of ourselves as cannon fodder. Student refugees from Germany were arriving.

Except for Panto Day, we wasted little time. We read widely as we had no special sources and information had to be gleaned from charts and statistics and verbose accounts of travel, all at the Picton Library. We sometimes went on excursions on Saturdays. All I remember of cliffs and rocks was the exhilarating joy of the African and Arab students when there was an unexpected snow flurry and the white magic was tangible. Easter week-long excursions were organised but confined to the British Isles as we could not afford the fares to the Continent.

Ireland was thrilling. In Dublin, the Trinity College staff joined us. We visited archaeological sites with the famous Professor McAlistair. He arrived looking dapper and dressed like a Free Church Moderator. He would put his polished leather attaché case on the ground, hook his furled umbrella to his waistcoat and lecture with such enthusiasm and detail that the earthworks were alive with their colourful past inhabitants. He graphically described how the foolish Irish got themselves to the top of their round towers to look out for marauders while the wily Vikings crept inland and behind them to light bonfires at the bottom of the towers, transforming them into efficient chimneys. I laughed. I wonder that I ever laughed again.

Our next Irish host was Dr Praeger, chairman of the Dublin Zoo. We had a lively time. The keepers opened the safest cages as we went behind the scenes. Then we came to the orang-utans. A nice, tame chappy was chosen and placed in the arms of a small blonde student. The delighted ape took all the hairpins from her coiled hair and spread it around her shoulders. Poor lass! Not fond of our ancestors, she was fainting when the keeper caught her. The Prof. must still have been thinking of zoos when he stopped us and lectured on racial characteristics and social habits as illustrated by a bewildered but remarkably courteous family of gypsies, eating al fresco. New Grange had entailed our wriggling under the huge, pre-historic stones to see the spirals, lozenges and zigzags carved five thousand years earlier. When we left, the Prof. needed safety pins for the skirt of his heavy overcoat. This draped effect and his inability to match up the rest of his attire made him an exhibition as well. New Grange was impressive. A local man said that in his lifetime the mound had still been covered with quartz chips. It had glistened in the sun; it could have been a beacon to the early men from miles away. We hunted and found a few chips and left them there. The man said the Americans had taken them away in handfuls. Our last night was a thank you dinner for our Trinity hosts. The talk turned from debate to acrimony and a Celtic feud in a Celtic fog.

Our subsequent Easter visit to Edinburgh was much less colourful. We climbed the battlements of fortress towns and trudged through wet heather to see glacial striations on slabs of granite. There met a glassy-eyed ram which identified the Prof. as the leader of his student herd. The ram stood four hooves square on the highest bank of the burn, defending his docile woolly wives until we wisely withdrew. The last Easter excursion, for me, was to the lovely Cotswolds. Even in 1933 I was disappointed when comparing the villages to my schoolgirl memories. In the sixties, I was there again and appalled at the huge damage by petrol fumes, staining and crumbling the lower walls while tourism impinged on the calm pride of the Cotswold heirlooms.

Varsity life was very happy and uncomplicated. We had turned against alcohol after our fellow student had ruined his degree through his addiction to beer. Drugs were unknown and cigarettes were our only vice. Sex was still tied to the safety of marriage; contraception untried. Staff told us later that students coming up in the mid-thirties seemed quite different and the dons wondered if this could be the effect of their being born during the 1914–18 war. We heard that coffee parties in hostel were exchanged for cocktails, and students refused to accept irritating restrictions. These observations were all very vague but it did seem we were amongst the last of a Liberal generation, defined as taking matters with responsibility for the general good.

We had the evidence of poverty all around and the conviction that our own future was bleak. We would be unemployed and there were student loans to be repaid, when we had qualified, to the local authorities who had been the sponsors. The lunchtime lectures given by Canon Raven from the Anglican cathedral were crowded out. His theme was that we were the unwanted generation, and we were glad to hear it admitted. We discussed the probability of war arising from the criminal disregard of the seizures of Ethiopia and Manchuria. We heard the continuous bleat of Germany for *lebensraum* and we bemoaned the follies of the Versailles Treaty. We did not know of the anti-Jewish evil fast developing in Germany. We were naive enough to hope that the friendships of different races in our generation would lead to peace and the rejection of war in favour of the conference table. The 1914–18 war had ended fourteen years previously. Now we feared a renewal of the slaughter. Internationalism needed urgent promotion and success. Mary Taylor, also one of our year, and I discussed our interest in foreign affairs. With encouragement from Roxby, we planned that she should take on the Secretary-ship of the League of Nations Society, while I started a social club to rope in the overseas students.

It behoved me to find a reason for staying up in the university. My parents were pleased to see my enthusiasm and I went across Abercrombie Square to an imposing building (compared with Geography's terrace house) which was the School of Social Science. The Professor was Carr-Saunders and I found him kind and approachable. My uncomplimentary request, that I be allowed to join the certificate course in order that I could use my energies to stop the foreigners being sidelined, met with immediate sympathy. I was rushed down to the ground floor and shown a pleasant, small, sunny room, cheerful with chintz. The Prof. rummaged in the white painted cupboards and produced a tea set and electric kettle, suggesting it might be a useful haven if I found students with problems. The news passed to other staff and some professors would greet me with smiling enquiries after my 'children'. I was free to launch our International Society.

It was necessary that it be seen as important and smart, certainly not as a do-good effort. I approached popular and successful leaders amongst the foreign students, explaining my motives. They grasped the idea at once; all agreed to be part of the new society and to encourage their compatriots to join. I told the Union porters, confidentially, that we were not going to be patronised. We would have tickets to all functions and I asked the porters to be alert to stop any gatecrashing. It was difficult for non-members to get tickets for dances, so the women students were soon clamouring to join and no foreign students lacked partners. There had been no intended colour-bar; Liverpool was cosmopolitan. The students simply needed reassurance and friendliness before they would risk a rebuff.

We chatted about our plans with Roxby as Mary Taylor and I went by train to a Sino-European conference in Oxford. Roxby was an Oxford graduate and had recently refused the newly established chair of Human Geography there, remaining loyal to the school he had founded in Liverpool. Mary Taylor enjoyed all things Chinese, as I did. With our welcome we were given labels to wear, translations of the sound of our names into Chinese characters. Each time a Chinese greeted me, it was with a broad grin or outright laughter. I asked why and was told 'Your name reads as "Lotus of the Dawn" and anyone less like a lotus blossom cannot be found!' Their humour was spontaneous. We went for a walk in the Botanical Gardens with four of the men. As soon as we reached the privacy of the glasshouses, they started playing 'tick' with gusto. One would touch another and shout, 'Your turn, General!' then career off out of reach. On the way back, we asked these boys, as we thought, why they used such nicknames. More laughter ensued. 'Oh! He is a general in the Kuomintang Army and this one is the Mayor of Canton.' Another was an engineer and the little shy man at my side was Shung Shi I, whose play, *Lady Precious Stream,* I had already seen in the West End. He was busy translating J.M. Barrie into Chinese. We wondered about being amongst such high brass but wondered even more at their lack of side and their ability to enjoy each small thing. In session, discussion ranged from the Japanese rape of Manchuria to the plight of young Chinese students lacking support from their disrupted government as the Kuomintang and the Red Army struggled for power. News was as sparse as it was disquieting. I met a girl called Hung Ming Liao who ranted at Chinese ineptitude. We spent more time with the Dutch and the Indonesian students. At breakfast we grumbled that our exam results were out in Liverpool, but we did not know ours. A kindly Chinese unwittingly told Roxby the sad tale. He then told Mary she had a First and I, an unexpected top Second. The Prof. had saved me at the external oral exam by standing between me and the examiner whispering the route as my trembling fingers wandered on the huge map of Chinese railways. He had seen me tearing my hanky to shreds under the desk and realised that I was scared to stupidity, despite my stolid looks.

Our train home left Oxford and I grabbed a meat pie from the station food trolley, which stopped outside each carriage. There was much chatter and I was so absorbed that I did not notice how tough the highly glazed pie was until, with the last bite, the invisible wrapping came off. I was very astonished and someone explained it was new stuff called cellophane! I digested all I had eaten. On the way down Roxby was most interested in a German student whose inclusion in the group had baffled us. She was the girl against whom the French tutor had been warned by the police when she took their passports to be checked, as required each month. The officer had advised Arlette, to her disgust, to read Rosa's passport on the way back. With much hesitation she did so and found that the girl we had known as a Plain Jane swot, was actually a chorus girl and obviously an agent. In Oxford, Rosa proceeded to chat up the Chinese, angling for invitations to China. She cajoled them into letting her dance at our evening entertainment. She appeared in a cleared space, diaphanously clad and with bare feet oblivious – or not – to Chinese etiquette that decreed bare feet to be the sign of a prostitute. The Chinese wives always wore rubber shoes when we went on mixed bathing expeditions; they were vastly amused at our naked extremities. In Oxford the German girl started her quite graceful dance. There was a tense silence and the embarrassment increased as, one by one, the Chinese eased themselves from the floor and turned around to resettle with their backs to the 'entertainment'.

Rosa returned to Liverpool in the autumn term. Three more Germans arrived and had little to do with her. Instead they joined our group and were enthusiastic internationalists until they found the coloured students were equally important. After we made it clear that the main drive was to welcome all colours and creeds, they hid their feelings and conformed. We were naive and reassured. We thought it time to experiment in weekends for French, German and British students. The enmities of the 1914–18 war should be forgotten. We were lent an old stone cottage in Llangollen and nine of us set out with useful supplies. We made a fire in the range, charred some sausages, reluctantly leaving a portion for two latecomers. A very brilliant light shone through our flimsy curtains and we thought the other two had arrived by car. We rushed out to welcome them and found a new world. About six inches of snow had fallen and a Hunters' Moon lit up the sky. The Germans stopped their romantic guitar twanging and decided a sleigh would be possible. We spread out the cottage blankets to steam around the fire and started a long tramp through the glistening snow. We slept all day and walked and tobogganed all night. It seemed like Austria, especially with the conifers weighed down by snow. We were happy and carefree; European peace seemed a possibility.

Early in 1934, there was a rumpus and Rosa was declared the enemy by the other three Germans. Hitler had come to power and she was on the wrong side. Even then we did not grasp that the three were Nazi agents and that

Rosa was on the wrong political side in Germany. Jewish students arrived in the summer. They described Hitler's oratory as mesmerising and admitted that they had nearly believed it themselves. We did not know them well enough to ask why they had left but they were certainly not going back. It was too early to hear of concentration camps but the vicious decree that Jews should be identified and demeaned by being forced to wear a yellow star was an early warning of impending pogroms. We tried another European weekend. This time we walked in spring sunshine and the Germans took photos of the canal, aqueduct, viaduct, railways and bridges. I dreamed we had a war and we were all killed by the Germans, ending up with a war memorial of a marble Liverpool tramcar! I told the others; they had been dreaming too. Nobody laughed. Seven years later the woman student was interned in the Isle of Man but the men were already in the German army. Our efforts had been feathers in the wind, but for that year we ignored our forebodings, forgot about the European antagonisms and enjoyed the friendship of the majority of overseas students coming from a larger world. Their closer links with university life was a progressive reality.

We turned to the town for wider support. First, manufacturers agreed that their foreign trade might benefit if students visited their plants for tea and talks. Next we suggested to certain professional bodies that the research graduates amongst the overseas crowd could be invited to join their clubs. This, apparently, was taken up to everyone's advantage on a continuing basis. Thirdly, the Quakers generously offered a bi-weekly social evening, a little marred by enthusiastic Esperantists blinded to the students' main ambition to learn English which was by then well on its way to replacing French or Latin as the universal language. Students were excluded from the Arts faculty by a lack of Latin or Greek. Prof. Roxby harangued the Senate on its narrow intake and Mandarin and Sanskrit were henceforth recognised as qualifying classical languages.

One day, an Indian came to a public lecture. As he came through the door of the Arts Theatre I realised he was 'new'. I tried telepathy and he walked slowly along the back of the theatre and down the tiered aisle to sit beside me. A friend of Prof. Roxby, an unfailing supporter, came to join us. She sensed some need in the young student and I left them to get to know each other. A month later when he had a sudden operation she took over his convalescence in her very hospitable home; telepathy probably helped us to understand the thoughts of students when their English was an obstacle.

Coloured students had difficulty in finding suitable lodgings. An Egyptian student showed us photos of his slap-happy landlady but he admitted her heart of gold did not provide the peace necessary for swotting for Finals. A Chinese geographer, conversely, was too isolated. On the day his excellent Finals' result came through, we found him in the town library and went over to congratulate him. He was pleased and delighted but we should have had a male companion to take him out for a celebration. We left him smiling to himself. The next day we were all horrified when Prof. Roxby was given a note. Chang had committed suicide that night. He had written to thank the professor for all he had done for him, saying he would never achieve such happiness again and he had decided to end his life on that pinnacle. It was, perhaps, too much of a victory to contain within himself. Also, turbulence in China made family news scarce and the future bleak. Chang had needed a friend.

At this time a deputation came to the small room provided by Professor Carr-Saunders. They represented the hostel for overseas students. The four dignified, gentle-mannered men were deeply humiliated and had obviously suffered a long time before they decided to make their position known. Apparently, the hostel warden when drunk was abusive, calling the students yellow swine and filthy dogs et alia. I went straight to the Registrar for advice. He was equally shocked and directed me rapidly to the vice-chancellor. After about ten minutes Mr Hetherington arrived, pleasant and approachable. I blurted out my concern; he promised and delivered a cleansing whirlwind of justice. The deputation of four reported next day that the warden was packed off that night. A lecturer took over for the remaining weeks. With hindsight I realise that the vice-chancellor had also spoken to the President of the Guild Council, Allan Kerr.

A few days later, Mr Kerr (as I would have addressed him), asked me to go over to the main Victoria building. He was much liked and respected and I ran down Bedford Street. He propelled me up the stone stairs to the vice-chancellor's quarters. He said, 'The Quinquennial meetings are on; you must speak to them. Every five years a few old men are selected to allot grants to the universities and they are here asking Guild what our priorities are.'

I was the Kitchen Secretary and I wondered if I was to talk about dining space.

'No! You are to talk about what is most important to you and I need not tell you what that is.'

At that, he pushed me in front of him into a room crowded with the top Guild Officers and sportsmen. Beside them, looking frail and alien, were three bewhiskered elderly gentlemen. At the sight of a dishevelled, apologetic young woman they showed real irritation and I sat down hoping to be forgotten.

The senior Ancient said fretfully, 'Well, let's get on. What does the cricket captain need?'

The said captain stood up and said, 'I will wait for Miss Jones to speak first.'

The old man snapped, 'If you've no sense we will hear the rugger and soccer captains. Where are they?'

Both insisted I must be heard; they must also have been rehearsed by the Guild President. At that, the senior inquisitor looked apoplectic and burst out, 'Well then, Miss Jones, where are you? Speak up!'

By now I had understood why I had been called and given a chance of redressing a gross neglect. I said we had a hostel for overseas students quite inadequate for their needs, segregating them from the main student body. A warden had abused his position and insulted the residents. A Chinese student lacking companionship, had committed suicide after successful results The university as a whole needed larger residential accommodation able to absorb foreigners on the same terms as the British. The crude speech drew snorts of disgust from the dispensers of wealth, but all the student representatives, despite their ambitions in sport, insisted that this was the first priority. It was an idea that had found its time. I slipped out. The new residential halls cleared up a festering disgrace.

The Guild of Undergraduates of 1933 and 1934 was interesting. Each academic school sent two members, a male and a female, in all fifty-six, representing over two thousand students, an important number for those days. It was the time of the 'King and Country' debates with Oxbridge in the van, sensing a coming war and questioning the morality of dying for one's country and the motivation of the rulers. We were still reaping the results of the 1914–18 war and recognised that 'glory' had become tarnished when the dead were counted and the living betrayed. We were deeply worried by the repayment of grants and a vista of unemployment translated into jobs as waiters on the Isle of Man ferry-boats. We would have been deeply shocked if we could have known the costly insanity of the betrayal of

Ethiopia and Manchuria and that the paranoia this spawned would bring us work through armaments.

Another octopus waved its tentacles, alcoholism. As larger numbers of women entered the universities they voiced their objections to the disagreeable consequences of drunkenness. This bore fruit. The Guild discussed the plans for the new Union. Out of fifty-six members only two voted for a bar. We went 'dry'. We controlled our own affairs to a remarkable degree for the period. The students had a professionally staffed office in charge of all sports and Union interests. I had become Kitchen Secretary, the job nobody wanted. I shared an office but had a massive oak desk to myself, which, when explored, revealed a Mouse Grand National, the little creatures leaping over drawer sections from a stable of white damask cloth. I gathered my predecessor had been uninterested in kitchen management. The Kitchen Committee now controlled a very efficient manageress and her staff. Fortunately for all of us, a former graduate, still retaining student rights, was a permanent member of the committee. He was Mr, later Sir, Sydney Jones, a well-respected city leader. Once, when a belligerent male student demanded cheaper lunches, as lettuces were a penny each, Mr Jones rescued me by stating cabbages were a penny but lettuces were in fact fourpence. But for him, the manageress would have had her salary docked and her staff decimated by self-styled economists, less concerned with the quality of the service than with the money leaking from their own pockets. As we were planning dining rooms for the new Union, I wrote to the other red brick universities for ideas. I was astonished to find that we were the only union in control of its own affairs.

For that year the Union had been homeless owing to the extension work on our old premises and we had been housed in 'Riley's Cowsheds', the then redundant architects' building. Professor Riley and his school had moved to a more permanent and pleasant place. Two long rooms were used as men's and women's lounges on one side of the oblong foyer, and the double room on the other side was my domain. Until then, men and women had eaten separately. Now there was only room for the kitchens and a huge new dining room, so breaking down the division of sexes. It also promoted integration of foreign students, who were directed to a big table where our society ate and where we proposed to welcome inhibited coloured students, it worked. Alcoholism was drowning; the manageress decided to serve school milk in bottles with straws. All the sportsmen took to these at once and the fashion was started. Very few now went out for a sandwich and a beer.

In the autumn term I had to justify my new certificate course. The building which housed the School of Social Science had been, I believe, the residence of a church dignitary, possibly a former bishop. The degree students kept aloof and we diploma-seekers were a mixed bag of motive, age and achievement, enlivened by two or three fashionable darlings who loved interrupting even Professor Carr-Saunders to create giggles and disturbance with little wit or wisdom.

The main course, taken by the Prof., centred on the shameful conditions of the day and the laws controlling them and the general public. Already I was missing Roxby's ability to weave Genesis or Sohrab and Rustum into a lecture on the timetable of evolution or the climate of the Pamir plateau. I was shocked by Carr-Saunders's justice. He advocated a betting system for the man in the street to equal the Ascot toff. Betting shops had not been invented; bookies employed runners, glad enough to earn a few pence. One saw them thin, eager and bright-eyed at street corners watching for punters.

The legal aspects of social work were well taught. Mr Caradoc Jones expounded statistics, introducing us to the mechanics of graphs. The varieties alerted me to the possible manipulation of 'facts'. His enthusiasm made his lectures enjoyable. Mr Simey, (later Lord Simey) was very young and carried the light heart of a recent graduate. Ogg's book on local government was discussed and peppered with irreverent remarks on our local government and parliamentary systems.

Casework was more important to us. My first weekly stint was a day of filing at the Men's and afterwards at the Women's Labour Exchanges. Luckily one knew one's alphabet and I was a dab hand at it. Even so, my attempt at interviewing brought tears. In the same term I was sent to a girls' club in the Chinese Quarter off Pitt Street. The police walked there in threes. I naively asked a local woman if I would be safe down the side alley. She laughed kindly and her assurance was justified. The club was fun. The girls, of mixed race, were often very beautiful but the Club Leader told me sadly that they dropped out when they were about fourteen, having by then found their way to the trade at the dockside. I was soon trying to trace an experienced child prostitute of twelve as part of my casework.

The overriding problems were unemployment, poverty and disgraceful housing. Liverpool was then a city of back courts, one unaptly named 'Rose Court'! In the courts, an oblong of houses crumbled around a trodden earth centre where a spine of broken down WCs made a quagmire. Water was usually confined to standpipes and even pregnant women would have to haul the heavy buckets of water up several flights of stairs. The houses accommodated families room by room. I remember one L-shaped room downtown was tidy and clean. One leg of the 'L' was entirely filled by a double bed accommodating eight, sleeping four heads on the bolster and four young ones sleeping with heads to the bottom. The other equal leg had the door, a chest, a table, chairs or stools, and the small kitchen range for cooking and heat. They were one of the forgotten families on the housing list. Another family balanced a bedspring base on the table, with coats for a mattress. Half the family slept on it until 2 a.m. and then changed with the other half. The houses in the once prestigious Bedford Street, now partly occupied by the university, had larger rooms. One which I visited had one corner as living quarters, a second for the bed and pram, a third for cooking and washing while the fourth housed the door. The centre of the room was occupied by a sizeable heap of coal. A basement in Bedford Street was rented by a woman with a toddler and a baby, her husband being in the Merchant Navy. She was exhausted trailing two children with her everywhere. She said the rats would attack the baby if she were to leave him in the pram while she ran to the corner shop.

Poverty engulfed everything. One afternoon a man joined me on Mount Pleasant, begging to walk and share his pleasure with me. After four years he had just been offered a labouring job by the nearby Labour Exchange. Cloud Nine had never had a happier passenger!

At, this time, the Rowntree Scale had just been dreamed up by the Yorkshire philanthropist and we were asked, as an exercise, to work out how we could buy a week's ration on the seven shillings and sixpence (thirty-seven pence) per head which marked the theoretical poverty line. Shopping in the cheapest streets behind St John's smelly fish market was loathsome. Our dietary knowledge was scanty. For carbohydrates we listed old potatoes, stale white bread (brown unknown) and broken biscuits. Porridge would help if cooking were possible. For stews there was disgusting meat, black with exposure, smelling worse than the slimy bits of fish. The vegetables, apart from the hefty swedes, were battered, and fruit was bruised and expensive. Rice and pasta, a stand-by now, were a bit exotic. We recognised the impossibility of producing a sufficiently nutritious diet, the lack of which would mean illness and lassitude. We realised that Liverpool families survived the totally inadequate provisions through the inbred gut strength of pre-war Merseyside.

These conditions were well illustrated when the women decided to run a camp for women, parallel to the camp for unemployed men which had been organised for several years by the male undergraduates. We thought it was as important for students aiming for the professions to learn about the appalling average life as it was for us to provide some help to the down and outs. We, therefore, planned to take ten students and twenty women at a time, giving a fortnight's holiday to the women. We worked for the three months of the summer vacation. We borrowed a house in Wales and begged food, fuel, toiletries and equipment from factories and local authorities. The Guild porters were amused and almost dismayed as the stuff rolled in. They agreed that we were the biggest scroungers to date. We spent the end of term scrubbing, painting and organising furniture. Finally, the beds were made, the kitchen put to use and the students were welcoming twenty anxious-looking women from their bus. They had been chosen by the Labour Exchange from the ones longest unemployed, often for many years. There they were with swimsuits in their luggage and dreams of promenades and shops decanted on to a neglected drive before a forbidding stone house. The famous seven winds which made the place so healthy and so bleak brought their own rough greetings. The ten students rapidly steered them into a sparse but genuine welcome and tea. Meals were a revelation; there were real tears over meat and two veg and a clamour for bread and fish paste which we had not anticipated. Friends rushed up with fresh fruit tarts to enliven the milk puddings and we all settled down to sleep: night and day. For the first week these too long exhausted, completely wrung-out women from eighteen to fifty years old, ate and slept. Then they livened up in the second week. Our University Chancellor, Lord Derby, passed the place on his way to golf from his annual health spa holiday, and was kind enough to call. He was amazed at the somnolent sitting room. He mistook a student for an unemployed guest. To his kind enquiries, she told him we were being very kind to her. Later he met the real and frailer guests.

The second week found them eager and cheerful. One group went on an unforgettable jaunt, dressed only in swimsuits, down the country road to the shocked village; they were hoping to swim. Thereafter, the church took an interest, offering a small tin of home-grown raspberries brought daily. The vicar's arrival triggered a dash to the sunny garden: 'Girls! Get decent, for goodness sake!' It was a ritual tin of raspberries, his entree to the show. On the last Thursday we judged it safe to invite the men's camp to a dance. The gramophone was nearly drowned by chatter. The smell of rancid margarine replacing fashionable brilliantine was overwhelming but 'a good time was had by all'.

We soon found that several of our older guests were chronically ill. A delightful white-haired woman who spent her days, despite our demurs, polishing the brass and copper articles we had brought to lighten dark corners, had cardiac trouble. One day she walked through a bedroom door as the whole heavy mahogany architrave fell around her, harmlessly, but giving a warning of the state of things in neglected old houses. Another visitor smuggled herself in for a second holiday. She was full of smiles but helpless-looking. I met her three years later in a wheelchair in Walton hospital. We hugged each other before she was whisked away. They told me that she had an advanced case of multiple sclerosis. How glad I was that we had kept the stowaway on her second spree. Lord Derby, on another visit, wanted to help a young girl hardly able to move with arthritis, but she insisted she had been given long treatment at Buxton and told nothing else could be done. We must have missed opportunities for doing more, as we knew so little of what was available at that time.

Lord Derby was ill-repaid. He was jolly, kindly but overweight. We had carted up a large strong chair, as we knew he would call if he was in the neighbourhood on holiday. When he did, the cleric with the empty raspberry tin was sitting in it. I begged him to get up from the special seat when a scout announced the Chancellor was coming up the drive. The clergy have special social status, so he wouldn't budge. Lord Derby was in the room looking for a rest by this time and to my horror sat on a collapsible spare bed got up as a sofa. It is not easy to forget the awful efforts to get our benefactor to his feet.

Handling our teenage lass from a barge was also unforgettable. She was a likeable, retarded bumpkin. Her non-stop conversation with each of us thoroughly covered two subjects, the time of day and whether or not one had any 'babbies'. Food that was new to her took a little mastering and we decided it would have to be all hands on deck for bath-time. Our plumbing produced only cold water, so we made a fire outside with coal from Gresford pit, under a long stout cylinder which boiled water, once the fire had been lit. We carted the hot water upstairs and provided two baths per week for each guest. Our young lass of the barge was brought into the bathroom. She gazed at the steaming water and 'stranked'; that is, she had a screaming panic. Then, somehow, she was in with soap and sponges and it was just as difficult to get her out until she was promised another in three days. She discovered when her next bath was due and was in the bathroom before us. The bath was empty; we were having difficulty with the famous local wind and the fire was hard to keep alight. The second strank, when she thought she would be cheated out of her new luxury, was worse than the first.

Afterwards, the students who returned to the university held small get-togethers with the girls and reported that the majority had had work interviews and obtained jobs. We were glad the Labour Exchanges had followed up the girls they had recommended. I used to think of my diploma as a 'Horlicks and Milk' diploma. A little help with food settled a lot of troubles and was often enough to get the proud and resilient Liverpudlian coping independently. A little extra nourishment for a tired mother who pushed her share of food to her family would build up her energy for the daily struggle.

The sociology students were all sent to the Personal Service Society in Stanley Street. It was a plain and purposeful building, crammed each morning to the pavement with the hopeful hapless. An assistant of strong personality and perception heard each client's needs and sorted out the crowd for interview upstairs. In a large room, four assistants divided Liverpool's problem families and the aspiring students into areas. A typing pool occupied the top floor, working grimly. I was given two files by two tutors to take up to the pool. 'Who wants', I looked at the labels, 'Sage... and Onions?' But they were too fraught to laugh at the coincidence.

It was not a light-hearted office; work was unceasing. Miss Dorothy Keeling, in charge, suffered more from stress than anyone, with unbearable migraines. I had to report my first case to her. I assured her that the pious old hypocrite I had visited would not misspend a grant. She had impressed me with her dislike of drink and waste. The scorn was corroding as I heard that was precisely why I should have been alerted. I learned.

I did improve. A smart, youngish woman had told us that her mother had delusions and should be 'put away', as she asserted she was being helped by an unknown man, a man to whom she would or could not introduce the daughter. A student had visited and concluded that the young woman was right but the tutor doubted the daughter's motives. I found the old lady cheerful but frail. A blind man whom the daughter had judged useless, was unloading the shopping he had undertaken for his neighbour and I was glad to hear the kindly exchange of assurances. He left and I sat down. 'I'm glad to see you have help,' I said.

She smiled. 'Oh! But I have another friend who does much more for me.'

Her serene face told me the rest. I put my hand over hers and said, 'Isn't He the Friend we all have?'

She nodded and we grasped each other's hands with understanding. I did not have the chance to re-interview the daughter. My wiser tutor gave the rebuke.

Our efforts with the women's camp had left us exhausted, because a youth movement failed to occupy it for three weeks, as arranged, and we had to carry on with few students. The 'girls' came with alacrity.

I was hauled off, without protest, to Llandudno by my parents for recuperation. On the second morning the *Liverpool Post* stated that the Gresford Pit was on fire and that two hundred and fifty miners had been lost. That pit was about two miles from our home. The men had tramped past us to work, singing hymns and songs in the night. The voices had comforted me in early childhood, when I found the darkness around my bed full of menace. So we paid our bills and packed. Next morning I went to the Gothic pile of the Police HQ and Courts to enquire as to my possible usefulness. Unwittingly, I had gone upstairs to the administrative hub and met the two Secretaries. One was the able and forceful Clerk to the Denbighshire County Council, Mr William Jones, and the other the forthright, efficient Clerk to the Magistrates' Court. They suggested I should understudy the committee clerk from the Rural District Council and so serve the committee. I was the only woman in the administration but no one noticed; neither did I. Later, a chagrined lady who had offered her services and been rejected on the grounds that no women were employed, challenged the decision by pointing out that I was there. With some spite, she told me that Major Roberts, the other Secretary, said, 'She does not count as a woman; she has a man's brain.' That satisfied me, as feminism was not a big issue, then.

The set-up was fascinating. The Secretaries jointly organised the rapidly expanding business of funds and grants, informing rather than consulting the chairman of the committee, an elderly and respected landowner, fretful about neglecting his farm and the new stockyard walls being built. Before the end of the week, my sympathy with his predicament had resulted in agreement that I should telephone him whenever anything needed his special attention. It never did. The committee, I believe, was composed of elected Rural District Councillors; the town's mandate did not cover Gresford. With them came a few RDC employees, including the committee clerk. Wrexham Borough lent their treasurer and his deputy and the County Council its Clerk and his secretary. All the small staff of the colliery office were there and the Midland Bank was in charge of donations rolling in with every post. The bank remained busy and aloof, the three administrative units kept up their historic vendettas, and the colliery team was too cowed to say moo. Each group was isolated in silence. Within two days, I was found useful; the RDC clerk retired to his own work and I took his place, as clerk to the committee, and so directly responsible to the two Secretaries. They too, had their own urgent business and were glad to delegate to me on finding I had a glimmer of procedure gleaned from my stint as University Kitchen Secretary. Work was achingly slow as members deliberated on grants to alleviate distress and on expenses for families moving lock, stock and barrel to be near relatives who could give them moral support in their grief. I minuted the grants and the members present. I read the minutes out on the next day and this produced a sudden sense of responsibility. It was then that the borough treasurer confided his worry that grants were out-stripping donations. As no group was on speaking terms with another, communications of this sort could not be conveyed, especially if they implied criticism. At this point the deputy treasurer advised me to smoke, as a cigarette in the mouth stopped an expletive. It was 1934; at twenty-two I no longer believed little girls might be seen but not heard. After the next day's list of disbursements, I read out the balances and caused a small flurry. I realised I was the only neutral worker.

In the absence of the Secretaries, whom I could contact by phone, I had a powerful position which I, fortunately, did not appreciate. Instead, as my desk was the actual 'Bench', in the smaller courtroom, the clerical staff teased me with a good-natured nonsense of 'court rise' when I made my morning appearance.

We were all there as volunteers to channel help to a very shocked, bereaved community. Some wives still haunted the pithead, although reason debarred hope. Others, with their children, waited with quiet dignity and uncomprehending grief in the corridors and on the stairs to talk to the committee. Their mutual loss was a shared understanding. Grief therapy had not been invented but each bereaved family gave the others honest, direct support born of unutterable community sorrow.

Two months earlier, when spirits were cheerful, we had received gifts of Gresford coal for the women's camp the students were running. Two miners from South Wales delivered it in their own truck. They said they had come north for better work. When they had seen conditions in Gresford, they realised that a disaster was imminent. They looked for work 'on the surface', and set up as delivery men; hence the second-hand and rickety truck. The students were disturbed and questioned them. The men explained that as coal was extracted, wooden pit props were hammered in to keep the roof up and then the space was filled with debris. Some days later, after it had settled, more debris was needed for firm repacking. This was not being done and the rocks of the tunnel roofs were creaking ominously. They had made their judged escape from the colliery about two months before part of the roof fell in and a raging fire completed the unspeakable slaughter. These men were unaware that, the escape route was little more than a drain through which a very few men later wriggled on their bellies to safety. Neither did they know what the enquiry revealed, that the highly inflammable coal dust was not being properly covered with stone dust to prevent fire.

When the enquiry was on, I searched out the two men to encourage them to testify before Stafford-Cripps, who conducted the proceedings. The miner said he would not speak. It had already been made clear that those making trouble would be blacklisted and refused work in the collieries around. It was still the time of the deep depression and scarce work of the thirties when miners marched to London and choirs from the Welsh pits stood on the edges of Oxford Street pavements. The rape of Welsh coal brought them no profits.

There were many tales of men who had been convinced that death was waiting for them at the bottom. They had told their wives. Some had left their work for good, others had had a sudden premonition and stayed away from the night shift which crushed and cremated two hundred and fifty of their mates. Their stories did not reach court either. We heard of the shame of the entombing escape route and the fact that HM Inspectors of Mines had not spent enough time below ground to find out this criminal negligence. The haphazard dusting and the careless repacking was highlighted but the office records had happened to be down where the fire was and got burned; the manager was desperately ill; and the enquiry was, after all, being conducted by the Ministry of Mines itself. This was what I was told; I heard nothing to quench my anger but lessons were learnt.

Meanwhile, we began to bring order to chaos. Two centres received and apportioned the torrent of spontaneous gifts sent from the heart, rather than the head, by a shocked public. Generous packages of kippers jostled children's bedroom slippers. Hand-knits challenged a shelf of shirts. Money came from poor and rich but the big, money-raising events had yet to be organised. There was, however, already enough to enable the plight of the living miners to be considered in addition to the widows and fatherless families. Unemployment benefit was inadequate and the committee determined to supplement it. A foolscap form of family details was prepared for each miner and served also for recording payments each week. Over two thousand forms were filed alphabetically by the colliery office staff and left in loose piles. A voluntary worker, unused to the alphabet or confidentiality, was charm itself, as he whisked papers from one pile to another, endeavouring to impress enquirers with the organisation! The committee varied the grants erratically and the Secretaries agreed to a proper scale and had it minuted. My father and I sat up that night until 3 a.m. applying the scale to each form. Next morning, a councillor proposed an increase for miners in his ward. He had not seen the minute. I was in charge and said 'No!' For the only time in my life, I saw a man jumping with rage. The committee stuck to the scale.

This precarious situation of bewildered workers, vulnerable piles of claim forms and long queues of recipients in the main courtroom was attacked every few weeks. A body would arrive for the coroner's inquest and would be laid on the Judge's Bench next to the only telephone. It was in wraps, but using the telephone was a discourtesy and a nightmare. Modern inquests appear more discreet. Each time a body arrived, a very influential member found us alternative accommodation in the RDC offices, across the road. We all streamed across, usually in gusty, wet weather, twenty or so clerical staff grasping sections of our loose paper records, the typewriters and much other paraphernalia. We docked in the RDC council chamber, only to be shuttled back when it was needed for meetings. The influential Mr Topp inspected his arrangements at 4 p.m. and found me alone, the men having sought liquid nourishment elsewhere. He decided that I, too, should go to the ball, and told me to order tea and cherry cake from the Clerk whenever I was in the RDC offices. I did not like cherry cake but Cheltenham manners required gracious thanks. The next day, at 4 p.m., I knocked at the Clerk's door – no thought of going to any underling – and went in. He was an elderly, handsome man but, at the sight of an unknown female, looked very irritated. I said I was now ready for my tea and cherry cake. He leapt up, shouting incoherently, and grasped his desk for support. I said, 'Mr Topp told me to ask you.' Collapse of spluttering official into apologies and promises that I should receive this sumptuous repast whenever I visited them.

I was enthralled by Mr Topp. He was a great spinner of yarns which he had come to believe in himself. School had taught me the value of a blank expression, so he thought I believed them too. There was the story of his promise to meet Lord This-and-That by 9.25 a.m. in the foyer of the Strand Hotel. The appointed hour arrived but not the Lord. At 9.27 a.m., Mr Topp told the hall porter to inform His Lordship that he, Mr Topp, had gone to the conference. A few seconds later the message was given and the nobleman rushed to the policeman on duty in Trafalgar Square to ask if a man in a bowler hat and brown tweed coat had passed him. 'You mean Mr Topp of Wrexham?' said the alert officer, 'He went across that road.' Obviously the constable did not know the member of the Upper House.

There was also a time when Mr Topp was sitting alone in the gods. Down in the stalls was an even more important noble with excellent eyesight. He spotted Mr Topp and called out from the stalls, 'Mr Topp! Come down. We have a spare seat.' Seeing I was rapt, Mr Topp embroidered further. After the theatre, his wealthy friend confided that his wife and daughter led a very dull life while he frequented the House of Lords. He would be deeply obliged if Mr T. would escort his family, now and again, to a theatre. Unfortunately, sovereigns were no longer available or a purse of gold would have been flourished; instead a few large crisp white fivers were rustled into his hand.

As time wore on, there were fewer applicants to be seen and the tales got longer. We got down to the nitty-gritty planning of the First World War. The railways ran effectively in those days. I remember long minutes as empty or full trucks were pulled through the station, banging each other in a music one remembers. Wrexham mines were heaving out coal and Brymbo was digesting scrap metal in its furnaces and sending back steel to waiting factories. The Royal Welsh Fusiliers sent their men in crowded carriages from the main platform and slow, quiet trains pulled in on the side platforms. There the wounded men disembarked, now in Reckitt's blue uniform signifying their hospital treatment and escape from carnage.

In this story of about 1917, the importance of the station lies in its proximity to Mr Topp's home. There was a short cut, up steps, to the parental home. The thundering Great Western train would disgorge the premier, Mr Lloyd George himself, on the platform from whence he hurried in the midnight hours, apparently equipped with a latchkey, up those steps. He ended in a bedroom. 'Move over, Ken,' he would say as he slipped under the blanket to discuss recruitment or the supply of munitions with his indispensable friend. The best story was of General French. Did I know him? Well, I once wagged a paper Union Jack in his direction when I was five. I had been on the wall of the kindergarten and he invisible in a military car. Good! I knew him, I would understand! It was the height of the war and the High Command needed the best advice. The General had mounted his white horse in desperation and galloped from London to Wrexham, doubtless up Watling Street. Now for the authentic touch! 'You know where my house is? Well, there are railings outside. The General found the house, dismounted and hitched his white charger to those same railings. He knocked at the front door and asked if Mr Topp was at home. "No," said my mother, "I'm sorry my son is out. Won't you come in?"

The General entered the front room and saw a Bible on the table. "Aha! This is what has made your son such a very great man! You must be very proud of him."

Mr Topp wilted a bit but finally decided that General French had remounted his unlucky horse and galloped back all the way to London, having received neither advice nor a cup of tea. We could have lost the war.

It is odd we retain trivialities from such a tragic time. They were the relief one needed. The sadness was no less but the lamentation quieter. The nation was now heavily involved in small and large donations and public interest was well aroused. It was time for the press to investigate. One day, at lunchtime, a horde of reporters, led by *The Times*, descended on the offices. The committee and most of the staff were hunting for lunch and the two secretaries out of town. I was on my own, on a self-imposed watch. I was aware that the journalists would be expecting chaos in the hitherto unknown, small Welsh town. They would be hoping for leads into mismanagement. I suggested they should see how money was being handled. They were eager and gathered around to see the assessment forms for the miners and verify the regularity of payments and signed receipts on the forms. I explained that grants to families were minuted daily and recorded by the borough treasurer. The bank looked after donations. It was all very dull and the press melted away with no scandal for headlines. The committee returned an hour later. They were aggrieved I had not retained the press a little longer and that they had had no individual publicity. The Secretaries were relieved and content. We made no waves.

Actuaries had been appointed from the commencement. They had done their work well and the funds were wound up, satisfactorily, in the late eighties. I wondered many times what happened to families bereaved in small accidents when the nation had less opportunity to be generous. The Fund now needed a permanent secretary and clerk and its own offices. I needed to finish my certificate in Social Science. Mr William Jones, as one of the joint Secretaries, persuaded the university to count my service to the Gresford Committee as the balance of the hundred days practical experience I had been expected to perform before I qualified. It was then that I attended a lecture on unemployment, addressed by the Secretary of the Welsh Council of Social Service. I was impatient of talk after my experiences in Liverpool and the revelations of Gresford. At the end of the lecture, I asked abruptly what effective action one could take. The following week, I was invited to meet a young woman of my own age. She was stimulating and knowledgeable. I did not realise she was evaluating me until I was invited to apply for a post with the settlements of the South Wales valleys. She had spoken of settlements as a possible employment, badly paid but a good social experience. I was grateful, and as we got to know each other I valued her humour and friendship. She had considerable knowledge of Welsh social needs and her input was appreciable. I wished I could have helped her as she had helped me; eventually I drove some of the voters who elected her to parliament in a nearby constituency.

Part Four

A River Combining Sources, Work and Training in Settlements, Charitable Organisations and Hospitals

In a short time I was examining my sparse but pretty bedroom in a charming, small Oxfordshire manor. I washed the railway grime off in an antique and inadequate blue and white basin on a corner stand and went down, when called, to meet the committee. There were four, including my pleasant hostess. I sat centrally on a high chair balancing a slice of fruit cake on a plate on my sloping knee and a cup and saucer in my hand. This justified my lessons in Cheltenham on unhappy Sunday afternoons. I was being offered the post of organiser of women's groups at a Monmouthshire settlement in Risca, run by the town of Oxford. The university ran a better known settlement in the western Welsh valleys. The interrogation was frustrating. What experience had I had, they asked. 'None.' Did I sew? Or embroider? Cut out? Certainly not, but my replies were politer than my thoughts. While I sipped tea and took pinches of the pyramid of crumbs on my lap, eclipsed for me by my intervening bust, further hopeful questions and my unhelpful replies did nothing to lighten the gloom. We must all have been desperate, I to find work and they to find an organiser for fifty pounds per annum. The committee sent me out of the room and invited me back as their new appointee to Risca. I accepted politely, abandoned the cake crumbs, cold tea and committee and streaked out for the nearest phone box to sob out the news to my mother.

A week later I got off a short steam train at a small station. Two others descended and disappeared leaving me and a tall, austere man pacing in opposite directions up and down the platform. It was very dark and grey. I addressed and somewhat affronted the man by announcing my name in the hope that I was what he may have been expecting. I obviously wasn't, but he did admit he had come to meet me. We drove to a small brick house with a hutment nearby on the side of a hill. I got a warmer welcome from his neat, alert wife, Ruth, and was then escorted to lodgings up the hill which was overshadowed by a huge earthwork known as Twm Balwm. I was to pay one pound per week for B and B out of my fifty pounds per year.

Next day I met the rest of the team. David and Ruth Wills, rooted in a steadfast Quaker tradition, were the wardens. Their deputy was George, a Ruskin graduate from Nye Bevin's Tredegar. He quickly assured me that I would always be useless, born as I was with a silver spoon in my mouth instead of the regulation coal dust. Cyril, possibly a Jewish refugee, had not yet found his niche. Winston was the sports and crafts organiser. Our housekeeper, tall, thin Mrs Skinner, was very kind and gentle but looked worn out. Every day she made the best of our poverty by scooping all the crumbs from the table into a clean tin. On Fridays, with a little cheating, jam and Bird's Custard she produced a trifle – very palatable after endless lentil cutlets and cabbage.

It appeared I was to supervise five or six sewing groups, one each day up through the valley, keeping them supplied with materials. Then I watched Ruth buying materials from the Manchester traveller. We bought attractive and varied good cotton ginghams, deep coloured cotton damask window curtaining and horrid summer cotton dress material, a pattern of sliced hard-boiled egg on a tartan background. I demurred but Ruth insisted it was the natural bad taste of the clubs that demanded it. We sold for the price we bought with farthings rounded off to halfpennies.

Next time, I did the ordering and was relieved when my hunch for subdued cretonnes and quiet dress materials 'as worn by Princess Marina' were warmly approved in all the groups.

A Swiss teacher had been promoting weaving in another settlement. She told me that after fourteen years she had only found one woman with a natural appreciation of colour. If other peoples like Arabs and Ukrainians, living in wide, simple landscapes of sand or pasture and snow, produced lovely patterns and colours in embroidery and mosaics, was this because they needed variations of form and colour to offset their scenery? So did the Welsh find their landscape sufficed? Did the ever-varying beauty of hill and river discourage local art? Or were poverty and isolation to blame? Welsh culture concentrated on poetry and music with the splendid new hymn tunes of the Nonconformist revival. Neither art needed costly equipment and both were easily communicated nationwide.

I was taken to the groups with my materials. There I found a local lady presiding, in every sense, over three or four of the groups in turn assisted by a treasurer to sell material. To my relief there always seemed to be someone able to help with patterns and cutting-out. I was busy enough taking orders for the next week. One dreadful night I forgot the handbag with the payments in it. I had driven since I was sixteen but I still hated cars and had made no attempt to drive in Risca. I woke early knowing that if I had lost the money the group would hear and insist on making it up, all of fifteen pounds, a very big sum in an area where there had been no work for eight years. I braced myself and decided to tackle the Austin 7, the newest and safest of the cars. It was in an unlocked garage. I found the keys and drove gingerly up the valley. The valley was narrow. Terraced into the hill, the road was at the highest level, the railway was next down, then the canal and, at the bottom, the river. That day, before I achieved calm, I came to a landslide and had to edge past it, looking down on the other transport lines. I reached the church and found my old handbag behind a pillar, as yet unnoticed by any cleaner. The journey back was a little easier, as men were moving the soil and stones from the road blockage. As I reached a village nearer home I saw George and jammed on the brakes. He came up and saw my white face. I was taken to a café and *heard* my first espresso coffee. Such a fuss and noise, it was an honour to drink the brew. We became good friends over that Austin, until in the summer I found a long hill with a wide new road and determined to be the first to hit 60 mph. I drove it at 58 mph to the top and could go no faster until it began to bounce its way down, completely out of control. At the very bottom, triumphant but chastened I began to apply the brakes. The men were furious they had not thought of the wheeze first and never quite forgave me.

The meetings were usually in church halls. One belonged to the 'Second Comers' who, believing in the imminent reappearance of Christ, kept their hall swept and garnished and were washing our dust from the floors as we left. They were very kind to us.

Six women were asked by the Oxford Committee to undertake the making of a patchwork quilt, an almost lost art at the time. They spent two years working in pairs on a frame, fitting tiny octagons of printed cotton from Oxford attics around templates and then, with minute, invisible stitching, clustering them into a lovely ancient rose pattern. It was fit to sell in Harrods. The committee member paid the group of six women two pounds! After all, they had been happily occupied. I wondered if it was the same person who smirked at the trifle, decorated with 'Hundreds and Thousands', the tiny sweets bleeding their pretty colours into the Bird's Custard, especially enriched with a tin of condensed milk for a welcome to our honoured guests.

The settlement ran classes on woodwork, drama, PT and music. It was frowned on by the local communists who had not yet been discouraged by eight years of inertia from hoping for a mass rising. The do-gooders were blamed for the political torpor. 'Depression' is an accurate name for such periods. One Sunday in spring, I was sitting on Twm Balwm's central mound, looking along a wide green road which may well have been an ancient Ridgeway. A middle-aged man, a member of the settlement, climbed up and sat beside me. He had been unemployed seven years and he was too old to get work in England. He told me how he loved his wife but felt himself a millstone preventing her taking her education and talents over the border; if only he were dead. Within an hour, when I was alone again, the wife joined me. She felt herself to be a handicap to her husband. A very happy marriage was now a bog of despair. I doubt if my words of inexperience were any help but listening has its uses.

About this time, the first stay-in-strike took place at Nine Mile Point Pit. The men stayed down the pit in protest and the wives fed them with sandwiches and so on, apparently letting down baskets on very long ropes. A new group had started in the area and I was visiting on a winter afternoon, using a settlement car with low batteries. I parked facing downhill under a lamp-post, on the wrong side of the road, visible but illegal. Soon a very tall police-men was knocking at the club door. Excitement was high in the valley. The police had been drafted in from Birming-ham and the women had noted that they seemed specially chosen for height in order to cower the colliers of lesser stature. 'Give us one word, and we'll stone him.' I thanked them for their concern and managed to convince the Bobby that although I was wrongly parked and my lights illegally turned off to save my batteries, I was also doing my best in poor circumstances.

The cars were dreadful. A large Rover with a long nose had to be driven out of a side street well into the traffic before one could see what was coming! I took this same car to another new group up a very steep hill. Then I found the seat had slipped away from under me and I was clinging to the dashboard and wheel. My shoes were off as the pedals were too slippery so I got a toe-grip as I steered her back at an angle into a wall at the bottom of the street. I had become used to driving cars uphill in reverse when the lowest gear was useless but this was an appalling joke.

Our work was extending and Ruth and David encouraged me to organise my groups democratically. I learned a lot from David at this time; it was invaluable in the refugee camps later. David would call his committee together and produce an agenda. He managed to get them to discuss problems and make decisions without any guidance from him unless an unknown factor needed to be mentioned. He waited patiently until someone made the right suggestion and then made encouraging remarks. The women's groups then held elections and produced chairmen, secretaries and treasurers. The inhibiting deference accorded to the former president evaporated and the clubs became lively and more enterprising. Patronage had done its best but not enough.

We borrowed an empty house in Llantwit Major for a summer camp. It was sparse, but we enjoyed the sun on the lovely small beaches, picnics in the overgrown garden and Sunday attendance at the tiny church of St Donat's. This was privately owned by Hearst, a newspaper magnate. The castle hidden in the woods behind the church was a place of legendary parties, well-screened from our curiosity. When the Risca folk had enjoyed their break, a group from Senghenydd arrived. Their mining village had suffered a major colliery disaster during the First World War. Four hundred men had been killed and the women still relived it and felt it gave them pre-eminence amongst other clubs.

Our recent but smaller disaster in Gresford was not worth a mention. I found the group manageable and reasonable until on one very hot day I decided to bob my hair. With the loss of my bun I also lost my dignity and control of the group; I was, after all, young enough to defy. They fizzed into noise and laughter instead of silence after lights-out.

Two volunteers from the universities arrived to help; they linked up with my past. A delightful South African girl was full of concern for the racial problems of her country. She had been in Cheltenham after my time. The other, christened Shi-fa when she was born in China, was the daughter of a professor of Chinese. We spoke of the shrinking world and wondered if, with her background and my links through Professor Roxby of Liverpool, we would both know any Chinese nationals. We found none but on the last day I let sand run through my hands saying, 'The Chinese are like sand, they will never unite.' I turned to Shi-fa and said, 'Hung-Ming Liao said that in the Oxford conference I went to.' Shi-fa sprang up and said she was her half-sister, reared with her as a child. So, it was a small world.

I had a great respect and affection for Ruth and David Wills. Some months after my appointment they had attended a meeting of the National Council of Social Services. It was held in Cardiff to discuss government funding and salary increases for staff, now possible with extra grants. The various categories were considered and I was alone in glory as being qualified but inexperienced. My fifty pounds per year was to be raised to seventy-five. The Willses remonstrated that it was grossly unfair. A month later I was invited by the organising secretary of the NCSS to lunch with an attractive young man and a theatre to follow, all for the purpose of offering me one hundred and fifty a year with the dizzy prospect of a more exciting life if I joined them. I refused to leave my friends in the lurch.

On my return they told me of the pointed decision that had been made to leave me with less than other workers. We remained firm friends while life lasted.

By the summer, David and Ruth were looking for residential work with teenagers. He was given an opportunity to organise 'Q Camps' for young delinquents. I visited them. The 'young' had been screened by others and turned out to be mostly out of their teens and some even in need of long-term medical care. The theory was to build a settlement, involving the group from the beginning. In this way, pride of achievement would create team spirit and promote a commitment to the care and upkeep of the camp. Ruth told me the first night had been spent by the group in the open field which they now owned. Cold and damp as they were, no one in the group would cooperate in lighting a fire, so they all did without. Next day a fire was lit and hot drinks were produced in a communal effort. Before dark they had decided it would be worth erecting tents. A whiff of autumn weather encouraged real enthusiasm for building semi-permanent wooden huts. When I arrived in summer, several huts were complete with bunks, chests of drawers and cupboards. They ate at long tables with benches. No one, however, would add handles or knobs to the furniture; each man carried a pocket knife and plunged it into the soft pine to open doors and drawers.

Meanwhile, in the Risca settlement a more difficult regime was being experienced. The team spirit had gone when David and Ruth were replaced by another couple. We were visited soon by three very influential Welsh women with important political connections. One was my friend who had introduced me to the settlement. Typically, we were not told of their coming. They were to enquire as to what the settlement needed. It was a long, hot afternoon and perhaps the warden lost patience; he ended up by telling these Welsh patriots that the valleys would make splendid reservoirs for England and, as far as he could see, drowning the valleys and all within them would be a good solution. He made a poor impression! Irritated later by some difference of opinion on my part, he said I was only there for the money. I resigned promptly but I did not explain to the bewildered Oxford committee chairman why the work had turned sour.

By this time, I was convinced that the apathy in some of the groups was closely linked to ill health. Undernourishment and tuberculosis were obvious problems. I decided that a better understanding of health matters was essential to a career in social work. I had heard of hospital almoners and I applied for admission to a training course. In those days women pioneers had started the new professions by their own enterprise. They were educated, and came from families who could support them while they tried to prove the worth of their work. This always entailed raising enough money for the worker to be self-supporting. The salaries were inadequate; the idea of social work being performed by moneyed women did not die down until the Second World War. Thus 'lady almoners' assessed patients' means and their ability to pay for treatment. Octavia Hill found her housing managers approved because they collected rents and bad debts. The reward was in having access to helping those in need. The theory that social workers would work for ideals rather than for money persisted even to the sixties. By that time women were showing themselves capable of pioneering and of holding posts of increasing importance. It was very hard to obtain good working conditions and staff salaries. I was to find out that women had become a threat to the professional classes and were to be kept firmly in their place by lower pay, committee carping on supposed extravagances and even by deliberate dirty tricks from parallel professions and obstacles to progress from chief officers who could deny access to information and put a tourniquet on the flow of financial support and appointment of staff. This was not a concern of mine as an unpaid student or subordinate staff but it did affect one's comfort and even health. I lived as poorly as I had done in Liverpool, walking to save a penny bus ride. I never disclosed to my parents how little margin there was. I was too aware that I had never ceased to be dependent on my allowance which had to be increased to cover my rented bedsit and food.

If I was to understand the effects of ill health on social problems I needed more training, and the course for Hospital Almoners appeared to be what I needed. I returned to the Liverpool School of Social Science and asked my previous tutor to accept me as a student. This done, I was sent to the Charity Organisation Society (COS), in London. My allotted area was Westminster.

I chose a hostel because it was labelled 'International'. It was not. Breakfast brought a hilarious exchange of the marital romps during the previous night. Seeing that that made no impact on the rustic in their midst, they asked me if I found London thrilling. As I had experienced two introductory sessions of COS, my reply that I found it less progressive than Liverpool in its conception of social service, produced a stunned silence. I was written off with no invitations to cocktails with the glamorous. Next day, a fellow student arrived and we went to look for two bedsits.

We found a Georgian terrace house with two empty bedsits on the top floor, pleasant and affordable. We had no idea it was a red light area but we were very fortunate in our choice. We fetched our luggage from Paddington nearby and arrived as a man was being hustled out by the police. It was said that he was a conman. Next day, an Arab student wearing a hairnet was being resuscitated on the staircase, apparently having tried to gas himself. It was all less daunting than the hostel we had left. We liked Mrs Mason, the manageress. She had a daughter of our age. Mrs Mason was firm and frank and we accepted her warnings about the metropolis. She told us that she had to support her daughter financially, as most of the girls in the fashion store where she worked eventually had to accept a man's 'protection', or more bluntly, exploitation, as none could live on the mean wage. Certainly it seemed that women were fair game and nearly a universal sport.

On our landing was a diminutive dressmaker, often smart in the generous spare cloth after cutting out. She adored two Siamese cats and with great courage would chase her mischievous family along the roof past our high windows within the Georgian parapets. The other neighbour on the top floor was a film extra, getting up soon after dawn to wait for hours on the set, usually in great discomfort, as she was, she said, nearly welded to a long rubber garment, meant to slim her as she sweated into it. Loo calls were an excruciating calamity. She was away a lot, so her room was once let to a large Germanic type of man, ostensibly polite but on the prowl. He tired of trying to wake me at 3 or 4 a.m. to borrow my radio. His secretary was on a lower floor. Mrs Mason was kind. She told us the poor secretary was terrified of her employer.

A Quaker friend came to a gas-ring supper and, as she thought I would never be involved, unburdened herself of a difficulty at work. A German colonel had contacted their organisation and brought excellent references, but a telephone call from Berlin had warned them to stall on his demands for assistance. I could not resist suggesting his name and to her horrified surprise warned her to be quiet as he was next door. After he left, another coincidence occurred when one of the other tenants brought a pair of shoes wrapped in newspaper from the cobblers. He had idly read a small paragraph reporting that this German had been cleared by a French court of any complicity in the death of his secretary, who had fallen out of a fourth floor window in a block of flats in Marseilles. His alibi was proven by his insistence that he had been playing his radio two floors higher up than his weeping secretary. He now needed another secretary and the following week wrote to Mrs Mason suggesting she should persuade one of her other tenants to take the vacancy! Despite severe unemployment, it was hardly a temptation.

Oxford Terrace was a convenient and pleasant area to live in, notwithstanding its reputation and the horror of the almoners at St Mary's Hospital special clinic when they knew our address. It was certainly lively; one never knew what would happen next.

On the night of Edward the Eighth's abdication, my wireless programme was interrupted by a call to the phone on behalf of my absent friend, Ella. A man's voice announced his recent return from America and his disappointment that Ella was out. I had a blurred memory of a friend who bitterly regretted losing a US friend so I suggested he came round to wait for her. Our sensible north country housemaid looked aghast as she announced a hefty Wild Westerner in urban clothes to my small room. He produced a bottle of whiskey and announced he did not know 'my' Ella but another Ella who had occupied the room. He had been on visiting terms, taking her out to dinners, paying her rent and even paying for lessons in speech. I remembered the dreadful scented emerald soap which she had left behind! By this time our king's wireless announcement of his abdication had ended and the man had found my medical books. Ha! I was a nurse, was I? Then I would probably be interested in taking over my predecessor's role, (the nurses were as grossly underpaid as the shop assistants, despite their skills and their real devotion to duty). I sat on the bed and laughed helplessly. I addressed an uncomprehending face. 'You would not even have to pay for elocution lessons. My father would give me a good deal more money if I needed it to stay straight.' It scared him and he grabbed his wide hat. I stopped his bolt down the stairs to return his whiskey. About three days later, I was sufficiently lonely and depressed to think that even he would have been better than my own company. The need for friendship might be as big a factor in promiscuity as poverty was. In fact, another student confided in us that her tutor tried to help her despondency. She had been given a small grant and bought a red dress and lipstick. Suddenly, men were making overtures to her and we hoped her happiness was prudent, as we were all students of the Charity Organisation Society.

I worked with the Westminster COS, cocooned in Edwardian values of gentility and respect for wealth and titles. The office was supervised, voluntarily or for an honorarium, by a thin, elderly gentleman. He had a kite-shaped face, dwindling from a broad forehead to a wisp of a mandarin's beard. Worse, though one did not wish to stare, he had lost an eye and remedied this by getting an artistic friend to paint a staring eye on the unusable lens of his glasses. Even if he dozed off, we would have been under supervision – of a sort. Other voluntary workers trained us, not always helpfully. As we wrote endless begging letters to the rich and good, a student asked how a Countess should be addressed. 'Good gracious! Haven't you any friends who are Countesses?' We should have withered away, but we were both Celts and I had to wait until after the next war to collect such friends and avoid the title for myself.

We were given casework in easy stages. Unlike Liverpool Personal Service Society, assistance offered was measured not so much by need as by the qualities of being deserving and properly thankful. Men, if not bald, should have pulled their forelocks. Women should have curtsied or at least 'made a bob'; it was almost possible. Two of my first cases were tenants in the cellars of beautiful, porticoed Georgian mansions on which discreet, small brass plates indicated the noble occupier. One cellar tenant was a seriously depressed teacher from a language school, far beyond my experience to help. Another was a very sick man with a young son. He apparently suffered from sleepy sickness which distressed the boy. They were hungry, damp and penniless. They had very little furniture and no comfort but they paid five shillings a week for it while I only paid thirty shillings for a warm, well-lit and adequately furnished room with baths and a daily breakfast tray. I was astounded that eminent people should collect rent from such pathetic families for such poor facilities. Perhaps the butler had sub-let on his own initiative. Today, we would welcome such shelter for the pavement sleepers. Today, it would need a very trusting landlord to harbour such tenants.

Other poor accommodation was to be found in expensive restaurants. One, where suckling pigs were banked six or seven layers high on a silver trolley and cream extravaganzas quivered on cold tables, had a waiter in trouble. For privacy I was allowed to his room which was furnished with a chair, iron bed and his own cardboard suitcase. I had to interview a film star's wretchedly poor aunt, a refugee from Germany, in a nursing home in Vincent Square. She was making silk lampshades. We sat on the stairs. This establishment was patronised by royalty and the matron was suitably grand, in amethyst silk with an ecru net veil falling to her waist, and of little hygienic value. I was intrigued by a frail woman asking for convalescent care after discharge from hospital. She had suffered from a broken rib or two and I pursued this to see if compensation was involved. No, it wasn't. Her husband had taken a flat iron and bashed her ribs in. She impressed me further; it was the eleventh time. I stolidly took down the details of each hospital admission and rang them all up. Each was confirmed. We helped her but she would not take any action to prevent the next occurrence.

I was to be rewarded for good work by being sent to a special pensioner. Each month we dispensed allowances awarded by London charities to very worthy recipients. To my astonishment, the great achievement of my client was to have been at one time the housekeeper of the Duchess of Portland. Living on neighbouring estates, the housekeeper had curtseyed to Queen Victoria as her carriage raised the local dust. It was a hot, dusty day as I walked along endless streets of terraced houses. I felt neat but overwarm in a navy pinstriped suit and good hat. At last I knocked on the immaculate door of a very respectable terrace house. It was opened by an erect and severe lady with white hair strained back into a high bun. She invited me in wordlessly and stood disapprovingly. I was aware of my sins of etiquette as, without invitation, I sat on a hard seat. She was now grim. After a two-minute rest I got up to hand her the envelope. 'Thank you. And what is your name? Ah! Will you please inform the Charity Organisation Society that this is the first time I have had to accept my pension from anyone without a title!' I should have offered to take it back.

My next 'treat' was more interesting. Another of these pensions was to be handed to the widow of a Chelsea Pensioner. She was a kind, welcoming little lady in a cosy flat with many photos. I picked out the most important frame and asked if it was of her husband. 'Oh no, dear. That was my fiancé, but he died. I have always been true to him. I vowed I would never marry anyone but him.' She confirmed innocently that she had never married her Chelsea Pensioner and indeed had never let him kiss her. The COS were very quiet when I told them they had for twenty years wrongly paid the pension destined for a widow. I'm sure the pension was continued.

At last I finished my COS stint and returned to hospital experience. I had already had two samples of almoner's work before coming to London. The first, for six weeks, was at Liverpool's huge Walton hospital, tutored by a delightful almoner. She told me she had had a dreadful time when training and wanted mine to be happy. They had never had a student before. The first occupation suggested for me was to drink a cup of tea with every brew made in the office. It was made thirteen times a day, against the rules, steam rising mysteriously from a screen of ring-bound files. The tea was very strong. I didn't like it. I was too polite to say so and I got tea poisoning, according to my doctor. I nearly had a nervous breakdown. I was given a revolving office chair and each person gave it a spin as he passed. The men were the old poor law officers, doing their best to cheer up our dull days. Perhaps I was owed some teasing as I made dreadful mistakes. Everything had to be done in triplicate. The entry forms for each patient were date-stamped in triplicate and every mistake meant taking the little machine to bits like a watch. We each carried a huge board on which were two-page wide sheets, in triplicate and interleaved with large sheets of blue carbon paper. To fill these by the bedside of a suffering human, and then transfer them to the bottom of the pile, all while standing, left the almoners as woaded as the Celts confronting Caesar. This was not all. A certain woman councillor had once opened the door to a white-coated woman and found to her humiliation and disgust that she had not assisted a doctor but only a struggling social worker. Her principles of equality were affronted and thenceforth, since she held sway on public establishments, the almoners dressed in green overalls for the walks along corridors and hurriedly changed to regulation blue-blotched white medical coats in the foyer of each ward!

I was proudly conducted around the kitchens by the hospital administrator. He took their soup daily for his lunch, a good safeguard. The chefs were preparing meals for the three cancer blocks of beds. Individual patients, suffering from cancer, were to be tempted with anything they fancied. Even in those days of stringency, this included poultry and salmon. Then I saw the three hospital blocks of dying cancer patients. They were nearly all bedridden. Most appeared very old and many seemed deranged by their pain and bad experiences in life. It is hard to realise how little medical knowledge was then available to help. They were disoriented, abandoned and lonely. Some curled up painfully, crying and clutching a handkerchief full of half-crowns. Their pension was paid to the hospital for their keep. They were mostly women over sixty without insurance cover, I believe. A half-crown was given to them each week as pocket money, useless with nothing to buy. We were to start a scheme of buying trayfuls of little things for sale. It was worth trying but it was unlikely to be a success. Another block of wards was the maternity department of three hundred beds. It was sparse but modern in treatment. They were given self-administering gas, known to the public as 'Twilight Sleep'. I was very surprised that most of the mothers were feeling well a few hours after their babies had arrived. I believe Robin Watson was in charge. I met him as a famous obstetrician years later.

It was in Walton that I met Gertie again. She had been on our students' holiday twice by a ruse. Now she suffered from multiple sclerosis. She was in a wheelchair and could just raise herself a few inches to hug me, chattering and full of hope. I missed an opportunity and did nothing to help her before I went to my next posting in Birkenhead.

Here I met an almoner who informed me that she had had a rotten time as a student, adding mirthlessly, 'and I'll see you have one.' I did. She had a narrow cubby hole as an office, demonstrating the medical contempt for social work. Behind her desk I was given a card table which collapsed every time I stood up in the narrow space. Even this did not dissuade her from demanding that I stand up each time she appeared. She was soon seething with frustration at the mix-up of forms on the floor.

These hospitals had not prepared me for the out-patient department of the Royal Free Hospital where I landed next. The mosaic floor camouflaged small cash dropped when we were assessing patients and taking payments. We groped around for tiny threepenny bits. They said I wasted time. A fellow student was perceptive and knowing I had had a bad report, advised me to make more noise, to clatter about in high heels and bang the filing cabinet drawers. I was an astounding success thereafter.

In a few weeks I was in Daniel's den although there was only one lion. Transferred to the in-patient almoner I found a taskmaster reared on the African Veldt but frustrated without whip and saddle. She revelled in toughness. It was January. The oval, high-ceilinged office was a tiled, one-time operating theatre. The several huge windows were also high and draughty; a half partition kept the typist in her place. There was no heat anywhere. It was odd that the typist's frequent tears did not freeze on her cheeks.

Again I sat at a card table. On the first morning I was handed nine files prepared by the out-patient almoners for patients who would be admitted in due course. The almoner told me to listen when she told me what to do in each case before we went to the wards. She exploded with scorn as she saw my hand creep to a pencil. Before I could note anything down, she gave me about a dozen orders for telephone enquiries regarding hernia belts and crutches and so on, and as I tried to be coherent, polite but firm with the several suppliers, asked me – telephoning – further questions. 'Yes, on the right hand... No, she has three... thank you... children. Will you deliver tomorrow? Yes, her mother will help...' It cured my poor memory. The scuttle across an open courtyard to the wards and back through driving sleet to the icy room did not cure my cold. I had to remain in my green cotton overall, soaked as it was. My nose flowed each time I bent my head to the letters I was now allowed to write. More scorn should have withered me to warmth. On the seventh attempt at a simple note I passed the first effort back to the autocrat. She praised it and asked me why I hadn't done it before. By the second day I had decided to challenge the bullying and we got on better. After three months my successor at the card table fainted at the pressure and I had to endure three more months there as each department depended on student labour.

Finally, I left for St Mary's, Paddington. The gentle head almoner took me into her in-patient department. She enquired carefully about my dreams and possible worries. My replies were short and reassuring. She then told me that I had been passed to her as my last posting had declared me mentally unstable. It was a pot calling the kettle black! Years later a young almoner, who had experienced the same thing, chuckled as she described her pleasure when, as an air raid warden during the Blitz, she had recognised our lady dragon covered in dust and applied iodine to small cuts made by flying debris. Her temporary power over the famous bully was unforeseen reward for bravery in air raids.

As I toured St Mary's wards with Miss Wetherall, I suddenly spotted an elderly patient for whom I had recently arranged convalescence while in the Royal Free. I went to her bed to enquire after her progress, realising also that this was someone working the system; warm hospitals in the winter and hop picking in the summer. The ward sister was puzzled next day when the lady announced she had had a telegram calling her to a sick relative.

Suddenly, Miss Wetherall became ill. She told me I would be in charge of her office but that all it meant was opening the post and distributing it to the other almoners. One day I was particularly pleased with myself. A tired clergyman came in to offer his church's Harvest Festival. I agreed he should bring it on the Monday. I saw it lying along the corridor – limp flowers, wisps of straw, bruised fruit and bleeding beetroot. Miss Wetherall returned that morning also. She was met by a furious matron and there must have been loss of face over the useless and order-defying compost heap. I was told firmly that food had to be fresh for patients though the nurses, it seemed, never found themselves in so privileged a position.

I transferred to out-patients determined to make good. It was possibly the busiest OPD in the whole service, and run by an almoner whom one respected. There were several *honaries* (consultants). We prepared each patient's form before he was examined by the honary. We were warned it meant two-and-a-half-minute interviews! As the patient came tentatively through the door of our long horsebox, an encouraging smile and a beckoning hand mobilised him as one said, 'Name? Christian name? Married? Wife's name? Please sit down. Any children? Ah. Yes. Address? Employment? Wage? Rent? Other 'outgoings'? And then, 'What's been troubling you? Oh, gastric trouble... as a driver you don't get regular meals. You will see the doctor and then you will be told to go to X-ray. Please follow the yellow light and if you have to go to the pharmacy, follow the red light afterwards. Thank you. Goodbye. Next please.' At the end of the session we had to secure the medical notes and find out whether our diagnosis of symptoms had been correct! Into all this pressure, which went on for two or more hours, there sailed a Welshman, undaunted by the rapid business of his reception. He was Dickensianly splendid in a frock coat, flowered waistcoat and even a square bowler – immediately removed. His kind face was surrounded with fluffy white sideboards and his eyes were blue and quizzical. He asked *my* name! We were both Joneses and indeed we were both Welsh. He was used to preaching in Hyde Park 'on a soapbox' and he could sing, which he did!

The lovely tune, *Aberystwyth*, (composed for my great-grandfather's Welsh translation of Wesley's fine hymn, *Jesus, lover of my soul*) rose and wafted over the top of my partition to the surgeon interviewing next door. My consternation was writ large and at last Mr Jones sat down, more subdued. Hoping to please me, he answered my questions, but inaccurately. I had diagnosed a hernia and told him to return. When he did, I went over his circumstances and assessed him to pay sixpence a week from his pension. A handshake and directions to the surgical belt supplier about finished my morning. Next day a frail but determined elderly lady came in. Her fashion was a little later than that of Dickens. Her skirt reached the ground and she had a neat jacket with 'leg-of-mutton' sleeves. She even had a veil on her small hat. She had found me from amongst the other students and staff and came to the point. She said I had been heartless charging her husband, Mr Jones, sixpence a week. He could not possibly pay it. I fished out the form and pointed out that their rent was half a crown only and they had two pensions. Did they spend a lot on heat? She smiled a little. 'I cannot light a fire. The room is full of bits of manuscript as he tries to write music. But, you see, we do not draw pensions. My husband will not accept charity. I go out to a Jewish household on their Sabbath when they need a goy to light the fire and do some housework. They pay me five shillings. With this we have a good Sunday meal for two and sixpence each and otherwise we have tea and bread and butter all week. I have a gas ring. My daughter in Yorkshire sends me the rent, tea and butter and, sometimes, a little extra money, each week. We just haven't sixpence for the hernia belt.' I thought how long she had loyally put up with poverty and how many years she had kept those clothes brushed and ready for such appearances. We had a glimmer of hope as we parted. I sent for him when he came next week for a fitting. I looked sad and serious and told him he had got me into hot water. I lied. I told him I had checked with the Post Office and they had said I had been wrong in my report on his pension, and now they would tell the hospital and I would be finished as a student. He was upset. He had been too proud to own up to poverty. I told him he might save me if he went to draw their joint pensions immediately and then I could say I had been right. On his last visit he appeared again with his wife on his arm. Could he introduce her? She had said she would like to meet me. Our handshake was particularly cordial.

My last posting was to be the VD department. Miss Copewell was pleasantly efficient, shored up for exhausting stretches of work by a jar of barley sugar sticks. The specialist had a bell and for a while I thought it meant 'next patient'! Although we started interviewing new patients before he arrived, the bell was so frequent that there was not even the two and a half minutes allowed for each enquiry in out-patients. He was seeing patients already known. The treatment for syphilis was longer than for gonorrhoea and lasted for twelve weeks. In either case if not completed, the horrors of locomotor ataxia or general paralysis of the insane were the final stages. I slogged hard but it was a quest bedevilled with handicaps, the worst being that no patient could be told what was wrong. Some were children, some quiet, dignified women. None could realise the urgency for treatment for 'debility' as we called it. Miss Copewell was pleased I did not shrink from the patients but three months later her conventional upbringing prompted her to unease that I was not showing any sign of condemnation at all. We made home visits in the afternoons when I was told to dress so that I would not be noticed arriving to beg some patient to resume visits. I was chuffed to bits when a cheerful cockney said, 'If you're a friend of the family I'll nip round and open the window for you. They will never open the door.' I made no disclaimer. The same day I felt an eyesore in Belgravia and was delighted when no one answered that bell. It was at this time that I was frightened by a widespread rash after eating fish. Mrs Mason, the manageress of our flatlets, was a sensible strong support, rightly enquiring after my diet!

Moorfields Eye hospital was my next training ground. It was well planned. The young almoner was friendly and taught me very efficiently. We were in a new wing with a modern restaurant available to staff and patients. There was enough money from the societies for the blind so we could afford to give proper help and even, on a hot day, produce a cool drink for a child. Professional dilemmas occurred; one was the knowledge that a very successful conman had completely changed his appearance while having his eyes straightened. One week great excitement prevailed. One or two doctors shared a secret with us. A refugee, I thought Hungarian, had arrived with a new invention. He had brought contact lenses. The doctors became involved and soon trays of lenses to cover part of the eyeball appeared. I think fitting was painful and specks of dust under the glass, torture.

Before I went to Northampton I had a brief spell as an almoner, paid, in a Staffordshire hospital. The placement was organised from London. It was a disaster. We three junior almoners lived in the YMCA. There were no men there. Indeed, there had been no one until they let women apply, all probably hoping that eligible men would liven up the place. My bedroom was called the Crypt, accurately. I was told to send for a dress for a dance the next day. I phoned home; the dress arrived next morning, as was then the postal custom. At the dance, I was not introduced to anyone; introductions were necessary then. So I sat by myself, watching the others. I tried to find a phone but the hospital in the dark was a mystery as yet unexplored even in daylight. An honary's kindly wife roped me into her supper group. I was numbed by my colleagues' discourtesy.

At work I was given a shy new secretary. We could get no help with any lists of agencies and medical staff. They must have jeered at both of us but we pulled together and she turned rapidly into an efficient clerk. I had refused to gang up on the head almoner, so they ganged up on me and reported me for holding up the work. This was easily refuted. I think this was the very hospital where they were so short-staffed that I found an interviewee dead while a tiny nurse struggled with a deranged man. As almoners we had no privacy and no right to eat in the canteen. The hostel supplied us with a small packet of brown bread and, I think, an apple. One cold day we bought a tin of soup which a nurse warmed in a steriliser for us. We had to eat our snacks standing outside the female toilet area in the white-tiled corridor. I gave my notice in. I was then told by the head almoner that she would block any move I made to get another post. She wrote in wrath to London but they advised her to let me go!

Next, I played golf and got bored until I went to Northampton as a locum. It was amazing. Mr Barratt, a wealthy shoe manufacturer, had endowed a new hospital for special maternity cases. The consultant gynaecologist was Robin Watson, previously in charge of the three hundred bed maternity unit in Walton Hospital, Liverpool. The Welsh sister-in-charge there now supported Mr

Watson in the Barratt Home. She understood how to run a caring staff and he needed this. Watson was sure that Nature did not intend women to be barren; it was possible to achieve a live birth, if not by the first confinement, then by the second. I was told he had been there for two years and had never lost a mother, nor I believe had he failed in his ambition of producing a baby by the second confinement, usually succeeding at the first attempt. The Barratt Home, as it was called, was attached to the General Hospital physically, but its administration was different. Only residents in the counties of Bedford, Buckinghamshire and Northants were able to benefit from its services. This would be confirmed to me at a later date, in UNRRA, when a colleague said that her relative married into the Royal Family, purchased the necessary residence and in due course became a happy mother. In addition to childless wives, women over forty years old, having their first baby, were admitted. Younger mothers were not considered at risk unless there was a specific problem.

Charlotte, the head almoner, took a risk when she went on leave and left me in charge. Mr Watson was a workaholic. He was totally absorbed in his crusade to bring fulfilment to the barren. He exhausted himself and would stumble out of the operating theatre and, blind from the theatre lights, weave his way to his office in the corridor. Having tried to waylay him with urgent forms, I would slip away until the morrow. We ended up in confessing that we each had nightmares about the other and about the intrusive paperwork.

The only patient I did not interview was Mr Barratt, the benefactor. No! he was not pregnant, but he considered his heart condition should be treated in his Home. He trundled about in a dressing gown and a wheelchair, creating consternation among the heavily pregnant and unwieldy women. All was forgiven; they had reason to be grateful to him.

I enjoyed being part of this very special unit. When Charlotte came back, she asked me to stay on as the in-patient almoner. I accepted happily. I had decided to take a post for a year, to prove I was capable and then to try other social work. I was dissatisfied with almoning as there was no time to pay home visits. One saw patients, usually clean and in their Sunday best, perhaps giving a wrong impression of their difficult lives. Every patient was seen. I was glad of my training in the out-patient department of St Mary's, Paddington. A mere almoner, guessing the likely outcome of consultations, sounds horrific! It had its uses. For instance, travellers snacking irregularly could discuss healthier eating with packed lunches; mothers, anxious about their families, had delayed seeing a doctor and needed advice to encourage them to continue their treat-ment if admission was necessary. Husbands and children had medical provision at work and school but women had no funding. They often came to hospital weakened by long-endured pain and afraid of the cost or by anxiety that they were suffering from cancer, much more terrifying then even than it is now. Arrangements for the family while they were in hospital needed careful discussion and convales-cence was, to them, unthinkable, with problems of dwindling money or a selfish husband's reactions sapping their courage more than the knife. The cancer funds gave meagre financial support. There was, however, a splendid network of voluntary insurance societies, helping with surgical appliances, diets and convalescence. Most men paid into these but the wives needed other help which we had to find. We provided treatment through the innumerable charities in Britain, listed in an efficient handbook. Once I had to arrange two funerals during one weekend. There was neither kin nor cash, but a village arranged a whist drive to avoid a pauper's funeral for one; I found a charity for the other.

Sometimes I interviewed a patient coming in with severe head pains. I followed the patient's progress daily with the sister, on my ward rounds. Meanwhile I had informed Queen's Square Hospital, London, that we might require a bed for a patient with a brain tumour. Recovery was rare but the magnificent work in the special hospital offered the only chance of help. When the diagnosis was reached, the young houseman, acting on the surgeon's instructions, would come pounding down to my office to beg me to put the critically ill patient on the London waiting list. I was never blamed for having pre-booked a bed on my own amateur hunch. Once a houseman charged in from the casualty department, stuttering, 'Can you see a mother for me? I was supposed to take a boy's tonsils out and I've done a circumcision instead!' In came a pleasant woman. I explained as well as I could that the young doctor had performed an operation which had not been requested. She said happily that she had hoped to find we could do it next. The houseman and the hospital were in luck that day.

I interviewed all the patients to be admitted after their consultation and again on their actual admission. I kept a small folder on each and jotted down a description or a sketch as an aide-mémoire. One lively young woman of about thirty, with dark curly hair, came to tell me she was to be admitted for the removal of her appendix. A relative would look after the children, there were no problems. About three months later I interviewed a grey-haired woman, looking old and tired. Her hands were misshapen with swollen joints. She gave the same name as the dark girl and insisted I knew her. I did not. I fished out the file and asked her Christian name; it was the same but the address was different. She said she had moved since her first appointment. I said, looking at her hands, 'Is your new house damp?' She looked puzzled and said, 'No-o.' I persisted and asked if her clothes were damp or even mouldy. She replied they were quite dry as they hung them away from the walls but their best shoes were mouldy sometimes. She agreed that the walls were cold and moist but was, at first, puzzled when I said the house must be damp. Then she understood and said, 'There's a stream in the living room.'

'How can that happen?'

'Well, it comes in through a hole in the wall and goes out through the door.'

I said, 'The floor must be of earth, not tiled?'

'Yes.'

She agreed they were tenants and I did not ask who the landlord was but I told her I would report it to the Sanitary Authority. A few days later, the hospital administrator was demanding apologies. The landlord was a benefactor of the hospital! The inspector probably found other poor tenancies on his estates. I did not kowtow; I was soon to leave. Possibly Charlotte had a difficult time but the war disrupted everything. Nothing could have recompensed the woman for her loss of youth and good health. The husband might have worked on the estate and as a tenant of a 'tied house' with no choice of where to live. No one would have thought of compensation.

I met strange people. A magician cum tea-taster was outshone by a delightful nurse, caring for all the bargees who docked in the large basin nearby. Her clinic was free, as were her services; her father paid the costs. The bargees adored her and she fought well for their health. She dressed superbly with a navy silk nurse's veil and a scarlet-lined, navy cloak which she swept out for a wonderful curtsy, good-naturedly mocking my title of 'lady almoner' when she paid her welcome visits. A man brought in his friend in the late and incurable stages of cancer. I felt their strong, deep grief and realised that this was, in effect, a homosexual marriage. I had no comfort to offer to them or others.

On Wednesdays, we admitted many children for 'Ts and As'. They would stay after the removal of tonsils and/or adenoids. One day a bright, pretty tam-o'-shanter cruised around, level with the top of my desk. The little girl was also bright and pretty and I enjoyed the chit-chat before she went in good spirits to the ward. I had no words, I was too numb to help the mother next day. The little girl had died in her sleep, swallowing blood that had not clotted, so that no one had seen the young life seep away. It was then I asked the out-patient almoner, Joyce, what she said to the bereaved. They came from her room with peace on their faces. She was embarrassed, unable to answer me. She believed my Nonconformity prevented my understanding. I knew I was inadequate and wondered if religion would enlighten me also.

Joyce had kindly, but unwisely, introduced me to her lodgings. Our tall, spare landlady appeared dottily hatted in the early morning chill; sometimes with a peaked gnome's cap, sometimes with a Victorian confection of violet velvet and pansies on her head. On my first lonely day in August, my gift of ice cream started a battle in generosity, capped a year later with a final gift from her of an orange spotted cover for my gas mask case, which one carried everywhere! She was a superb cook and we dined on pheasant, turbot, delicate pastry and many exotic dishes looking all the more exotic when our fellow lodger, a school inspector who demanded to be served first, sent the dishes out with oysters shivering, plucked from their warm sauce blanket, and the Charlotte Russe quivering from the slashes of the spoon. Joyce and I dined together and then each night returned to the hospital to tackle the writing-up. This was the final check on old case papers to ensure all had been done and to note it down. Our only outings were to the local repertory theatre when they had a rare new production and to a Left Book Club meeting, each month, where we found the discussion as dull as the young medics found us. My half day was only Friday afternoon when I had my hair shampooed for five shillings and bought a coffee and cake for one and six. My one hundred and twenty pounds per annum was almost consumed by two pounds per week for my good lodgings. The fare home had to be guarded. The cost of a crêpe de Chine tennis frock at three pounds (when I could not find my size in cotton) scotched my purchases of lingerie. Hospital staff still expected us to patronise every raffle. We nearly needed one for ourselves. My weekly coffee drew my attention to the fact that a coffee and sandwich would be covered every day by the paper cost of our hospital lunch which was part of our remuneration. This lunch comprised disgusting cod and mashed potato. I went off on my own to interview the hospital administrator and suggested I should be given the cash and buy my own lunch. Though young, his face went purple. I went out quickly and fell over a posse of housemen who had heard of my enterprise and were also going to ask for their money if the keyhole revealed that I had won. We were, nevertheless, promoted from the cleaners' dinner to the housemen's and thereafter had salads with radishes cut into water lily shapes!

While I was a locum, I had gone alone to a cinema one afternoon. As I entered, the newsreel showed Chamberlain alighting from a plane, wagging a little piece of paper and saying it promised 'Peace in our time'. I had shouted 'Boo!' before I could think and then had the sense to crouch in the dark by the entrance until the ensuing hubbub had died down. The imminence of war filled our thoughts. When I went home for leave in May, I heard of a local post and decided it was my opportunity to look after my parents in the event of war. The town clerk was rudely indifferent when I called to see him, a revenge for my teasing when my parents entertained him. When, however, I said I needed an interview soon so that I could give three months' notice to my employers to find a replacement, he decided I had a possible value. The post was the town's first housing officer. Almost immediately I was called to an interview.

I climbed the decrepit, dusty stairs of the Wrexham Guildhall, a rambling building which had been a grammar school. The council chamber was housed in a one-time art school over the fire station. I was put in a tiny ante-room with about eight middle-aged women in it. There was a hiss of held-in breath as I seated myself. I smiled around and they started on their questions, gabbled in haste. Had I lost a leg or an arm? Was I a widow? I said 'No' to the last and showed off my sturdy limbs for their benefit. There was relieved muttering amongst them. I was called in to the council. The chairman asked me to outline my qualifications. I made it clear that I was not an Octavia Hill-trained housing manager and they made it clear that that was what they were trying to avoid as they believed such a one would demand assistants! To their relief I said my degree was irrelevant though my social work training was not. I was then allowed to ask what my duties were. They didn't know; the chairman answered adroitly that anyone they appointed would know without being told. Was I satisfied? Yes! I was whipped out for a medical. I asked the doctor, whom I knew, why the women in the ante-room were worried about my legs and arms. 'Oh', he said, 'they are applying for a job as lavatory attendant and it will go to the most "deserving" case.' I found later that pity for the underdog often influenced the appointment. Fortunately for me, I was the sole applicant for the new experiment of employing a housing manager for the town estates. I got the post and returned to Northampton to inform Charlotte that

I would be leaving on the 7th September. It would be the first week of the war.

The last months were busy. Patients were being called up quickly for operations and wards were overcrowded. One very excellent and dependable ward sister was shaking with distress. She needed to talk. For days and nights she had tried to run a big ward, overfull with very ill patients, one of whom, herself seriously ill, railed in a high pitch through all the hours. No one could sleep. Patients were being weakened instead of recovering. The sister had increased the already prescribed dose. She had done her best for her ward, but she had also hurried the last hours of a mentally ill patient in her care. She was surprised and horrified at herself but believed she had taken the only course in the interests of all.

Soon we were in a period when I decided to warn relatives that war was imminent and in that event they would be asked to take their relatives home and the hospital would be cleared for war casualties. Within two weeks this was official. The authorities decreed the radium must be safeguarded and all treatment on cancer patients stopped. War was declared on Sunday, 2nd September, 1939 and for the two preceding nights I was on duty, following the irrational decisions of the administrator who was dishing out gold stars to be put on the medical cards of those too ill to move, and instructing me to get all the rest – all but a small minority – home, whatever their circumstances. The Sunday work was hard. My sensible, loyal clerk had come in to see what she could do. Together we slogged away at the list, interviewing relatives, already alerted to the patients' discharge. A very good houseman made lists of the serious cases being discharged and began an endless succession of home visits to ensure they had medical supplies and to assist their GPs in the follow-up. A sort of hysteria overtook too many of the staff. The company from the repertory theatre brought in their enthusiasm and left their sense behind. In no time, the new office wing had tar dripping down the walls from blacked out windows. The wards were left to move their patients into the busy ambulances.

Next day I awoke at daylight to see a fleet of buses, occupied by pregnant mothers from some London hospitals. An hour later the first air raid alarm went off. We huddled under the stairs with the school inspector until the 'All Clear'. I left for home on the 7th September.

Part Five

The Tide of War Engulfs the Past in New Work on Housing Estates and Youth Clubs

In the hubbub of the second week of the war, I started work as the first housing officer on the Wrexham housing estates, of which there were five: two big, two small and two sample-size. There was no office room for me in the Guildhall; I was given a flat in the best estate on the outskirts. The council had assumed that I would be glad to live there, but I needed both rooms, one as a waiting room and one for an office. That winter an elderly woman, less than four feet tall, tramped every Wednesday night, sometimes through deep snow, to make sure I still had her name on the housing list. She walked about three miles each way, as the office was on the edge of the town. She brought me bribes, at sixpence each from Woolworth's, although I urged her to buy for her home instead.

Grace was aware that sixteen flatlets for single persons were being built. My first duty was to assess the four hundred names on the housing list to choose tenants for the flatlets and for the two dozen ground or first-floor flats being built on the same road; it was the only housing project of the war years. I enjoyed this. Contrary to past practice, I started with those longest on the list and who might be suitable for flat life. I interviewed them and successfully paired them off as likely good neighbours. Then one flat became my new office. It was central, near the houses given to tenants rehoused from a sweeping slum clearance project. The sixteen flatlets were an experiment. There were two blocks, each with four flats at ground level and on the first floor. Every flat had a big bedsit, a WC, a sink for toilet or kitchen use and a tiny pantry. There was an open fire with an oven on one side and a small oven above. The fires were supposed to heat their back boilers, and pipes were laid to produce bath water in the one bathroom which served each set of four flats on the floor. Only men could design such a source of inevitable controversy. I was, in the end, inclined to agree that the flat nearest the bathroom did all the heating. Open battle could have resulted but I had been prevailed upon by the rating officer, a gentle, wise man, to house Baldwin as sole man amongst the female flock. My fears were assuaged. Half Baldwin's face had been shattered in the previous war and he was no longer handsome or young. He was soon each woman's knight errant; they adored him. He was fed by good cooks, and his clothes were fought over for the honour of doing the repairs. He was the answer to all bickering. But New Year arrived. He had promised everyone, including little Grace, that he would bring good luck to each with a piece of coal for first-footing. But everyone also expected to be the first he visited. He ran like a trembling, hunted hare to my office. I subdued the flashing eyes and shrill denunciations as the waiting room filled with angry ladies. Sadly, they were forever disenchanted with poor, kind Baldwin.

My appointment had been governed by the fact that, in attracting grants for slum clearance, the authority had to appoint a housing manager. They had questioned other councils who said that professionals trained by the Octavia Hill school were too expensive. Octavia Hill, at the beginning of the century, had achieved her mission for social workers in the slums, by training them to collect rents and bad debts in the hope that there would be time for social work as well. I was very lucky. The council would not disturb the rating officer and his rent collectors, so I was free to promote social work in any way I chose, providing it cost next to nothing. One chore remained; I was responsible for the welfare of all those from the former back courts and dilapidated terraces who had been rehoused and so attracted rebates on their rents. These were usually the families with problems. Soon I knew them all. Many were quiet couples, grateful for peace and pensions. But the big, young families became my chief concern although the town clerk believed that, by magic, I also knew every family on all the estates. It is now much, much larger but it was then quite enough work for one social worker.

Before the year was out, there were two of us. Do not fret for the council; it cost nothing. She was a volunteer. By November, I was falling over children, milling about in the blackout. Home was theirs until father came back from work in mines, steelworks or the leatherworks. Out went the noisy clutter of children to fend for themselves and get into mischief.

At the end of our road was a very majestic tithe barn, built in the late seventeenth century. It had curly, stone-edged gables and solid brick buttresses and it rode high and proud on the top of the rise. The local school held nursery classes here and I got permission to use it at night. I had a few friends with enthusiasm and like me, with no knowledge. So we went ahead and invited in the girls aged ten to thirteen on a Monday night. We would each teach what we knew and liked best. We launched the club on a tide of PT, sewing, music, drama, French and flowers. No class lasted more than forty minutes, the endurance span for one subject; it was successful, when we could be heard! The doors had been protected by steel sheets and the windows by heavy gratings; this gave good opportunities for efforts in percussion from the outside. I faced the shindy. These were hoarse little boys, red in the face from shouting. It turned out to be anger that the girls had something they did not have. Okay: we would try. But there was already a budding rumpus among the teenagers to get separate girls' and boys' evenings. Two capable and friendly conscientious objectors and their wives came to the office. They said they wanted to put all they could into the war effort and they thought I needed more help than anyone else in town. Sydney and Rex soon had the junior boys happy and controlled on two nights a week. Connie came to my personal rescue; she was a good typist and better, recognised need and was sensible on remedies. Her happy companionship in the office was a literal Godsend.

The autumn of 1939 was the period of the phoney war. After my first air raid warning in Northampton, I didn't hear another for a long time. We waited with unease and did our ramshackle best. Brown paper tape was stuck across the windows to prevent flying glass. Our blackout curtains went up and the new air raid wardens grew important. We practised in small local groups, something to do with buckets and a stirrup pump. 'Water on! Water off!' was barely comprehensible at the end of a tiring day. I was never on night duty, but others trudged around warning that light showed through cracks. Father, in his seventies, joined the ARP – the air raid precautions team. He felt he was useful in another bit of Dad's Army. The air force was being efficient, close by. They had fixed lights in little grots in the lovely Eglwyseg rocks above Llangollen and around them. It had to look like a badly blacked-out dock area; the German air force bombed the Welsh moors with gusto for three days, or perhaps four. The heather roots caught fire and glowed enticingly. Thick, acrid, black smoke rolled heavily down the hills from eight or ten miles away and choked the town. We cowered as the planes groaned with their heavy loads overhead. We had no defences but had been told to get into cellars, under stairways or just by the strongest bit of the house, the chimney. People were digging semi-underground shelters in their gardens and risked chills rather than death by occupying them at night. A very few bombs dropped near houses but the ensuing accidents were rumoured to be caused by twit-brained heroes kicking the bomb to show what they thought of Hitler. We were lucky and Liverpool had a respite. The Germans, I believe, found the docks again in May. We were bitterly ashamed to listen to the bombers grinding heavily through the dark, over our heads, sometimes causing conflagrations which lit the distant sky, and then to hear them return, lighter. Our only danger, while Liverpool burned, was the odd bomb to be jettisoned before the return run to German bases. Our relief, as each night passed, had been paid for elsewhere by many people.

Liverpool was 'defended' by 'blimp' balloons, trailing long tethers to trap aircraft. The anti-aircraft guns were far too few. It was then that the evacuees arrived from Liverpool. My father was early in the queue, as we thought two teenage boys would be the easiest to manage. They were cheerful. Peter, the smaller, older one was full of the importance of having a Lord as his grammar school headmaster. He interviewed the gardener as to his satisfaction, or otherwise, with his wages and conditions of service, but got short shrift from the young cook and the housemaid. (The heavy industry of the region resulted in a surplus of female labour so that many intelligent girls opted for housework. It could be a fair preparation for marriage.) Apart from the plentiful fruit being stuffed down the sofas by the human squirrels, we got on well. On request I helped with homework. They shared the local grammar school with the local boys on a half-day basis and the Liverpool girls' school shared with the Wrexham girls.

The Women's Voluntary Service, not yet acknowledged by royalty, took on the initial distribution of evacuees, but the volatile nature of the problem and of the carers brought trouble and I was the obvious solution. Then Connie showed her splendid quality as a social worker. She was now paid a government grant as a semi-salaried official caring for evacuees. She also kept to her full working week on a voluntary basis.

Evacuation taught the community that there was a very large, inarticulate, urban population not reached by any fair distribution of housing, good schools, clinics or work. However, the men were being called up rapidly, and before the new prosperity from jobs in armament factories could bring them a more sustainable life. Homes in town or country all suffered. The soldier's wife drew thirty shillings for herself and for rent, heat and light. She was given five shillings to feed the first child, three shillings for the second and if they had been rash enough to have more children, one shilling each for the rest. That was for food, clothing and, worst, shoes. Many could not afford to buy their rations even when eggs were reduced to one per month, per person; talking of which, I once tried to comfort my office cleaner. She was wet-eyed. Not knowing what tragedy the war had brought her, I enquired carefully. She said that she had broken the three eggs her family was entitled to each month. I asked if they were still on her shelf, which I knew would be spotless. They were; I suggested she scrambled them. She went white with anger. 'I may be poor but I can assure you I have never scrambled an egg in my life.' I told her of the scrambled eggs with boiled rice in school and their price in restaurants. I think she readjusted.

It was indeed time to start a women's group. We had plenty of good second-hand clothing coming from America, especially golfers' plus fours which must have gone out of fashion. My mother, of course, helped. We had a 'Make and Mend' class. The plus fours made hard-wearing, skirts and children's trousers, and dresses were easy. The poorest families were soon sure they were welcome. Then my good cleaner made me think. She had insisted on telling me of an employer with *very* dirty habits. 'She has an old saucepan full of old bones and even puts eggshells in it.' So I talked about stock pots and the addition of stock to vegetables for good nourishing meals. I thought that perhaps extra flavour would be necessary. I advised her to get small tuppeny packets of soup powder. Two weeks later she was bubbling with triumph. 'I've done what you said, and I've added a packet of chicken, one of tomato, one of celery, and a packet of mulligatawny. Will that do for me and the two girls?' At that I went to the ministry of food office and suggested they gave a demonstration to the club. I warned them to be simple and asked for a special lesson on soups and stews. They came up with their equipment and showed us how to produce... lettuce soup! Then we went on to vegetable pie with breadcrumbs browning on top, and they capped the meal with the delicate feat of inside-out rhubarb dumpling. The acrobatics involved cooking the stodge of suet in a basin lined thinly with short lengths of rhubarb and, with considerable skill, decanting the white blob with the stringy fruit still clinging to the exterior. All was tasted and duly applauded, after my little speech of thanks. As they went out, the women rushed at me in one swoop, like a lynching party. I faced them bravely. 'How do you make breadcrumbs for the pie?'

By now our working group for the girls' club was really enthusiastic. My mother, always a second backbone to me, prepared hot snacks each clubnight and we trooped in to laugh and to plan. More joined us. There were no distracting amusements and we enjoyed our night out. They agreed to open a club for the over-thirteens, and two or three ran an extra night for drama which occasionally entertained the parents. The senior boys by now trusted me enough to wait with a little patience. I launched a senior boys' club on two nights per week; I was foolhardy. We started off with ten volunteers, enough for good cover. Within a fortnight they had all been called up. I was alone with forty young colliers. I held endless committee meetings to discuss football fixtures! As soon as I stopped they were climbing high in the lovely old beams, hurling darts at those below. I managed to get some equipment and occasionally a helper with an interest in boxing. Then I started football matches. The visiting team changed in my office, down the road, and our boys, now equipped with red shirts, in the little cloakroom in the barn. The first time, I prepared a tea. We could get bread and margarine, and my mother made a tasty paste from cod roes. Also, there were some sticky buns. Our boys changed first and wanted to scoff the tea before the guest team came up. Our barn team was furious as the others were older and the captain was married. We lost and they choked when I insisted on 'Hurrahs'. This tea was a great lesson. Our poverty was obvious and the visiting captain made a speech wishing us well, and then produced three pounds for club funds. That was untold wealth and the goodbye cheers were genuine now. After that, sportsmanship was under-stood except that in time we won all the matches. Superior club leaders reproached me for hiding a Blackburn Rovers forward in our team. I called the club together and we all enjoyed a laugh. There was this short, fair-haired 'boy' – 'and he's married, Miss, with three children' – playing with the team. I appointed the good-tempered Jim as my first steady male youth worker; unsalaried, of course. We had no grants or sponsors, so the whole club had to be responsible for its upkeep. A night in semi-darkness, until the next night's takings could buy a bulb, ensured that the whole group took care of our equipment. When a small bully tried to blackmail me by 'telling the council so that you'll lose your job', I closed the club for three weeks until they understood that it was all unpaid work in free time. It was also resented by some councillors, who thought I was wasting my time. They also had to understand that it was my time and not theirs!

Gradually, youth clubs became important. A county officer was appointed, and the Barn made an application for equipment. A would-be Apollo arrived, looked at the young colliers, dubbed them 'rednecks' and refused to help. We did not qualify; our classes did not go into boredom time – the full hour. So my lack of male help prompted me to apply for a paid leader. Sadly, he was appointed to two youth clubs. He was much happier at the old, established club in the town centre and found our rough and tumble too demanding. *And* he persuaded one or two good players to join the other club. Before his advent, a part-time leader and his wife had undertaken a weekly summer camp on the hills. Conditions must have been difficult for those adults but they were much appreciated by the older boys. When I first opened the club, the senior boys' section was left without any men to help. A strong young man appeared and I welcomed him hopefully. 'Good night, Miss,' a boy said.

'You've only just come! Where are you going?'

'Good night, Miss. Early shift, Miss.' And the refrain went on until the twenty-five boys had all gone. I was very disappointed and bewildered. The man said, 'It's my fault. I'm a detective in the police force and I know every one of your lads for some offence or other.' They were all there again, next time. Eighteen months later, the first probation officer for the courts was appointed. Again, I hoped for help and invited him in on the grounds that all the boys would be on his books. He had never heard of any of them. In fact, those who came did not get into trouble. Two evenings a week and a football match absorbed their spare time and energy. This was also the effect on the juniors.

Directors of Education soon decreed big was beautiful. Junior clubs were closed ruthlessly, small local clubs discouraged. The opportunity to win achievement by moving from junior to senior club and then perhaps to the facilities of a big centre was lost. Before long, the clamour of the younger group for recognition led to senior clubs opening their doors to juniors. With that, affronted older members left. To survive, the clubs amalgamated boys and girls and later I became involved in these.

Clubs were a side issue. My daily work began with visitors to the office at 9 a.m. and my bike brought me in hailing distance of others' houses as I passed. I called at one to suggest the husband sought work, which was now easily obtained. He could then save up six pounds to buy his wife a set of dentures, women not being covered by any medical schemes. He seized the opportunity to quote the scriptures. 'Consider the lilies of the field, how they grow; they toil not neither—' Inspired, another Biblical quotation flashed and I interrupted with 'Go to the ant, thou sluggard; follow her ways and be wise!' He was nonplussed and showed me respect thereafter. Whether or not his wife got her dentures, I do not remember.

The unreasoning fears of the war surfaced when a frail woman, whom I had sent away for convalescence after a major operation, reported danger in the tinned soup I had recommended as an easy diet for a lonely person. US relief had come in. 'I opened the tin,' she said, 'and there it was! Lots of letters of the alphabet! That's how they send messages to Hitler.' I tried to reassure her that the pasta was better down her throat than down the drain. I seem to have been 'in the soup' for much of my time. In fact, British restaurants now took over our lovely barn. There were really healthy, cheap meals for all who would come; a great help to the elderly or people with a single ration book. Even children sometimes bought the good soup although more often they were hoping for uneaten bread on the table. At home, I remember enjoying lentils, usually with curry sauce, at least twice a week. We made cake with liquid paraffin; we did not need cake, but it was one of those gestures to say we were holding our own. Everyone dug for victory... cabbages in rose-beds. Then the government commandeered all the railings, uselessly if they were cast iron, to make armaments and a mess of the parks and streets. They could have taken the unlit street lamps we bumped into in the dark. The lights had gone out all over Europe.

Our club life was finished when the lovely old barn was commandeered for war work on the kitchen front. And the United States front was also to advance into our midst. The town was won over without a single shot being fired. The US colonel invited all to a dance and to a mind-boggling buffet of chicken drumsticks by the hundred, such as had not been envisaged by us since our Bible readings of the quails raining down on the Israelites. Our teenage girls were soon beguiled but reassured me, 'We only go out with the black ones, Miss. They treat you proper, not like the white ones. And they come home with us, to see the family.' I could vouch for the pleasant manners of the six black GIs in our chapel, whom we invited to tea. They came a week later. What a tea! We had so little. They took a toasted bun each; one bite and it was left on the plate. We hurriedly passed our best sardine sandwiches and then a sponge made with liquid paraffin instead of margarine, but cheered with raspberry jam. After a sample mouthfuls all the remains rested on the edges of the plates. In despair we passed our oat biscuits around and we paused. They glanced at each other and then ate the whole lot while we filled their cups again. Two years later, I presented my partitioned meal tin at my first American mess. I went round in the queue and was given spam, pickle, sliced peaches, custard, baked beans, iced cake and a fried egg roughly in that order. While, with horror, I tried to separate the food out, the GIs were cutting the whole lot up with knife and fork and then ladling it into their mouths. No wonder our guests had been nonplussed. They were kind and came back with oranges for us, but we had not the grace to accept; we were so indoctrinated on equal rations. But that never stopped my mother shaming us by getting the odd pound of butter from Montgomeryshire, an area too rural for the transportation of farm produce which would not keep fresh. The party was a good start but soon we were trying to get help from the commanding officers when other GIs enticed our young teenagers into their camps, hiding them away for days on end. It is so easy to blame the girls. The two or three I knew of never bothered with any other method of support after that bit of education.

Wrexham had opened a citizen's advice bureau early in the war. The hard-hit soldiers' families were in danger of losing all their hire-purchase furniture. War service grants dealt rapidly with the problem. Extra help was given to pay the debts and prevent most families being stripped of beds and tables. My chairman had no difficulty in ensuring my involvement on such a matter. The bureau was organised by the former town clerk and a rota of volunteers. On Thursdays I was asked to inspect their correspondence and files and to deal with any problems. An Austrian refugee handled the Red Cross mail. As the town lacked social workers, the bureau was soon involved in complicated cases. The four desks were manned by loyal but elderly and inexperienced ladies. There was no system of useful notes from HQ; all answers were limited to common sense and what could be gleaned from telephoning local ministry offices. We were so pressed that neither I nor our hard-working inspector noticed we were never registered as a bureau.

We were helped by our fortnightly visits to Chester. We felt small and shabby. Chester had many sources of wisdom. Each session, we had a lecture on the wartime legislation affecting a particular ministry, such as food and fuel rationing, health and grants for special needs. After waiting for the Chester organisations to put their questions to the officials, we rose from the back row and shocked the rest with the complex matters we had come across. By the third meeting, Chester found our problems so interesting that we were made to speak first. The visiting officials also appeared astonished. The town clerk was told we were being inspected and he asked me to arrange a dummy run of the bureau acting as an emergency centre in the event of an air raid.

This proved a very exciting Sunday. Remembering the Liverpool Personal Service Society, I installed a central desk where two lively workers would sort out the requests and send them to the seven desks spread across the two floors. The desks were manned from the ministry HQs, using the experiment to test their own responses. Recalling St Mary's, Paddington, I decided that each person, probably unable to take much in after being bombed out, would be given a coloured card and directed to a desk with the same coloured identification notice. Then the fun began. I was able to recruit seventy Dramatic Society members to each of whom was given a name and family details together with the effect the bombing raid would have had on the home and relatives. I simply copied out details from old notebooks of families I had visited elsewhere. Everyone responded splendidly. The clients clutched several cards but were easily channelled to the less busy desks. The cases showed up many difficult questions and the ministries, despite war worries, went on trying to solve them by post, many weeks after the exercise. The town clerk was so pleased with it all that he decided that, in the event of an air raid, I should be in charge of the rest centres, in addition to the advice centre. I was to go to a weekend course immediately. I said I would resign if he sent me, as the whole thing was too absurd and I was desperately tired. I was sent and I resigned. And he still did not believe me. The council tactfully did not press me for my reasons. I could not tell them that their chief officer had lost a wager.

The actual conference was important to me despite its being the most stupid I have ever attended. The lectures were chaired or even given by a large man whose pomposity seemed to have been spawned in very shallow waters of intellect. His organisation was designed for show. We were each given four small flags, of different colours, mounted on thin bamboo sticks. These were to be waved by the small audience to attract the chairman's attention if the speaker could not be heard, or on a point of order or in order for a question to be put. What the fourth was for was not divulged; perhaps the chairman was too delicate to suggest it was for permission to leave the room. The other seat of my double school desk was vacant and I was joined by the Welsh Office representative on emergency training. We were soon quietly hysterical, trying to make good use of the flags to cheer up a frustratingly elementary homily.

Matters livened up with visits to youth clubs which had already made their contributions towards setting up emergency beds and canteens for local people made homeless through bombing. I was interested in the development of the settlement at Risca which, with the extra grants we had once been promised, had provided excellent premises for PT and drama. During our meandering surveys, I was approached by Dr Roberts of the Welsh Board of Health as to whether I would be prepared to join his inspectorial staff. I was flabbergasted to think of myself as fit for anything so grand, and refused. He pressed me for reasons and for my future plans and, because he was kindly and dependable in appearance, my mind crystallised its ambitions; I told him I wanted to be free of any work contract, so that when the war ended I could go abroad to assist with the refugee problems. He took this seriously and remembered it.

It was, for me, the goal of the prayers I had made as a five year old that the First World War could last until I was old enough to help the soldiers. The Second World War concerned civilians as much as it did troops: and there were far more of them.

In Wrexham, the various voluntary organisations were confusing each other and, incidentally, wasting resources. The charismatic miners' leader took the chair at a meeting to coordinate their functions. We were all there. In the front two curates guarded an empty chair. The meeting readily agreed to the setting up of a permanent coordinating committee and started to select representatives. The door opened and there, breathless and flushed, was my old acquaintance, the Girl Guide commandant. 'Sorry. Mr Chairman. I'm always late. But now I have my MBE, Must Be Early, you know. Must try but I've got one hundred and four committees to attend, so it's very difficult. Ah!' She had spotted the curates and went to fill the empty chair. 'Now! Where are we?' The chairman did not, as she expected, give a whole résumé of the meeting but said that we were electing representatives. Then the two curates sprang to life in defence of a great Anglican supporter. They proposed that the newly honoured MBE be on the committee. The chairman, with exquisite kindness and tact, said, 'I'm sure you do not want your name to go forward; you have just told us how overwhelmed with work you are. Any other names?' They were all chosen, and because I was a local authority social worker, the convening of the meetings fell to me. As I had found out that the technical college cookery department had to use real eggs and butter and dried fruit for teaching purposes, I was able to convene meetings there with tea and cake. No one ever missed!

During these years from September 1939 to the spring of 1943, I managed to squeeze in some self-development; I attended very elementary classes in Welsh. I went to chapel. Again I was reminded of the emptiness of my responses to grief when my very pleasant office neighbour fell dead. His wife had come in bewildered. Her husband, standing on a low stool, had reached up to change the light bulb and fallen to the floor. He had not moved again. I went in. He looked happy and at peace, but I was as inept as ever and I too wondered if he were dead. I phoned the doctors' busy surgery and asked them to come straight over as I feared my neighbour might have died. It would have taken them less than five minutes. I phoned again, twice, and three quarters of an hour later I told them I would have to telephone for the police. Then they arrived. I think an ambulance could only be called by a doctor. The man had died. Good neighbours were soon comforting the widow. I was left with the mundane business arising.

I had made no spiritual progress. I now attended chapel regularly and looked forward to the pastor's sermons, straightforward theological talks on the quality of the Godhead or the expected Christian response to the needs of the time. I recognised his function as a battering ram, the fortified gate being my own mind. I just sat and decided nothing could or would make any impact on my logical defences. I was still lofty but I was beginning to appreciate that faith was worth achieving. Time passed, probably two years... I said prayers every night, as did most non-believers when the noise of enemy planes overhead grew loud and menacing. My prayer was simple: 'Please make me want to believe in You.'

One summer Sunday, I went as usual to chapel. My neighbour whispered that the preacher was a missionary. I prepared, as I had done in my Liverpool days, to listen carefully for any denigration of the 'natives', in this case the people of Assam. I glowered at this short, plumpish man with the disarming look. In no time, I was giving him full marks for lack of condescension and for a proper respect for all persons. We came to the reading, 'What went you forth for to see? A reed broken by the wind?' I suddenly confronted myself. I had been loafing around, arrogantly waiting for a special sign to convince me that the historical Jesus was – as Peter, the rough blunderer, perceived – 'that Christ, the Son of the Living God.' I wanted reason and logic to dignify the capitulation of my intellect and my pride to the concept of the Living Son of God. I would not be responsible for the abdication of my will.

My mind was digesting the disconcerting text... Why did I think I was so special? My favourite uncle was preaching in my parents' church and I had promised that I would hear him that night. I went to him to say I felt I should return to Trinity, my chapel. He said I was right to go; he thought it was important for me. The chapel was packed as usual and to get a seat I had to inconvenience a woman who was wearing a calliper, stepping clumsily over her stiffened leg. I listened to the service and would have gone out at the end but could not disturb the woman again. The elders held an after-meeting, more intimate and less structured than the service. I had never stayed for it before, being a non-member and regarding it as private to the regular congregation. I had often sat through such a meeting in the Welsh chapel but without understanding what went on.

I sat still as a third of the people drifted out. I was aware that I must take a positive attitude... and then David Edwards, the missionary, gave me the English version of the little speech I had heard so often in Welsh. 'Is there anyone who has stayed behind to give themselves to the Lord Jesus?' I had often laughed at this evangelical ploy but that night I knew the answer was vital to me. It was time I acted, because I had read of the sin against the Holy Spirit which was unforgivable. I decided it was probably the sin of denying Christ within myself. So I stood up. I was aware I was making a spectacle of myself and I thought, 'Well, you've done it now!' My whole life was now the price for achieving my faith and I could not ask for safeguards. I could only go forward, trusting in help to stay upright. I was edging to a feeling of relief and satisfaction when I felt a sharp, unseen slap across my face; the Spirit was a Reality. The shock told me that I lacked humility and awe. I had to lose my self-esteem to become acceptable. I sat praying quietly until the service finished. David came over and smiled. So did a kind but obtrusive elder who started saying how well I worked and what a good member I might be. I told David that work had been my defence against a committal to faith. He understood and we were left in peace.

Next day, I had a letter from David telling me to have no doubt that my experience was real. He came to see me, and reassured me that I would not lose what I had found after so long a time. He also advised me to read the Bible, for the first time, on my knees, so that I would remain uncomfortably awake, and to read it from the first verse of Genesis to the end of Revelations without missing out a single 'begat'. Once I began to pick and choose, I might miss a dull but valuable passage.

It takes about two and a half years, reading a chapter each night, to read it all. Eventually one gets an idea of Purpose being achieved, slowly but inevitably, and with it the comfort of an ubiquitous, everlasting God. The bloody-mindedness of the Old Testament eventually reveals a conception of mercy and prepares the way for the incarnation of Jesus. The Virgin Birth is splendid poetry and is a possible stumbling block. There were many such. I do not worry about them. I haven't an intellect to satisfy nor the time to waste. One can only accept one's salvation with simplicity... the meek can inherit the Earth and its Maker. For a few weeks, life was much more intense. Colours were brilliant in the garden and I felt myself part of a beautiful world. Of course, pollution was not yet a buzzword. I read St John's Gospel for the first time and it was sheer poetry, besides being a lucid account of Christ's teaching.

The most unexpected outcome was that I no longer had an outsize need to be the one to help. I could take myself out of the middle of my little world. David encouraged me to wait for opportunities and not to make them. My mother's anxieties, that I would charge around and off to befuddle some luckless tribe, were allayed. I took on a Sunday school class and then gave it up – my lack of decent piety created too much laughter. I helped another Sunday School on the housing estates. That was better. The children ignored the doors and came in through the windows. Two or three of us tried to deal with more than a hundred. My sketches of Bible stories were the answer to overwhelming noise and, as the assembly was very vague as to what the Bible was about, I did little good and also little harm.

My new outlook made few difficulties for me. As a child, I had felt God to be at hand though He was not asked to rescue me from my nightmares. My grandmother spoke easily of 'talking to the Almighty'. There were stories of my great-grandfather being accompanied through dangerous places, when he rode to preaching engagements. The quiet companion who protected him came from nowhere and disappeared before he could be thanked. My great-great-grandfather had been famous when a bare-footed teenager, walking alone for a day and a night to obtain a Bible printed in Welsh, inspired his conception of the British and Foreign Bible Society. This last fact had subjected the family to a lot of hypocritical adulation. Tall men had pumped my hand when I was small and called it an honour. This had devalued for me the considerable contribution my forefathers had made, alone or with others, to Welsh Nonconformity through the Sunday school movement and through theological writing, I was more impressed by the visible provision of Bala College and Aberystwyth University College, built by my great-grandfather's and great-uncle's fund-raising efforts. Edward the Seventh actually thought it fitting to honour the Bible Society Centenary with his presence as Prince of Wales. He lifted little Evelyn up to cut the huge cake. Evelyn was my mother's youngest sister and the least pious of all. She had made fun of everything; her derision covered the preachers and their services. She related their peccadilloes with gales of laughter. Only a minority would be involved; nevertheless, it was hard for me later to respect an orthodox religious background.

My new belief brought me peace of mind. I tested my contract of surrender to God daily and, occasionally, hourly. Whenever I was in doubt as to what I should do, I said a quick prayer on the lines of 'Thy will, not mine, be done.' I was not shirking responsibility; it is very difficult to identify one's own wishes and discard them so as to be receptive to better ideas. Soon, I conceded that I was avoiding mistakes. Years later, staff said I was convinced I was always right; an irritating trait, but not such a bad prop in a lonely post. All my working life was to be stressful; understaffing, long hours of overtime, unending demands for attention and grave decision-making left me exhausted each night. But I could sleep soundly. I had read CS Lewis and others and I had come to understand the power and the economy of the Lord's Prayer. By the time I had 'forgiven those who trespass against us' – including my own mistakes – I could believe there was nothing to prevent my communing with a power outside myself. I was – and still am – convinced that my worries were shared and that I should be able to face whatever was coming. I could put my head on the pillow and obtain refreshment of body and spirit in untroubled sleep.

Early in my Christian apprenticeship I thought I was in for a spot of temptation. The husband of a delightful Canadian cousin came over with the Canadian Seaforths and was duly invited to a nearby aunt's house for Christmas. Mother properly decided we should also welcome him and I was furious to find my short weekend deflected into entertainment. I was sick. A little pale, I was in the welcome parade, and horrified to find a handsome, sparkling-eyed and very self-assured man of my own age. Quite unused to any non-business relationships with men, I decided he was mischievous and that he was too attractive by half. In seconds, I decided, rather deviously, that we should do our best to interest him or he would soon be lost as far as my cousin was concerned.

As customary with visitors, we set out, by bus, to show Bob the Roman remains in Chester. By the time we got to the city, Bob had said he had dreaded coming and he too had been sick with apprehension. My aunt had warned him that I was a bluestocking, meaning I was a very boring intellectual. This produced laughter and a good relationship. My annual five days' leave in May was spent with Bob at home and visiting the aunt. We walked across the moors and took a bus ride. We carried a present of fresh fish and a picnic. We kept the cider cool and forgot the fish. On the bus we found out what the abominable smell was and kept straight faces when we duly presented it, like two naughty children. Our friendship was established, firmly.

Our next annual holiday was spent with a good friend in mid-Wales. We cycled around on bicycles we had brought by train. We were stupid enough to go straight up the face of Cader Idris while experienced climbers hollered at us from the Fox's path to come down. We could only go on up. Somehow Bob got me over the overhanging cliff edge.

The sea looked very beautiful as we turned to look at our path up through a dry waterfall.

Our hostess thought we would be safer driving around her area where she dispensed relief. We went to her office and could hardly believe the scene. She selected a hat from her filing cabinets, clapped her hands and two sadly humiliated civil servants appeared, one with her picnic basket and the other with her radio. Duly instructed, they put them in her little car, which she called Julius, and we followed. The three of us breezed off to see superb scenery. Better than scenery was her visit to a village. She was heralded by her own tooting on the horn. A white-haired pensioner dashed out of his cottage and elevated his decrepit hard hat on to his uplifted walking stick, waving it and shouting, ' Hooray for Miss Gwyneth Griffiths', until she halted. People loved her larger-than-life style but her colleagues bemoaned her mixture of administration and art when she wrote her quarterly reports to Cardiff in not so blank verse.

Over thirty years later, Bob came back with his second wife. There was no hitch. I was still fond of him, faults and all. He assured me that I had never betrayed my feelings when I had spent my time mulling over his photos and reminding him of his home. Then he astounded me. He told me Father had been so worried about my ignorance of men, my apparent lack of interest and my questions as to the wisdom of encouraging an impending and very unsuitable proposal of marriage, that he had asked Bob to teach me what he could! This commission had been a happy one for my 'cousin'. It had been a slow trailing of the quarry for him. There had been long, letters of gentle reassurance to counteract my deep dissatisfaction with myself. These had occupied him during the long wait for the second front. Father's judgement had been right. Bob had carried out the commission honourably and my naiveté had been demolished when I left for UNRRA. Before that, however, I had changed my job as housing officer to that of organiser for Girls' and Mixed Clubs. These were very different from the clubs on the housing estates. The National Youth Movement had good, but conservative committees, borrowed, well-ordered premises and sadly, a reluctant membership. I wrote newsletters and visited clubs by train and bus, humping a bicycle together with bags of craft materials and my overnight necessities. I had bought a car but my allowance of nine gallons of petrol per annum for the supervision of North Wales was a non-starter. I saved the coupons for an expected tour by the powerful national chairman and found I had lost them the day before she arrived. I went to the fuel office, and when it came to my turn, I was too choked with desperate tears to be able to speak. Officials were alive to problems and they listened and quadrupled my allowance – monthly!

I stayed with kindly committee ladies. Two were very wealthy benefactresses. Their home was now a service-men's convalescent hospital. These two sisters denied themselves any luxury, even home-grown tomatoes. The younger sister was deeply interested in the clubs which loved her in turn. Their shrewd and wise business manager had assessed my integrity. They ran a hostel for us... I loved its smell of slate floors, stored apples, wood smoke and cawl. Cawl was unbelievably good on a cold wet night: it was made entirely of root vegetables, doled out unceremo-niously by a fierce but very good-natured warden who became a loyal friend.

The North Wales Clubs borrowed the hostel for an American weekend demanded by HQ. The GIs were not getting the welcome they thought they deserved. So we were to spend a weekend trying to understand the inferior-ity complex of a people trying to build a nation from hordes of half-assimilated immigrants. Our party menu was to introduce their taste for weird sweet and sour food. Prunes stuffed with cheese! In fact, the prepared bumph in our leaflets did not lead to comprehension. It would have been asking for trouble to have asked for direct lessons from the GIs but doubtless we would have been well educated.

It irritated me that we should have to spend so much time on the American culture when we did not know our own, and I determined, despite HQ's opposition, to hold a Welsh Sunday evening. I found a wonderful school inspector of music, Cassie Davies. After tea, we sat around the room, about twenty of us, and she stood in the middle and asked who was Welsh. None. Who had Welsh parents? Grandparents? None. It was useless asking who spoke Welsh at home. I saw that the scorn of the English invader had affected these youngsters just as I had been damaged as a three year old. Wisely, Cassie began to sing. There was a piano; her voice was sure and sweet. She had a wonderful selection of little-known folk music, and beautiful harmonies for the harp. A very shy boy of seventeen, sitting by my side, was trembling with excitement, and forgetting us all, he leaped to Cassie's side and started to interweave his tenor voice with hers, as so many Welsh people do naturally when singing hymns. The atmosphere was charged. Most could now join in. When we stopped, there was immediate competition to produce Welsh relatives. Even parents profited by the new recognition.

We had run an earlier weekend in Llangollen. It had been a great success in a tall rambling house borrowed from the Liverpool clubs. The theme was to be fun and leadership. I was certain that we could not ignore Christ as our Leader. I planned a simple service and hoped to get someone to take it. Queasy, despite my agony of prayers, I had to do it myself. It was just bare bones but my young friends understood and respected it. One of the girls went to a National Assembly of the clubs and insisted that they had a short service which she led. She was brave and she was well-supported. We were very proud of her because such a stance is never easy. The club members were now enthusiastic, eager for new challenges and prepared to consider serious subjects. New members were joining. I reported our future plans and inevitably the committee was chilly, pouring cold water on the proposals. It was then that an ideal post was advertised in my own area. I applied for it. When the committee was informed, all the funds I had needed for development were suddenly at my disposal. Still, I advised them to start advertising for my successor. I was fond of my chairman, Lady Wheldon, and the secretary the minister's wife from our church, and I was sorry to withdraw my support from them. I realised, however, that even they could not stop the older committee members frustrating the growth of the movement. I believed the clubs were in good shape and that a new organiser would be encouraged by their liveliness. I felt free to go.

Part Six

The Ocean Has Now Swept to the Coasts of Europe; to Human Tides of Soldiers, Victors and Vanquished

UNRRA, Training, Assembly in Normandy and Across the War Zones to the Saar

The almoner's post being advertised in my own county involved special work with patients in TB sanatoria, on venereal disease clinic lists and with the blind in their own homes. I had had good training in the last two categories at St Mary's, Paddington and at Moorfield's Eye Hospital. I thought that my general encounter with poverty and malnutrition would assist me with the normal problems in tuberculosis. I applied for the post.

As always, I prayed about my application for the first work, available to me locally, for which I was qualified. I might as well have prayed to a wooden idol. I was disconcerted by experiencing the complete indifference of my Heavenly Father to my pet project. After a struggle with my thoughts, I had decided that I would not be doing God's Will if I persisted. I was finding it hard to distinguish between my own wishes and the obedience my faith required. It will always be a tricky business, demanding an honest squint at one's own murky, mental depths and, after discarding one's preferred action, waiting in disciplined stillness for alternative ideas. My new thoughts, had, by then, become a conviction, very late in the day. I telephoned the appropriate official to say that I would be withdrawing from the interview the following day. I was taken aback to hear that, as the only applicant, the post was already mine; I did not change my mind. Later I told my mother that I was uneasy at having chucked up one of the few posts that would ever have suited me. We never talked about faith, but she assured me I was right to follow my strong sense of being guided, to wait for another opportunity. I was surprised and heartened by her support.

That night, I did not toss or turn though doubtless I snored. Around eight o'clock in the morning, a distinct voice ensured I was wide awake with the words: 'Leta! You will get international work today.' I had been a bit other-worldly since putting my beliefs to the test with my resignation from a guaranteed post, so I accepted this message and got quietly on with the day. In the late afternoon, the phone rang and someone from the Welsh Board of Health Office introduced himself and asked, 'How would you like to go to Germany?'

With no hesitation I said, 'I'll go.'

'Hang on,' the voice said, 'You don't know what it's all about!'

I replied firmly that I did not care as I was going anyhow. I was then told it was an application for UNRRA, of which I had not heard, and the next day was the last day; I had to take two references to his office immediately and fill in a form. I seized the references for my cancelled job and rushed there, explaining I had to start that moment to keep a speaking engagement in Montgomeryshire. The form was filled in and signed by the sensible chief officer. He had been rung up by Dr Roberts of Cardiff who had suddenly remembered the woman who wanted work with refugees. I was on my way to post-war Europe.

With the enormous sacrifices of our new ally, Russia, and with the flood of US weapons and troops, victory for the allies had become a matter of time, prayer and sheer determination to hold on, taking whatever came our way until that day. Not that it amounted to much in my case. I paid monthly visits to club HQ in London and never experienced an air raid. My friends, noticing my luck, took the risk of a good night's sleep in bed, without recourse to the air raid shelters, whenever I was in town. On the other hand, I remember travelling home in a crowded carriage. One woman aired her mild misfortunes and the rest talked of small privations. Having listened patiently, another woman said calmly, 'I've just been to see my old home. I was told it had been bombed. It had; there was nothing left to rescue.' We asked where she was going. 'Oh, back to Birmingham. My mother's there with my baby. We were sent out of London to billets, to be safer. We've been hit by incendiaries, though.' She smiled at the irony. Our interest extended to the rest of her family. She told us her two daughters were evacuees in Cornwall where she thought they were safe. Still smiling, she said she was hoping that her husband would get leave from the worst of the battle zones in Italy. Our small grouses had dried up as she made light of her troubles.

The UNRRA interview was interesting. It was held somewhere near Broadcasting House. Dozens of excited and very 'with-it' young women loudly indicated self-confidence. They surged around the mirrors in the cloakroom with sideways looks and giggles at the fat rustic in camel coat and Henry Heath felt hat. In turn, said fat rustic went into the room where there were three pleasant people on a dais.

'How does your experience fit you for UNRRA?' they asked. At my reply, 'Well, it doesn't. I have never experienced complete chaos,' they broke into laughter and said to one another, 'Neither have we.'

The chairman, more gravely, said, 'Do you realise you will not have a telephone and be unable to get advice?'

'I have got a telephone in North Wales but there is no one I can ring up!' I answered and the mutual laughter covered the next question and my exit, confident that when I did hear from them, I should be going to Germany. They called me up to join the first teams, but I had promised the youth service that I would work an extra month. The club HQ staff bitterly accused me of leaving them for the sake of money. My pastor said I was leaving God's work, to which he considered I had been guided by Providence. I felt unable to disappoint him further by asserting that I was, in fact, obeying a clear directive. David Edwards understood it instantly.

A hostel in Reading was my first posting. Here I met Brits and Poles and Americans, all of us being incubated on an intellectually nourishing diet. The real diet included suet puddings like roly-poly and plum duff. The Yanks were ecstatic about the cooking and wondered why such puddings were not served in the better hotels as a tourist attraction. We ate on benches at trestle tables and slept in wooden-cubicled dormitories.

Our other diet was dished out by a wonderful, quiet, small man, Arnold Foster, consumed with concern for all nations and devastated one morning, when he told us that Roosevelt, Churchill and Stalin had signed the Yalta Agreement. It was difficult to find words for this callous treachery but we all understood the shattering consequences with which we, too, would have to cope. The problem would be that of enforcing repatriation to a dictatorship which was also an official ally. We had lectures on the state of war-ravaged Europe, on the refugees and slave labour all on the move, and now known as 'Displaced Persons' – DPs to us. When Foster told us that the Dutch were very weak physically, from undernourishment, and that Britain had decided to send their fleet of Queen's Ambulances, donated during the war by all the colonies, to

Holland immediately, an American stood up in high dudgeon and asked wrathfully what right we had to export our royalist views. Foster replied softly that the Dutch might think it referred to their own queen. In Aldershot, we had talks on flies and disease. Later, in US camps, the posters were not on the same subject though the words were the same. Aldershot taught us how to dig latrines and to run a field kitchen... in theory. In Reading, we had more lessons on the background and on the social and political character of various nations. We ended up with uproarious and vitally necessary charades on how not to treat the DPs who would be in our care.

It was two weeks well spent and I had developed a very high regard for Arnold Foster. On our return to the London hostels, I accompanied two US women to St Paul's. We were on the gallery round the dome when a doodlebug whistled overhead. We scampered down with everyone else but once again St Paul's escaped. We huddled over a cup of coffee somewhere in Fleet Street. The two Americans looked at one another, lowered their voices and said, 'Tell us what you thought of our lecturer in Reading.' I praised him unstintingly. 'But he didn't wear a suit! And he had...' (agonising pause) '...carpet slippers!' I was flabbergasted but managed to remind them he was living on the premises. I told them suits were not the general garb for university lecturers, especially in wartime. It was useless talking of clothing coupons and shortages. They were puzzled but relieved, saying, 'American professors always try to look smart and we thought he was deliberately insulting us.' Quite small variations in national manners could apparently build up to a deep misunderstanding. Very few US citizens had any grasp of how four years of war, disaster and rationing had changed our own attitudes. London hid its wounds well behind high hoardings covered with bright paint and posters. Debris from bomb and fire was cleared up as rapidly as possible. These devices kept up our morale but did little to enlighten our new allies. Bombing raids were now infrequent, supplanted by long-distance rockets, less accurate and less damaging.

As we left the café, a policeman caught up with us. It was surreal. In the middle of the war, he had spotted the foreigners and walking down Fleet Street began to tell us proudly of Fleet Street's fame. There was the Cheshire Cheese where Dr Johnson bemused the assembled gentlemen. Dickens had used such and such for backdrops to his stories. He was quoting and reminding us of classics – meaningless and boring to my American companions. They pulled down a mental safety curtain to save themselves from a perceived surfeit of culture.

In Reading we had begun to learn from one another. The Poles, and two Czech doctors in particular, told us quietly of the tortures the Nazis were inflicting in Middle Europe. I still cannot understand how little I knew of the extermination camps and the cruelty accompanying the German drive to be a pure-bred *Herren Volk*. It was nauseating to hear eyewitness accounts of civilians stripped and pushed into swimming baths of icy water amongst Alsatian dogs trained to bite the genitals of the terrified men. The statistics of defectives, dissidents, Jews and handicapped people being driven into concentration camps became a ghastly reality.

London was still being bombed, but now by doodlebugs which were meant to be psychologically demoralising; they whistled their way overhead, stopped whistling and dropped devastatingly... no one knew where. It was less damaging than the huge bombing raids and the incendiaries, both causing tremendous havoc, spreading fires in the earlier years. We had yet to deal the death blow to an army which had once looked victorious to everyone except the dogged British, upheld by Churchill's courage and oratory.

One night, we had bedded down in our cubicles and some rumble made me draw back my blackout curtains. I'd never seen anything like it and I called out, 'The Milky Way has turned red... all the stars have gone red...' and in a choked voice: 'I think it's the taillights of aeroplanes.' We were in the path of an enormous air armada going to the Saar or Cologne or Dresden, in the most terrible of onslaughts. Later, I was to see in Saarbrucken only one room left with four walls and a ceiling in a town of rubble. In Reading we thought of the danger to our pilots and the anxieties of their families, who never knew what mission would be the last for their men. A time comes when a price has to be paid for victory but the price is not confined to the transgressors and their people. A whole conception of life in Europe needed to be confronted by all the Western nations and whoever from dominions and colonies, shared their anger. No one can be clean of that blood who benefits now, as well as then.

Early in the war, I knew I could no longer say I was a pacifist. Whatever we ate sapped the lifeblood of the crews of the convoys. From Anglesey, I saw a huge convoy moving to Liverpool, covering the sea to the horizon. Big ships shepherded small cargo boats – and we wondered how many were missing. German submarines refuelled in Eire, I was told, and the food chain was vulnerable to the end of the Atlantic crossing, reaching the Mersey docks.

We all returned to London for more lectures. We were equipped with khaki uniforms, badges displaying the world emblem and eventually passports describing us as 'World citizens'. A little bit of paper, in my case, now announced that I should have the status of a lieutenant if taken as a prisoner of war. I was thrilled to belong to the world and not to any particular country; I had not yet encountered the drifting misery of the stateless created by two World Wars. Doodlebugs still whistled and dropped in the sudden quiet, leaving us guiltily thankful that we were still alive. One of the last bombs that dropped near Tavistock Square blew me out of bed. Next day, we saw the demolished church and heard that the two caretakers had descended from their third floor flat with the rubble, still sitting, unharmed, in their armchairs.

The war was being won. On 4th April, 1945 we crossed the Channel. Four marines pointed their rifles at a dodgy-looking magnetic mine that accompanied the ship quite closely. We gathered our luggage together, landed and fell into a new train which the French had kept hidden from the enemy. The gleaming stainless steel and hot water tempted me to strip in the loo for what might have been (and was) the last chance of cleanliness. It was exhilarating.

Sitting in the train compartment I contemplated the other women, for we had segregated ourselves automatically. There was a strong-minded Russian who announced she was appointed a director and tried to recruit me on to her team, believing me to be a toughy. I was pleasantly surprised but was much too wary to join forces. Meantime, a once beautiful, auburn-haired woman was bidding for attention with a huge holdall of Elizabeth Arden cosmetics which gave her extraordinary satisfaction. I was amazed that anyone would expect to have time for personal grooming and glad my page-boy cut was easily controlled with a razor blade. Eighteen months later, she was still benefiting from the holdall when I was sent to take over her work.

The scenes hurtling past the train windows were of a bleak Normandy. Black, charred tree stumps, dead bushes, and the grim, pollarded willows, covered with soot and dust, separated smashed farms and half-destroyed villages. In the dining car (snacks only), a Frenchwoman wailed at the light weight of the new franc, symbolising to her that all France had gone ersatz... a word much in use at the time for everything from dried egg to shoddy cloth. We reached our headquarters in Granville, on the coast. It was a large hotel, stripped bare and pockmarked with bullet holes, many recently acquired. My train ablutions were justified, but our very minimum needs were met. We each carried a splendid canvas bed, easily mounted on low W-shaped rods. We would spread our sleeping bags on the strong canvas and at night were too weary to stay awake.

Each day we jostled at the noticeboard to find if we had been posted to a team. I was lucky being pulled into Team 32 within two days as deputy director to an ex-Indian army colonel, now appointed as our team director. A medical officer of health, near retirement, and a half-Flemish welfare officer came from the UK, while a sparkling young Czech nurse and two bored French drivers made up the team. I learned that no teams ever got off in time as the tyres of their allotted lorries were stolen. I got our newish tyres, and as the French drivers refused to guard them, carted them one by one up to our dormitory and slept on them. We were amongst the first to leave but only after the excitement of a German raid from the Channel Islands.

We were told that there had been a raid the previous week, accounting for the newer bullet holes. Among the few UNRRA personnel captured was my previous boss from the settlement. Some were lamenting his ill luck but, remembering his dislike of the Welsh he had undertaken to help, I thought the DPs in their turn had been lucky. The Germans came for us too. A raid warning sounded and we were herded into a semi-underground room from where a spot of shooting could be heard. Towering over us, standing on a bench, was a GI with a loaded gun which he was waving about while he shouted angrily at our laughter. As the Germans retreated, he was the greater menace.

The weather was idyllic. We sweated in uniform on the soft sand of the beach and then went slowly back to the compound. It was only then I realised it was Easter Sunday.

Four tall GIs of African blood stood together singing spirituals. Strain and general tension had made my senses taut and I shall never forget their expressive, reverent singing of 'Were you there when they crucified My Lord?' It was the only reminder that human endeavour was not enough for our enterprises.

Our team was ready to go. The director was a man of integrity and courtesy but rigid with army discipline. In the previous war, he had been made a prisoner and escaped after recutting his uniform to a German pattern, backstitching the whole thing until it looked machined and tailored. He had managed to walk through Germany to freedom. It was all he divulged about himself on our formal evening strolls. The doctor was furious that a chit of a girl was the deputy director when he was obviously the more able. I pointed out to the director that we would not have a smooth-running team until I had another title and the doctor became his deputy but my advice was unwelcome. The welfare officer did not trouble us much as the army later gave us an aeroplane (and pilot) and he took off back to the UK for unspecified welfare supplies. Our Czech nurse was busy learning English, and was greatly puzzled by the doctor's mischievous play on words. She told me a long story about having saved her mother by sacrificing herself, perhaps it was a half-truth. She was very efficient at ensuring medical supplies. We owed a lot to her friendships with the US medics, well supported with the plentiful brandy we were allocated.

Meanwhile we left Granville and the rich American diet of the refectory. A diet so rich that the average Brit was suddenly looking like a severe case of high blood pressure. As for me I could not face a fried egg without bread and when the waiter refused to give me any, something (my conscience and upbringing) snapped. I stood up as the waiter passed to the inevitable high table and snatched a white roll from his tray, biting into it before he could snatch it back. It was a new moral laxity which had its uses later. We started our journey in two surplus-to-requirements fire service lorries from the Manchester blitz, i.e. clapped-out light trucks with canvas curtains and gaps in the floorboards through which spurted the thick dust of the roads, the mud having dried out in the gorgeous weather. We opened our equipment; the rations were poor and the bread entirely mouldy. Doubtless, the good bread went daily to the Norman households. We had a very elaborate American cooking stove from which some essential pin was missing; it was quite useless. The simple instructions we had received in Aldershot were more to the point. We had been told to create a barbecue of bricks, sloping two pieces of roof gutter to meet at the base, feeding one with water and the other with used engine oil, both drop by drop. Ignited they produced fierce flames. We never had to test either the stove or the barbecue. We were near enough and overfed enough to be able to wait for our first landfall, which was Rheims. The nurse and I were to sleep in a commandeered house exactly opposite the lovely old cathedral, apparently not badly damaged. We had been housed as high as the newly freed bells, celebrating their release each quarter of an hour. Fatigue ensured that we slept, some of the time.

There was no time to look around, nor was it sensible to wander alone. We set off in the mornings to find an army canteen rather than eat our rations. We washed in our flattish British Tommy helmets, making hard decisions as to whether we cleaned our teeth or had a general wash-all-over first. In the middle of the day we would have what are now called comfort stops. By now we were in the war zone where notices of MINES SWEPT TO DITCHES confronted us. The men were cheerful on the edge of the road but Erica and I received little sympathy for our need to get over the ditches into the bushes. I remember two of our canteen stops during our journey through the north-east of France. The first was a US camp. We broke their monotony and were given a big welcome with an eye-boggling meal of fried eggs piled high on a platter, probably four each for the seven of us, a truly nauseating sight to Brits used to one egg per month. Our second stop was nearer the battle zone and was, therefore, British. Our welcome, this time, was from an unsmiling and over-worked soldier. The food was boiled potatoes and thinly sliced but well-cooked beef, served on well-scrubbed tables. We appreciated the meal and the reality of the situation. We were reminded that a big sacrifice had been and was being made for the impending victory, which was to be realised about six weeks later. The contrast between the camps reinforced the general belief that the British and dominion troops were given the spearhead positions against the Germans.

My letters home are no use in retracing this journey. No one knew quite where we were, route instructions were mysterious, we were not allowed to write our addresses and many of our letters never reached the UK. We found that mail from home had been held up for about two months because the local army unit thought that UNRRA signified reds under the beds. We did stop at Verdun where the director was anxious to visit the memorial to the soldiers of the First World War and to read the Book of Names. There we found a small stationer's shop, and the director fell happily on a pile of yellow typing paper, the colour of egg yolk. He told me to keep it carefully. It was to be his quite useless ammunition to draw attention to our team at headquarters, easy to spot and throw away.

We spent a rather horrid night, Erica and I, billeted with a woman who appeared to be being punished as a Nazi sympathiser by having people drafted on her. She was very hostile and we went for a long walk to escape the atmosphere. The town was on the bend of a river running through a narrow gorge. We scrambled up the escarpment overlooking the river and the road. At the top, we found a German defensive line of huge guns on steep tracks, able to thunder up to the edge of the escarpment from their concealing shelters and then to inflict terrible havoc on their enemies below. We were even more sober when we returned to the lodging and we wedged a chair under the door handle. Fortunately we ate elsewhere.

Next day, we were probably near Brussels or on the outskirts of some other big town, when I espied a notice: UNRRA HEADQUARTERS. We pulled up the two trucks and I was sent to reconnoitre. A large man whom I had seen in Granville was sitting behind a small desk with two phones, one in each hand, bellowing into one, 'Hold on!' and into the other, 'That's your team number? Where are you? You don't know! No, I don't either. Where's your destination? You've lost your instructions!' and in despair banging down the one telephone while I escaped to report on the hilarious situation then prevailing in the Belgian HQ of UNRRA. It was not uncommon. UNRRA had been preparing for the end of the war but the armies had found the chaos too unmanageable and demanded instant help. The director had been given a destination and a devious route, probably planned for our safety, avoiding battle zones and troop movements. Possible canteen stops had been thoughtfully provided. In the north, long under German control, we found no smiles, but when still in France we had rapturous welcomes. Brought to a halt at a level crossing, the handicapped son of the crossing control-ler slaughtered a lovely lilac tree to cool Erica and myself in the heat and dust of the second *camion*, as the French drivers called the truck. We two women, in the second, were choked with the dust of the first while the men squeezed in by the drivers in the airier cabins. Climbing in and out was difficult and I was once left hanging by my skirt, hooked on to a handle; my scratchy wool trousers were too inconvenient and hot. Khaki expunged the idea of gallantry! I tried to buy cool cologne at a *parfumerie*. There I was seized by the neck while Madame doused my khaki jersey with sprays of fresh and pleasant perfume... to the intense displeasure of the director. I realised that the Union Jack, sported on the *camion* bonnet, was now immensely popular and no longer carried our pre-war 'snooty' image; any Brits, anywhere, were the symbols of Free Europe.

It seemed as if we had been on the road for about a week when at dusk the protesting *camions* climbed a hill to a small barracks to report to the UNRRA team there. We were just another chore to them but we were welcomed to supper and sleeping quarters. After supper, the exhausted medical officer came in and I was delighted to recognise one of the Czech doctors who had been in Reading. I was asked to help the French social worker. She had a mission in life, to stop every woman wearing a headscarf and so prevent the proliferation of creepy-crawlies. It was a transit camp. Each day about eight hundred displaced persons were sent elsewhere and replaced by the same number of new DPs. They were desperately clinging to their relatives, especially to their young children, terrified of losing them and their very few belongings. Into this confusion the French girl tore, yanking headscarves off as she passed, yelling in incomprehensible French and only producing tears of fear and frustration.

She and I agreed on one thing, the stench from the barrack basements was putrid and promised disease. We harassed the men to investigate as we imagined some ghastly source of the foulness. It was then I met another Reading acquaintance, the most senior of the US social workers. The encounter was shocking. She also begged for my assistance, possibly to control queues? She had a pile of precious fluffy white towels, a stock of little cards and a babies' weighing scales. She only lacked the sterilised paper mats to be placed on the scales for each baby to prevent cross-infection. However, the towels would do. Now, where was the first mother? About four women were lined up with their infants and an elaborate charade took place to demonstrate the proper care of babies by US standards, which would prevail everywhere now that the war was nearly over! A snowy towel was laid on the cradle of the scales and a little underfed, poorly clad and unbathed baby was laid tremulously and lovingly on the towel. It was weighed and then, with elaborate mime, the date and weight were entered on a little card. Names were beyond comprehension. Little could have been conveyed to mothers who did not know the Roman alphabet. To make the hygiene lesson clear, the tall American picked up the towel as gingerly as possible and threw it into a corner of the room to signify it must not be used again. Poor mother! Her child had been shown to be unworthy and the lovely towel was not to be a present after all. Word went round and no one else attended.

There would have been two or three thousand DPs in this camp at any one time. They came in batches from farms and factories where they had worked as slaves. Their nationalities had been mixed as Hitler had overrun their countries. The whole place was in confusion but medical help was given by the exhausted Czech doctor. The DPs rested on wooden bunks and were given good food and clean water. And here was a miracle, better than that of Cana. At dusk the big American water tankers pulled in and throughout the night there was more hilarity than even freedom from Hitler would account for. An officer went to inspect the filling of the tankers and found that the DPs had already organised the Germans, via American rations and a few cigarettes, into filling the transport vehicles with wine instead of water.

Milk for the children came in the morning, uncontaminated. Later, in our own camp, we had trouble as the milk was sour every day. Officers watched the genuine fresh milk from spotless churns being poured into our equally sterile tanker and every day the milk was undrinkable. Eventually a Polish farmer suggested that the Germans were mixing fresh milk from two different milking times and he knew this would curdle the milk. Further investigation confirmed that he was right; the milk problem was solved... leaving us time to deal with water in the sausages!

Triers, with Five Thousand Poles under American and then French Military Governments

We moved out of the harassed transit camp to an American billet in Triers. I shared accommodation with American nurses in a smart private hospital, run by nuns, but now commandeered for the occupying forces. Water was still at a premium but I obtained an American helmet to use as a much deeper washbasin than my previous British one. One wonderful day we were all whisked off to a shower unit. In a large room were a few chairs to hold our clothes and three or four shower heads pumping *hot* water! We stripped and rushed in, showering and shampooing in one wild and rapid bath, trying to give the next lot their turns before the luck and the hot water ran out. At last, after two weeks, Erica and I were free of the grit of the Manchester fire trucks that had brought us from Granville.

We did not go out at night. The high walls of the hospital gave a little shelter but Germans were still firing tracer bullets across the gardens. In one street, I noticed a machine gun mounted on a stand and pointing out of the window. No one wanted to investigate it. The nurses were not allowed out, but no one had kept me indoors or bothered about my safety. Triers was deserted; apparently the townsfolk had fled into the countryside. There was no one to prevent the American forces raiding the cellars. They were packed with Moselle wine. The GIs seized the bottles and when these ran out, took the bungs out of the casks. The gratings above the cellars reeked as the wine flowed; it even ran down the street gutters. Later, in Bayreuth, an old Russian driver was more careful. He broached a cask and fixed a rubber tube to deliver wine effortlessly into his mouth while he lay alongside, swallowing. Death was averted when he was, by chance, discovered. The Triers citizens were cautiously drifting back. I remember a woman cyclist in black satin. Her backside, overlapping the saddle, stretched the dress until the seams were pulling apart. I asked myself why Germany had capitulated. There was no starvation to be seen there. We had been on a meagre diet that brought fatigue easily, but not despondency with Churchill to rouse us on the wireless.

On the first day, I wandered up a quiet street by myself. With screeching brakes, two lorry loads of GIs pulled up by me, the men jumping out and shouting 'Woman!' The unpleasant possibilities did not enter my head but I stood still, my pudding face expressionless. They waltzed round me, reading my epaulette. The more learned read UNRRA with hesitation and then one brightened up and said, 'Ha! She's a Ruskie. Better not touch her.' They became confident; sure that I would not understand, they made remarks about my big teeth and solid figure. They all knew they must not offend the Russian ally at any price, so I became a dangerous problem. They hurriedly climbed back on board the lorries and drove off. The next morning was Sunday. I spruced myself up with a modicum of make-up and trotted off to the service for the American troops. 'Good morning, gentlemen,' I said in clear English to the dumbstruck GIs, hoping some of them had seen my epaulettes before. I sat at the back. The sermon on Potiphar's wife had little solace for me. The Padre missed his wife and blamed the pin-up girls. The news-sheets carried cartoons of a very slinky

Jane, always in flimsy undies or shiny black satin, outwitting the enemy. It was probable that the curvaceous minx was an official antidote to homosexuality. I recalled the girls with Eton crops – short back and sides – and the flattened busts in all-in-one corselettes we called 'drainpipes' during my schooldays in the twenties.

By now, the director had met the military governor of Triers and been allocated a house for the team and a group of Italian prisoners of war, not, as ex-enemies, an UNRRA responsibility, so they were swopped for five thousand Poles in a caserne, or German barracks, about four miles from our house. Our transport was still limited to the two wheezy trucks. We were given bigger trucks. I was too short to drive them properly and could only control the slippery pedals by discarding my shoes. Cigarettes, however, bought us individual cars. One packet bought me a camouflaged Opal of uncertain, cross-grained temperament. While the men and Erica went to camp every day, I was kept at home, the director asserting that my prime duty was to make the team comfortable. My secondary duty was to type a daily report to HQ on the yolk-yellow paper purchased in Verdun. The task increased daily, as I had to list all previous letters sent and still unacknowledged. Our field phone in its leather case was never cranked up by its wobbly handle. We were as alone as was predicted at my interview in London.

The house was on the banks of the Moselle, a pleasant wide river, until one rowed on it and noticed the untreated sewage around the Germans swimming there. Water was a problem; the Germans had poisoned the wells and we were reduced to drinking the worst of the Moselle wine, so sour that a sprinkle of pepper improved it. We were in a quandary and my first task was to reduce the risk of disease through flies and mosquitoes. There were plenty of unpleasant smells but the doctor refused to be responsible for hygiene. I was given half a dozen Italian POWs whom I employed to clear out the fetid lily pond by our windows, the huge stone tanks in the great greenhouses and various utensils containing excrement which had to be destroyed. The worst smell of all was outside the kitchen door and the Italians had to dig this up under US scrutiny. They rolled their eyes and told me they were digging out bodies, something I half believed as we had found several discarded German helmets in the grounds. I think it was actually a very badly sited latrine. Our own latrines, consisting of three small tents for men, women and drivers, were far from the house. We grumbled when torrential rains came but by then the tanks were clean and soon filled with the good pure rain, solving our cooking and washing needs.

The house had belonged to a high ranking SS officer who was also a famous rose-grower. I purloined Nazi memorabilia, including a shoddy doorstop of Hitler's face surmounting his famous slogan 'Strength through Joy'. I also had half a horrid naval flag, the red dye of which smelled of fresh blood. I burned it when I reached the UK. On the rosier side, we left intact a small library of beautiful books illustrating roses and, in the garden, rows of good rose bushes from which we cut bowlfuls of prize blooms every day. The kitchen had an excellent Aga stove. The floor was of large black and white tiles. At night, when all was tidy, we squirted insecticide at the hordes of flies, probably from the old latrine, and as they fell thick and fast, the difference between black and white tiles was obliterated. The dining room led into a sitting room overlooking the garden. There was a very feminine, small, blue room with a painted ceiling, for Erica's use. Upstairs, we each had a bedroom, mine was the largest and doubled up as a store room, out of temptation's way. Each day a consignment of tinned goods, coffee, useful dried and diced vegetables, dairy food and chicken, all beyond our needs, arrived with a ration of wine in jerrycans and, very soon, a ration of cognac and liqueur. What a good thing my father had warned me at eight years old not to promise anything I might regret when I was older. I never joined the Temperance Band of Hope! The US army treated us very generously and we were now in a position to offer hospitality to our GI neighbours on the same site, and to the military governor's staff in the sophisticated HQ on the hill above the town.

Our garden adjoined strong-walled buildings with huge outer gates. The army contingent was based here and served to protect us. We were not as safe as we thought. When cleaning out the extensive greenhouses, I had noticed each day that there were fresh spent bullets about. Remembering the stench in our first transit camp, I asked the director if I should clean out the cellars, expressing my doubts about going down alone. He agreed immediately that to go down the long iron ladders backwards was an invitation to attack; there was a strong possibility that we were hosting a few Nazi soldiers in hiding. Some nights later, Erica and I heard movements outside and chivvied the very reluctant males to investigate. We went, too, and saw shadows behind the two parked *camions* but the men said cunningly that was just our imagination. The following morning we heard that the GI sentry on duty next door had had his throat cut. Our cellars were floored with wine bottles already opened and empty. Nevertheless, one of our French drivers could not resist trying to drain a few dregs from each bottle. He came out at a gallop and said there was a steady ticking there. At our request, the army investigated and found a live bomb had been placed there very recently.

Our menage was run by three cheerful and capable Polish girls. They cooked well, making fresh noodles and high sponge rings for puddings, daily. Excellent coffee was always simmering on the hob. One or two Polish soldiers visited and a young jolly boy offered to teach me Polish when I discovered that all I was learning was pidgin or DP Deutsch. I asked for the phrase 'Good morning. I hope you are well.' I learned it and went proudly around the camp administration, giving a grave bow and apparently saying, 'I love you, give me a kiss.' No one did. My serious demeanour was forbidding!

The girls attracted dangerous, unpleasant attention. We had been allotted three very competent young women from the Polish camp to run our house. Helena was a good cook and Regina and her younger friend undertook the housework and even flower arranging very competently. One morning there was scuffling in the hall and I found sixteen drunken GIs in a bunch at the foot of the staircase. They asked where the girls were. Fortunately, they were all cleaning out the bedrooms and out of sight, behind me. This was trouble needing a solution. I remembered, confusedly, a biblical instruction to speak with faith that the words would be right. I opened my mouth and was surprised to hear myself say, 'I like Negroes', which was more like putting paraffin on the flames. I was thinking how much better behaved than the whites they had been, back home. I could have been lynched but they were shocked and sobered up as they shambled out into the street. We bolted the door behind them.

Our invited guests were pleasant and delighted with our home cooking. We were all surprised at the ceremony our ex-Indian army director wanted. He and I presided at opposite ends of the table and Erica, as the younger and more beautiful, had to pour the coffee. A few liqueurs released our spirits and Erica was a great asset. In return we went to a happy evening reception in the gardens at the three-star general's HQ. It was delightfully organised by the aide-de-camp, a son of a one-time US ambassador to the UK. He was well-mannered and efficient, educated in

Britain and his wit and chit-chat a rare pleasure after the cobbled-up talk with various Americans with whom we shared few interests. He explained that the end of the war had brought a plethora of generals to his camp. To employ some of them, they had each been allotted one of us for supervision. Mine was so new that he failed to take his helmet off, like a felt hat, finding no grip on the metal. He was elated that I had never tasted Coke. A morning was wasted looking for a canteen, for a bottle and then an opener. We retired beaten, to crack the glass on the rockery and I reluctantly sampled the sickly fluid, possibly laced with glass spicules.

I had no part in the DP camp until it was obvious that the welfare officer had used our plane to make his UK 'business' trip a long holiday. Bored to tears, I insisted on taking over the welfare office. Our camp was neat barracks round a sandy parade ground. Barracks, by mutual arrangement, were not bombed, as troops never knew when they would be occupying each others' quarters. Homes, schools and shops were not in this category. The centres of Paris and Brussels had also been preserved as rest and entertainment areas for the armies, German, American or British.

The camp catered for Poles in temporary shelter, as they waited for special trains to repatriate them sometime in June. As the camp began to fill up, I made my first speech. For this, in addition to 'Alles Caput' (all bust up) I learned 'Leute' (people) and 'viel' (many). Thus fully prepared, I beckoned the camp committee to follow me to a dormitory. Here I said severely, looking at the ample space between beds, 'Viel Leute kommen. Sie mussen,' and my German was supplemented with a mime of toast, closely packed in a toastrack. To my delight it produced a chorus of 'Jawohl!' and the camp started preparing for an influx. Mime, English words similar to German ones, and a sprouting

German vocabulary gradually increased my powers of communication.

In the first few days, an interpreter brought six sobbing women into the director's office. The Pole said the women were afraid of being killed; possibly they had been collaborators or at least prostitutes. The director could not believe it was anything more than hysteria, nothing was done and we heard no more, which proved nothing except our inadequacy and general bewilderment. One thing, however, was being well organised... weddings! Brides somehow found long white dresses and sewed sprigs of green on to the gowns and had flowers in their hair. Arm in arm with their grooms they formed a very long procession around the parade ground, waiting for their turn in the improvised chapel where a priest married them in a short ceremony. About thirty couples would be sauntering around a lawn, the path taking the place of a church aisle. Two by two they reached the priest and presented themselves with dignity and reverence for his blessing.

We did not know the Poles as individuals as few could speak any English and interpreters were lacking. They were on their way home from army, factory, farm labouring or prison camp with little idea of the quality of life then to be found in Poland. Freedom and hope made any change a change for the better. Soon, Polish officers, eleven of them, appeared to ensure that this dubious UNRRA set-up was doing its best for their nationals. They were unfriendly and, again, we were to be individually shadowed. My opposite number was thin and grey-complexioned, possibly after many privations. His eyes glinted behind spectacles and when he sneered, one saw that his teeth had rotted down to their gold fillings which also glinted in turn. We were soon at loggerheads; I was trying to make life more comfortable for the women and children and they were determined all should be chaos to encourage repatriation. One tussle was over the bonfires now being lit all over the parade ground to enable the women to cook their special dishes with bartered German rations. They were tired of UNRRA soup and bread, amounting to twelve hundred calories per day. Tiny children were tripping over and being burnt on the hot embers, and the whole place was dangerous. I proposed to open a crèche and found some support and a suitable room. A few men were willing to make little stools and toys and women were prepared to undertake kindergarten work. Enthusiasm evaporated as each morning we found the previous day's work kicked to bits. There was a hippo-drome and I suggested it be floored. I had found dismantled army units in the hills with its huge sections of flooring easy to move. I put the scheme to the camp committee. 'We cannot use this place, it has no floor.'

'I have found plenty of flooring.'

'We have no transport'

'The Americans will lend us the trucks.'

'We have no nails.'

'I shall get them.'

But it was all useless, they had been warned not to coop-erate. Consequently, my next project, a sandpit for the toddlers, was also boycotted.

One thing was a success. The director complained that no work was being done and the camp was getting dirty. The Poles were the most obstinate of men and had refused to work for the 'funny money' (vouchers, in effect) that he was entitled to pay them. I asked what they could buy with this money as it would have no value in the German economy. There was nothing to buy, so the payment was valueless and there was nothing worth working for. A rare flash prompted me to ask if we could get permission to buy from the NAAFI canteen stores in the areas where the troops were being withdrawn. I was dispatched immedi-ately to Brussels with a truck and the more intelligent of the two French drivers. In Brussels we spotted a NAAFI sign and followed it to the administrative HQ and a dry welcome. I was told that the chief had just written a letter pointing out the lack of enterprise in UNRRA in ignoring the surplus stores. I had made the first enquiry and the letter would not be sent. I was then ushered into an Aladdin's cave of sweets, clothes and even toys. I noted the range of small things, cotton reels, hairgrips, soap and cosmetics, safety pins and Vaseline. With their encouragement, I left the NAAFI with permission to start a weekly wagon roll. The director and doctor took immediate charge of the enterprise and started a miniature Woolworth's, (in those days noted for its cheap, small merchandise) and were both as happy as children playing shop. They assured me they had no need of female assistance so I spent long quiet hours by the river, watching the poppies bud, bloom and wilt into the blood red that once made them the emblem of Flanders.

By midsummer there was growing unrest. The camp had been told the trains transporting them back to Poland would arrive soon. The Poles were to show their patriotism by being ready, with their families and few possessions, to board the trains when they arrived. At this time, a very sane British officer in mufti and khaki shorts out of Somerset Maugham visited us. He warned us that all was not well in Poland; the Russians were still running the country. There were great shortages and the people should be told the truth before they set off. Their country was not yet ready to absorb them. The situation was hopeless as, without unbiased interpreters, we could not convey this news. The Polish army unit sensed our misgivings on repatriation and our poor relationships worsened.

We had, by now, a small fleet of cars which were essential as the *camions* deteriorated further. The Polish officers were furious that we always had enough petrol. The petrol racket was a lot of fun. We would drive the short distance to neutral Luxembourg and indulge in ices in a pleasant tea room. The little town was calm, the people relatively well-off, the shops appeared prosperous and any shortages in window displays were disguised by the large, loyal photographs of their Duchess, flanked by suitable floral offerings. A little band, in blue uniforms, strutted importantly to a small square and played unremarkable music. The atmosphere was charming. Despite this, we had a surprise on our first visit. A group of young journalists waylaid us quite easily and asked us if we would like to see Radio Luxembourg. Everyone listened to this free station during the war with mixed feelings and some disbelief that anything so insubstantial could possibly go on functioning while most of Europe was a disaster zone. We all agreed to go and were whisked off to a long, low, modern building. As we entered we were adroitly separated and isolated in different small rooms where we were interrogated about our work and interests. The young men then compared notes and decided we were too naïve to be their quarry. They had actually thought that we three men and two women were the centre of a ring, smuggling not just art and other loot, but transporting huge American tanks, which were suddenly appearing over the German borders and entering France and Belgium for a price!

The road we travelled to Luxembourg was the one taken by the Eighth Army. The lorries of ill and completely exhausted soldiers, being sent on leave from the terrible last-ditch struggles of the retreating Germans on the Italian peninsula, rolled past our gate. The listless men had no energy even to be glad that victory was in sight, nor to stop and take up the boxes of ripe plums offered by the Polish girls and vouched for by my British uniform. Perhaps it looked like an enemy trap. On the other hand, immense suffering cannot risk the unmanning of kindness. On our way back to this road, from our Luxembourg jaunt, we would visit PLUTO. I had heard about the wonderful pipeline running from the USA, under the Atlantic and bringing the essential oil to the war zone in the centre of Europe. I was actually to see the terminus of this fantastic enterprise. It was an anti-climax; a lone GI was on guard in a little hut. He would challenge the infrequent visitors and was very bored. Our truck was packed with empty jerrycans ready for petrol. We showed identity cards and proffered a libation of whisky or cognac at the simple shrine, asking if we might fill up. Perhaps he assumed we meant the tank of our lorry. Erica, bright-eyed and vivacious, was sent to take his mind off the time it took to fill every jerrycan in the curtained truck and a happy time was had by all. This was the petrol that aroused such jealousy from the Poles. We did not try to understand their accusations and much less their demand for a share of it! One afternoon they broke into our office waving guns. I slipped behind the door, the men shouted at each other and the Poles left. Our relationships had not improved. I wondered sadly how such quiet, idealistic and honourable men as the UNRRA doctors I had met could be part of the same nation as our local brigandry.

Times became harder. The French replaced the Americans in their coveted Saar region. The area was still a shambles when they moved in; bombed sites were clogged and dangerous buildings stood tottering. Triers itself had been largely spared. Porta Negri, the huge black Roman arch erected by the Emperor Maximillian who had courted and married Helen in Caernarfon castle, still stood. The industrialised Saarbrucken, which we visited, exhibited no standing buildings. I thought I saw one room with a roof and four walls, sheltering someone with a candle. The townsfolk were living in the pine forests and had come to the market, a barter centre with stalls of odd planks, under umbrellas in the downpour.

When the French came, the havoc was confronted. Every able-bodied German was drafted into line, passing bricks and stones hand to hand from derelict sites into trucks for landfill elsewhere. Streets emerged clear of detritus, but we, UNRRA included, were not allowed on the pavements, all reserved for the conquerors. Wooden posts supported long strips of tricolour, strung waist-high, to prevent any Germans desecrating the paths alongside the offices occupied by the French army. The new Town Major was ruthlessly efficient. We were invited to a formal dinner at his Schloss, a small mansion in lovely wooded country. Our host was a Basque, aloof, erudite and musical. The well-chosen dinner did not break the ice and a return invitation seemed beyond our inadequacies. I was unable to learn anything of this fascinating and isolated Basque people. We did, however, meet a few of the French officers. We each received an open invitation to visit their newly installed brothel and a more suitable one to a nightclub. We sallied forth to the latter, the director leading. It was my first experience of a nightclub and remains the best. They had discovered a lovely German hostelry with panels and beams of dark oak. The floors were red-tiled and the round tables had glistening copper tops. The dance music was good, and a gallant Pole put me through the quickest Viennese waltz I had ever danced. The French female officers must have been chosen for their wit and accomplishments. One sang haunting modern ballads and others played intriguing music. The climax came when the colonel and a slender lass danced, leaping in unison from floor to chair and then to table top, still jiving expertly on the round copper surface. The applause and laughter swept us out and home.

A Frenchman called Plessis joined our team about this time. He was a quiet man of principle, finding the frustrations of our camp difficult after the efforts he made in the war. He proudly carried in his breast pocket a little note from our Air Ministry, acknowledging with gratitude, his considerable help in rescuing twenty-nine airmen after their parachute descents behind the enemy. On each of the twenty-nine separate occasions, he had risked his own life and also those of his family and sometimes friends, who had hidden the airmen, as he seized opportunities to push them to the Spanish border via the Pyrénées. I thought that that sustained bravery demanded a more tangible recognition, but he was of a modesty that is surprised ever to be recognised.

D-Day came. I was on the roof of a small building, encouraging a GI to mend the only public clock we had. Down below the DPs were idly grouped around a radio when the news of the German defeat began to be broadcast in one language after another. There were mild cheers as each group understood the broadcast but the DPs were listless knowing their lives would still be affected by war for a long time. I also could only think of the weight of problems to be tackled now that we would be more free to get on with them. The GI was exasperated that we could not share his joy at the thought of returning to the USA, though I did try. I left him to fire his gun in the air. His audience had had enough of gunshots. In London it would be different; they would be delirious to think there would be no more devastation and the servicemen would be returning. But there would be many also with too many tears for a celebration of fireworks. It was not the end of the war. Our soldiers were in the Far East, India and, worse, an unknown number had yet to be released from Japanese prisoner-of-war camps. I had, meanwhile, quietly told the British officer in mufti that I had no work and was longing to be useful. One morning I received orders to transfer to Karlsruhe, a staging centre. My director was speechless and hurt. I packed, hugged the girls and was off the same day. I was taken to a delightful pension run for UNRRA by an Englishwoman who had learned Austrian cookery. I went with her to buy food in a small town. The streets were clean and the high town walls hid big farms behind great double wooden gates. The farms in the town centre surprised me but they were the source of dairy food. One hot day, I strolled into the woods, relishing the aromatic smell of the pine needles on the trees and rustling beneath my feet. My uniform was very warm and I sat in the shade, listening to a distant woodcutter, and grateful for the coolness and the peace. Then I was aware that the chopping had stopped. There was a man walking my way below in the woods and, now alerted, I saw another making his way above me. I wondered if there was an Alsatian in the shadow with him. I walked quietly and as quickly as I could without showing panic to the edge of the wood. I had not been far from the road. My hostess said I had been wise, for there were still SS men and their dogs in hiding down there. My uniform endangered me. I thanked my guardian angel. In a week I was in Karlsruhe.

Landshut, Peace is Declared, a New Team Works in Bavaria in a Camp of Seven Thousand DPs of Forty-Eight Nationalities Organised into a Community by a Multinational Staff

My first memory of Karlsruhe is of meeting Ben Paxman, my new director. He offered me coffee and told me I would be his chief welfare officer. He asked me if I thought I should be able to get on with him. I looked at him carefully, and considered I could. He seemed calm and decisive, basically a serious and decent person; later, I found he was politically intelligent. He gave me a remote smile. He said we would choose the team together. This was an unusual courtesy. I told him that in the UK I had overheard two women discuss the selection of UNRRA personnel in their respective countries. The Dutchwoman said their officers had been chosen for integrity. I suggested that we therefore ask for Dutch warehousemen. We found four but were restricted to two when our Polish deputy was also cut out, as we were not going to a large camp. A Cuban doctor, Roig, had been allotted and he had chosen a Belgian nurse, Jaqui. We had the inevitable French drivers, Alex and Jean, and later a Dutch assistant welfare officer called von Henke joined us. The director then suddenly selected Johnny, a cheerful and wise cockney of twenty-two. It indicated trouble which never arose, as Johnny had a down-to-earth concern for his work and the DPs.

We were soon en route to Landshut, east of Regensburg and west of Munich. We also travelled in two trucks of respectable age and condition. It was anything but a direct route, going at first north, through Heidelburg, coming to a wide river, probably the Rhine at Mannheim, and crossing on Bailey Bridges, trucks and all. We then traversed a landscape, scattered with little hamlets and small churches with tapering towers, changing to 'Onion tops' as we went south-eastwards. We were bewildered by the huge clover-leaf roundabouts without signs. We often went back on our tracks. It was late August, hot and thirsty, we were tempted by the pear trees on the verges. A cycling nun smiled at our guilty looks... it was mild looting.

Eventually we reached our new quarters, two flats in a modest estate house. The swiftly running Isar, one of two rivers on which Landshut had been built in mediaeval times, flowed directly under the back windows. The house was clean, and newly colour-washed in pastel shades with floral strips applied down the wall by rollers. The furniture was sparse but adequate. A team of Polish staff welcomed us to a meal we were too tired to enjoy, especially as it was accompanied by a lady playing the piano accompaniment to her own high, too high, soprano. A US liaison officer, Langsam, had installed himself with us, and a Lithuanian, Joe Kepulis, presented himself as a chauffeur while Berkes, a Hungarian, thought he would be a useful interpreter. We now spoke four main languages round the table: Anglo-American by six, Dutch or German by four, French by three and, overlapping, Hungarian by two people; Alex, the French driver had lived in Budapest. If the director was missing, we played tunes on the glasses with our knives; at least we could do that in unison.

The next day, we went to the office. Landshut was a nearly unspoilt mediaeval town. We had been allotted one of their long-life buildings. It was tall, narrow and equipped with one seatless iron loo. Steep stairs and corridors were crowded to a standstill with docile but determined DPs until we were loaned a sympathetic and courteous German policeman. He was later withdrawn when we foolishly sent a letter of appreciation to the Burgomaster. Langsam had collared the best office and installed my desk. He had no intention of working but would supervise me on behalf of the military government.

The Burgomaster was active and correct. He saw the wisdom of collecting in all the groups of DPs squatting in farm buildings and guest houses. I was soon on my way with Dr Notel, my excellent Hungarian interpreter and personal secretary, to locate the groups and estimate the housing needs of the various nationalities, while Ben Paxman badgered the military governor for better office and DP accommodation.

The DPs had already been organised by an enterprising young Hungarian woman, Anita. I think she had probably found a local sympathetic German attitude to her own group and that of the Ukraines and perhaps Balts who had fought or served as German allies. They had been provided with good clothing, food and shelter. As 'ex-enemy aliens' the Hungarians were in tune with the population. The US officers had found, as we did, that they were excellent, English-speaking office assistants.

Our first duty was to open an office and set up a screening unit. Dr Postoiev was to be in charge. He was a Russian of standing, having been the head astronomer of the Tashkent Time Observatory. Under Soviet suspicion for attending an international conference on astronomy, he had been sent to the Siberian labour colonies for five grim years. He was just and trustworthy and spoke several languages well. His work was to ascertain that each displaced person was a genuine refugee and not from any ex-enemy group. The Americans, in whose zone we now were, were very agitated about the authenticity of Yugoslavs and Ukrainians, who individually might have fought on the German side, a most confusing issue. After our discussions in Reading, I was very anxious about the effect of the Yalta Agreement. I had a quiet word with Postoiev on the possibility of forced repatriation and the need to limit the uproar, struggle and many tragedies that would ensue. He was equally apprehensive and readily agreed to classify the Ukraines as 'Polish Ukraines' and 'Russian Ukraines' according to which side of the Yalta Line their homes had been situated. The DPs understood this action and remained fearful. There was a real advantage. The Polish Ukraines, devout Roman Catholics and fiercely nationalistic, with great pride in their regional culture, were separated from the Russian Orthodox Ukraines, more attuned to the old Tsarist patterns of rural life. About four hundred Soviet Russians were also accommodated. Postoiev understood their refugee status, though it was not until the end that we discovered we should not have supported them, owing to our ally's attitude to nationals resisting repatriation. A Russian liaison officer confirmed that Russians who had missed the Soviet trains in July would be shot when they returned. Stalin would not want the disturbing influence of those who had lingered to enjoy Western luxuries. In 1994 the evidence of massacres and mass graves for civilians was being uncovered in Russia.

A huge old building, used for filing all the precious individual archives for generations, was given to us. We occupied the Regeirungsgebaude immediately, throwing out the records, to the consternation of the Germans, and installing in their place four hundred and fifty Russians. As we piled the homeless in, we could not have cared less. The place was alive with amateur carpenters hammering two-decker bunks together while others filled US palliasses with straw. One room contained fifty-two honeymoon pairs in twenty-six two-tier bunks with much merriment. The kitchens provided good bean or pea soup, bread, potatoes and doubtful German sausage. The buildings were set around a small square garden. The staff had had two small and now waterless loos and these, together with dustbins for soiled paper, were the total provision for four hundred and fifty adults... until our splendid twenty-two year old cockney, Johnnie Potter, on behalf of the director, asked the Burgomaster's troubleshooter in. He, a little man ridiculous in Bavarian lederhosen (shorts), insisted all was well. What he meant was that it was good enough for the DPs. Johnnie was angry. He took the little man upstairs, told him to look inside one of the two loos, gave him a push and locked the door on him. After half an hour the Burgomaster's representative was released and the town provided better facilities in the central courtyard. It was a happy though Spartan camp and ran well with a young Pole as chief. They needed someone who spoke English. Joe Sekula left after some time and I had to select a new leader. The ten committee members came and stood in front of me. I chose Dimitri Poliwianyi, a stalwart man of fifty. He looked as if he had had a very hard life but his eyes were steady and wide apart under a good forehead. He proved a good and honest leader. He was working in the UK until he was eighty-seven.

We found a colony of Latvians in a comfortable, sprawling house in nearby Worth. It had ample room for other Latvians until we had room in the town where we were allotted blocks of flats which had belonged to Nazi sympathisers. Dr Postoiev informed us that we had seven thousand DPs made up of forty-eight national groups, the smallest being one Armenian! There was almost no bickering between the groups; this was probably owing to the type of accommodation. The DPs had lived for years without privacy. I met groups who were shivering because they used their only blanket as a curtain between their family bed and the next. The flats were a Godsend. We did not need big kitchens; a three-roomed flat would house three families who would work out a time-share for the use of kitchen and bathroom. The family was busy; they shopped by bartering rations, cooked family dishes and taught home life to their children.

The *gasthäusers* and farmhouses were emptied as the DPs occupied the flats. Just about this time Czechoslovakia took up the reins of government and decided on an experiment in ethnic cleansing. They expelled the Sudeten Germans who had infiltrated their country before the war or, more sadly, had lived there for many generations. Although they were not our responsibility, we met many of these refugees. They were not impressed with our lists of emptied properties as they were convinced they deserved priority treatment from the military and the German governments. I was not sympathetic as I saw they had their families, health and possessions; we were surrounded with people who had lost all three. The situation put pressure on the Burgomaster, a dignified, efficient and fair-minded man.

The last of our difficulties had been solved with the allocation of good, large-roomed flats, adjacent to the other blocks. They had been occupied by the wealthier Nazis, who had managed to hold on to them while less important people were being ejected to make room for the DPs. There were forty-six flats. With excellent cooperation from the Ukrainian leaders, families were rapidly installed in rooms of a limited but sufficient size for each. In no time the Burgomaster's troubleshooter arrived, looking very woeful in his *lederhosen*. Dr Notel translated the complaint that forty-six families had been evicted and replaced by no more than forty. The Sudeten Germans and indeed the town thought we were wasting valuable living space. I asked Dr Notel to bring the list of tenants in the new flats and to read out the first six with their numbers, and then go to the end of the list for the last six. That brought the total to four hundred and four, including children. The miserable little man was given the list to look at but he could hardly bear to touch it. He walked out backwards, in his embarrassment, with unhappy little bows. The Germans felt no debt to and no responsibility for the years of abuse the DPs had suffered in their enforced support of the Reich. They were despised as slave labour for the factories, peasants for the farms and as uneducated, uncultured and un-German. We had found them, ill and undernourished, unable to do more than survive, in barns or hay lofts of farms where they had worked for nothing.

I remember an attic, lit by one lantern, where an extended family of twenty-eight had lived in quiet dignity. The leader struck me as able; later he took on considerable responsibilities in my department. A celebration party had been held in a stable loft when they were told they were moving. It was my first invitation to such an event and I took my usual precaution of a cup of condensed milk before I went. The low-roofed room was narrow and small, the floorplanks revealed cattle moving beneath us and the acrid fumes of ammonia could not be ignored. Two of the Dutch men had come and I was greeted by a Lithuanian priest, Dr Vaisnora, who thereafter was my official escort whatever the nationality of the host group. With deference, they asked me to choose what they should drink for the first toast. I looked at the selection of bottles; most looked to me like unknown and dangerous vodka but there was a safe-looking bottle of egg-flip. '*Niet, niet,*' they chorused with great concern as I decided to choose it. I should have trusted them but I thought they did not want to let me off lightly, so I insisted. Down the hatch, from tiny glasses or paste pots. It was a sudden horse's hoof in the stomach. I looked at the rest; the men all had red eyes and were in various stages of shock, more or less according to nationality. I peeped in my powder-compact and saw my eyes were normal thanks to a stomach lining of cream. I apologised. Whatever it was, it was to have been the last toast after steady drinking.

We were now finding the smaller groups and lonely families, Russians and Russian Ukraines and later the Yugoslavs. The less educated groups might not have known the war was over and were anxious to hide themselves from the Soviet army. They would not have known that Germany had been divided into four zones: British, French, Russian and American... and that they were in the safer American zone. The US officers were sometimes a bit concerned that those who had been found in *gasthäusers* were people who could afford to look after themselves and who had fraternised with the enemy. They should have been excluded, but we had neither time nor language for investigations; hundreds each day needed food and security while they gathered their families together or started a search for them. That was sufficient for our UNRRA team.

Eventually, Landshut DPs were nearly all housed in blocks of flats around a large paved courtyard, safe for children, or in an adjacent block and a nearby terrace. There were also two large houses for small groups of Poles and Yugoslavs and two small, wooden-hutted village camps, already occupied by Polish Ukraines. We added a large farm camp in Ergolding for the Russian Ukraines, who hid many little horses from the GIs. A villa enabled special care for Yugoslav children near their parents' village homes. The

Regeirungsgebaude housed the Russians in the centre of the town.

Our offices were now moved to a group of garages and outbuildings which provided for transport, warehousing and workshops. The office block was convenient. I was installed in a suite of rooms with assistant welfare staff interviewing non-stop a clamouring crowd of DPs. A kindly German policeman had been instructed by the Burgomaster to control the DPs who were trying to visit the welfare department. It was nevertheless a great struggle to wade through the throng by nine o'clock as they kissed my hands and worried old women even tried to kiss the hem of my tight khaki skirt. I could do no work until von Genke, with better German than me, took over.

Across the forecourt was a cheerful canteen for the staff of the workshops, office and transport depot. Later we were given a very useful warehouse with a good loading platform and ample room for shop counters. It was adjacent to our main blocks of flats. This enabled the DPs to shop with their ration cards like the normal citizens of those days of general food shortages.

Our own quarters were soon settled except for the commissariat. We had not enjoyed the Polish cooking or the musical accompaniment which became an extra obstacle in our attempts to communicate when all four languages were being chattered at once. The Polish staff left us and a wonderful Jewish cook, who had owned a restaurant in Munich before the Nazi regime, made everyone happy. Unfortunately a blonde, teenage pro-Nazi was included in the military government arrangement. She taunted the older woman and I could not persuade her that she was missing an excellent training by her unkindness. She left when the cook was rushed to hospital after a heart attack. I had not been at home to see and assess the strain of cooking for all our differing tastes and of having to accept a stream of insults and insubordination. On my hospital visit, I heard something of her loss of sons and home to Nazi anti-Semitism. She was too ill to talk and she died next day. I had failed someone on our own doorstep.

The next assault on our stomachs was by a team of Hungarians, convinced nothing could replace goulash. They spent happy afternoons gossiping round a small square table, pulling gently at the stiff dough on the tabletop until a near-transparent pastry curtain practically reached the floor on all four sides. With this, they made endless apple and cherry strudels. The team's grousing increased; scorn from the French, pleas for nutmeg and cheese from the Dutch, a general Anglo-American revolt, and Ben simmering to a boil over no baked beans. Our tired efforts to talk were drowning in the hubbub. We called a truce, deciding the only relief from asphyxiation by language at work and at home was to resort to tinkling tunes on our glasses with our knives, while the glasses lasted. Good humour returned with *Jingle Bells*.

At this time Dr Vaisnora, the Lithuanian priest, was added to my staff as Russian interpreter, communicating with me through halting French. He was concerned and perceptive and asked if he could alleviate my extreme fatigue by taking on my household responsibilities for the team. He had been trained for eleven years in the Vatican in all things pertaining to the social side of life there. Certainly he could assemble, from the Lithuanian camp, most excellent cooks, supervisors and cleaners. The team, at last, was wreathed in smiles as the sweet-toothed men found, every lunch and dinner time, two beautifully decorated gateaux on the coffee table!

The team was expanding as our work grew. A Canadian social worker, a second Belgian nurse and Jac, a Dutch warehouseman of Jewish blood, joined us. An American transport officer, educated at Harrow, had served with the

Free French Forces and, being unable to digest his upbringing, crossed swords with all of us when he arrived. Soon
afterwards a totally unnecessary American catering officer
was sent. With only two communal kitchens he had
nothing to do and was always pleasant, bored and mildly
drunk. Ben Paxman was also feeling he had done all he
could and was transferred. He had become irritated with
the military government and at one party we gave them,
when they drank our cognac without responding to our
conversation, Ben, slightly tight himself, pulled Johnnie
and me into the room and said, 'The little fingers of these
two Brits are worth the whole lot of you!' We missed Ben.

Our next US director, Cameron, was a composed and
self-sufficient man. He came with two Dutch nurses,
charming girls. When he telephoned us to announce his
appointment, we were at lunch, and Langsam, the US
military link, conveyed a phonic welcome with a dazzling,
glass-percussion rendering of *Jingle Bells*. That scared
Cameron into requisitioning a cosy villa about seven miles
away. We hardly saw him; he missed the inspection by a
three-star general, luckily, as he did not know the organisation. He was replaced by a decent, well-meaning Texan
who, in turn, was replaced by Wheeler, the first, since Ben,
to be involved in the work. He was ambitious but we were
all well-entrenched and the camp ran so smoothly that the
next move was to consider winding up the UNRRA team
and moving out, leaving it in the hands of the very competent DPs themselves. It is necessary to describe how we
reached that administrative goal.

In my first post in a Quaker settlement, I had learned
something of democratic leadership. At the group meetings,
the warden brought the members into all discussions and
had the patience to wait for the right answers. We required
a democratic approach in UNRRA. I asked the busy
director, Ben, if I could hold meetings for the Lagerfuhrers,

the leaders of the various camps. He was delighted, as this was an unforeseen duty. We had twenty-seven large groups. I met the Estonian leader on my first morning. He came in, huge, solemn, faded-blond and tired, carrying a little grey, two-dimensional elephant in the palm of his hand. It was of leather, and blanket stitched along the edges in white cotton. We bowed our greetings and he presented the elephant without a smile. He might have disapproved of women in charge; perhaps it wished me luck or longevity or, more likely, wisdom with the hope that I would not forget the Estonians. We had, as yet, no hope of understanding one another.

This was being remedied with the appointment of Dr Notel, a Hungarian, qualified in law and economics and above all a magnificent interpreter in English and German. He was an ideal personal secretary, able to anticipate my needs and to forestall my ignorant, unintentional offences against custom. On Monday mornings we held the Lagerfuhrers' meetings. I stood up as the camp leaders came in, all a little apprehensively at first. It was very formal. They each kissed my hand and then found a seat in a semi-circle. Once, later, I decided I had put up with undemocratic hand-kissing long enough and I put my hands behind me. I remember their hurt and bewildered expressions and their enquiries to Notel as to their offence; I resumed the custom. The Lagerfuhrers were all well-educated, level-headed men and one very able woman journalist representing the Lithuanians. The rest had been headmasters or civil servants, farmers, one high court judge and one a director of education. There were 'engineers' whose standing and work eluded me. The Russian element joined us; their leaders were likely to be those who had suffered in Siberia for their enterprise and superior knowledge. They could not understand German well and it was then that I asked Dr Vaisnora, the Lithuanian priest, to be a second secretary.

Each Monday, I would deal with directives from Washington demanding speedy establishment of clinics, schools etc., followed the next month by counter-demands, intended to destabilise the DPs and get them moving once again across the national frontiers over which they had been harried by German troops, who finally had impounded them as trench diggers for their retreating armies. UNRRA in Washington seemed out of touch. The people still needed to eat and sleep in peace, to have medical and dental treatment and to have their babies in safety. Many searched through the Red Cross for their children or partners, and lovers married in a euphoria of hope. Above all, they were political refugees. The Soviet Union liquidated late repatriates and with mass immigration of Russians into the lands they had occupied, was ensuring a communist occupation. The Americans brushed the DPs' fears aside and only saw that there were thousands and thousands depending on costly aid. The Texan director, Currey, did his best for the US. He told the Lagerfuhrers that their people were lazy hangers-on and should be going home instead of eating American food, which, to him, was all that kept them in Germany. He knew nothing of Europe and its history, nor had he asked the DPs about their own sufferings.

He could have spoken to my Latvian typist, in the next room, who had had no news of her husband since he had been wrenched away by the occupying Soviet forces. She had stayed hopefully in Latvia but a 'Big Brother' regime brought her near a mental breakdown. Each day the Latvians had to attend propaganda meetings. If they had missed or looked bored, or worse, slept, they were interrogated at work the next day. Genocide was to be achieved by murdering all the males, flooding the country with Russian families, and intermarriage with the stranded females. Dr Vaisnora had spent a winter in a cell, flooded waist-high with icy water as a punishment for his faith. Even though he had been educated on 'Reds under the beds' in the USA, Currey could not appreciate that the main mass of DPs had to remain exiled because of this same threat. Germany, although hated and cruel, had appeared the lesser evil. It was as well that this had not been understood by the US. They might have branded the forced labourers as collaborators and stopped their aid. In this atmosphere of homesickness, nostalgia and a great longing for one's country – 'hiraeth' as the Welsh call it in one word – Currey ploughed on, interpreted by men who understood the implications. The twenty-seven camp leaders listened. The pain showed on their faces. To dismiss the experiences that had forced these intelligent people into DP camps and to label them idle layabouts, greedy for ten to fifteen thousand calories per diem, was a crass insult. I stared grimly at the window, fighting my anger and my tears. When I turned to Currey, he said, 'What have I done, Jonesy?' Perhaps the camp leaders forgave him but they had seen my blocked tears and I think it was this that welded our team and our displaced persons into one understanding community.

The camp leaders had been selected from each national group, possibly for their knowledge and experience but also for their ability to communicate with the Americans through English or, failing that, in German. They would report back from the Monday meetings on the directives we had received and the resulting changes to be undertaken. Their work was formidable. The meetings were an obvious necessity and soon became a very valuable communications machine, a place where complaints could be heard and answered. The frequent destabilising changes from Washington deeply concerned them. After I had read, and

Dr Notel and Dr Vaisnora had each translated what I said, sentence by sentence, the assembled leaders would throw up their hands in despair. Then I would say, 'You will continue as now to provide nursery education or special help for certain groups, but if an inspector appears from UNRRA HQ, you will explain that you know all about the directive and that you are planning your changes.' What a relief that was! I was devious perhaps, but the camp was peaceful and we did not experience any outbreaks of violence or crime as others did.

By that time, Washington was anxious to export more of its civilising influence and we were told to hold elections for camp leaders. Democracy was to be experienced. By the spring of 1946, we could be seen scurrying about explaining to national groups in their separate camps that all camp leaders should be elected and that elections should be free of bribery and fear. In the Baltic and Polish camps Dr Notel and I could explain this rapidly and arrange dates, booths and ballot boxes. It was a slower procedure with Dr Postoiev in the Russian camps, as they were used to elections by terror. His language was fluent; I had no fear that anything would be misrepresented and I then found I was beginning to understand the speeches and could even intervene if I thought clarification were needed.

We provided sealed ballot boxes, voting papers, pencils and booths to ensure privacy. We arranged for single candidates or party lists for election according to the voting customs in different nations. We were present at all the elections – which only took an hour or two – to ensure a smooth run. I then understood the fabulous ninety-nine per cent turnouts of the dictatorships; elderly women, for example, came to me in tears, saying their husbands were seriously ill, begging me not to stop their rations despite his non-attendance. It was not unexpected that many of the old tried to show me how they had voted before they placed their papers in the ballot box. I mimed a covering of my eyes and indicated the slit in the box. I do not know which of us was the more surprised! Once again the interpreters explained the purpose of free elections in Western democracy. Able people were elected, most of them the leaders we already knew and the Monday meetings were resumed with little change... except that by now I was beginning to talk my own brand of UNRRA language. Once I looked at the rain and told the amazed leaders, 'Es ist gwlib.' 'Gwlib' is Welsh for 'wet', but it sounded like 'It is love!' The explanation was a relief, the unknown language an astonishment.

Our UNRRA team 537 ran its administration on wages of funny money, i.e. a military government coupon acceptable as currency in our workshops and for the nightly entertainments at the Turnhalle. Employees also received a strict ration of cigarettes, a vital source of revenue for barter with the Germans. The Germans also flocked to the Turnhalle concerts (where they were relegated to the back rows!). This produced real German marks with which we could purchase machines and materials for the workshops. In addition to this the military government gave us requisitions from the Kreis, our local region, and valuable medicines, clothing, bedding and games equipment from their army stores, particularly useful for education and athletics for the young unemployed men.

It may be difficult to understand how the cigarette exchange rate worked. A packet of twenty would buy a car, two would buy a good one or a piano. Single cigarettes paid for meals, lodgings and utilities. Once, on a bitterly cold winter's day, I was sent to our Nuremberg HQ to fetch the camp cigarette ration. We had two huge American trucks and I squeezed into the cab of one with some of the team of eight Russians. They procured the cigarette ration while I tried unsuccessfully to get myself a pair of nylons in the PX, the equivalent, with trimmings, of our NAAFI. They called me a 'Limey' and refused to sell me my legitimate quota of sanitary towels which would have been a great joy to the lady typists. The PX man nursed a grievance that the USA paid fees for landing US aircraft in the UK. After all, they were awarded 'Purple Heart' medals for just coming over to the war zone... we had not appreciated them enough... now, the German Fräuleins, well... they were different. The Americans had, in his opinion, chosen the wrong ally. The grey day had got darker and colder. I huddled back in the truck, now fully laden with food and a great many huge cartons of cigarettes. I knew the value of the cargo but I did not know the men. I wondered how easily they could throw a carton over the hedge to retrieve it later. They laughed kindly and with understanding when I wrecked the privacy of their comfort stops by marching around the trucks to see there was no interference!

The DPs had no furniture and this was remedied by Dr Notel and myself going to individual houses, knocking at the door, making a speech about the shortage and explaining that we would take one item and give them a receipt so that they could reclaim the item when we left. Any unwise objection triggered a short reminder of what their government had looted. Thus I managed to furnish a pretty bedroom for Jaqui, the nurse who was young and unhappy. I got myself a psychiatrist's elegant wooden couch to serve as a bed and an antique skew-whiff walnut wardrobe where I hid my bedroll by day when the room served as an out-of-hours office for visiting DPs.

The UNRRA administration was soon well established. Ben Paxman, the director, dealt with the military governor and the Oberburgomaster. Johnny Potter, as Ben's aide, dealt with the little troubleshooter. Both UNRRA men were now becoming involved with applications for emigration, largely to the States. Applications to adopt were passed to me, if they had managed to get through the tight social workers' network in the US. The extended families valued their young people and cared for them and protected them fiercely. Very few orphans came our way. The director obtained the DPs' accommodation from the military government. He was relieved that unlike US social workers, I put the needs of the greatest numbers first, before I dealt with individual problems. The pre-eminence of the individual over the group has been imported to the UK with a loss of social justice, I think, in certain circumstances.

On the medical front, we were served well by Henri Roig, the Cuban doctor, and his two Belgian nurses. His secretary was Elizabeth, the widow of a Hungarian general and a most efficient administrator. Dr Roig's team was augmented by English-speaking Lithuanians, Georg, a young medical student, several nurses running clinics, and a fairy-like dentist who had to stand on a low stool by the clumsy, old-fashioned dental chair, requisitioned from the Burgomaster. I can vouch for the excellent fillings that were produced by feather-light skirmishes in my mouth, despite the uninvited and obtrusive presence of our official camp photographer!

A famous Russian paediatrician amongst our DPs arrogantly refused to join the medical team, as I had been unable to provide him with sterilising facilities and *six* new feeding bottles for each of the many nursing mothers. He said that only he should prepare the American baby food and the substitute milk feed. I recalled the month I had spent at a very busy Kensington children's clinic, learning to hold, bath, feed and potty-train babies and, eventually, will them to sleep, so that I should not distress DPs if I handled their children. The practical matron, realising war shortages, had advised us that a sterilised medicine bottle with a plug of clean gauze, firmly secured, would be a suitable feeding bottle. This advice fell on deaf paediatric ears.

Hospital beds for DPs were arranged, without political problems with the religious orders who ran the hospitals. One drawback amused me one very wet winter's day. I was visiting DPs in different wards around an open courtyard. (The hospital was largely a mediaeval building.) A young nun, in a wonderful starched cap with big swan wings of linen curling back from her small face, turned to me in near panic. She could not get through the downpour to her next urgent case, across the courtyard, as the rain would bring the starched wings flapping down over her eyes and nose in a wet curtain. The past was an impediment but the nuns were kind to all.

The big icy sheds of the warehouses were peopled by a team under the three or four Dutch men who controlled scrupulously fair rations and the clothing distribution for which I had to organise a ration book system. They had recruited strong, reliable men, mostly from the Russian and Russian Ukraine camps, to collect food from UNRRA HQ and the German agencies, apportion and deliver it to the camps in Landshut and the rural areas. It was heavy work, difficult in the icy early morning, fifteen to twenty degrees below zero, when trucks would not start and when kicking the vehicles was the first resort. There was much good humour and laughter promoted by a splendid young country lass and the rescued dog who was now the team mascot. At the end of a gruelling day, rich in mishaps and repairs, there was an appetising hot meal in the canteen bar near the sheds and a chance to thaw before walking back to camp.

As we settled in, more of the sheds were renovated and workshops were set up under the Russian Ukrainian camp leader from Ergolding, Miroschnitchenko. The majority of workers were Ukraines, not speaking German, but a

Latvian manager assisted the German speakers. New material and unsuitable clothing or uniforms were turned into children's stout school clothes, and shoes were made with infinite patience from thousands of grey leather nose protectors, due to be allocated for the German conquest of the Russian border. Wire spirals were fixed to concrete bases for illegal but essential small electric fires. Very skilled Ukrainian women embroidered ethnic designs on cushions and cloths for an expanding trade with American wives arriving in the late spring of 1946. These goods were paid for in funny money and a proportion in cigarettes, my compromise to prevent unfair prices which would have resulted if left to barter between the DPs and the army families.

The cultural side of the welfare department was organised by an able Hungarian, Lazlo, the husband of Anita, who had been organising DPs when we arrived. Lazlo had a quiet dignity and was pleasant, handsome and very popular as well as being a very competent administrator. We had obtained a large Turnhalle, once an army drill hall, later used for British prisoners of war. The huge building was cleaned and redecorated in one morning by the Germans using great ladders on wheel bases and jumbo sized rollers, unknown to us then, for emulsion paint. A stage and several hundred chairs were requisitioned and the national groups lost no time in seizing the opportunity to reawaken their cultural life and to introduce their young people to their own heritage through music and drama. News travelled fast and prestigious national choirs, orchestras and soloists pressed for invitations to entertain us. Theatre companies seemed the most frequent. I decided to attend every possible performance for my own pleasure and because neither the directors nor anyone else would have been willing to risk boredom. I had, however, been used to sitting through long Welsh sermons which I did not understand, so I was already accustomed to thinking out my own scenarios with no help from UNRRA languages, and I thought the team should show appreciation of DP efforts to reach back into normality. I was amply repaid. Night after night, they gave me a touching welcome to the front seats. There was good music, plays and ballet. I sat through the first act of a Chekhov play, unbroken talk on a garden seat. Act two – *action*! A post boy arrived on stage, brandishing an envelope, shouting, 'Telegram'. The kindly audience realised that this was the first word I would have understood; the play halted as half the audience rose and bowed in my direction.

Lazlo also arranged for the Munich Orchestras and their opera company to come. The presentation of *Hansel und Gretel* was, I thought, an unfortunate reminder of imprisonment and cruelty, but people, including the large German audiences who were restricted to the back of the hall, liked the music. The engagement would have been lucrative even for Munich. We now had enough money in the welfare department to buy sewing machines and other items for the workshops and equipment for education. This was all administered by Lazlo and the Dutch assistant welfare officer, van Henke.

Religious Practice and Churches

Funny money and welfare funds were spent on two large groups. The first surprised me. The choristers who sang the lovely church services were all paid and were all adults. In Wales it would have been honour enough to join a choir without thought of fees, but the Ukraines practised hard and the Orthodox services lasted five hours, so their life was not so easy. The next group were the teachers. There were good professional teachers in the kindergartens, primary and secondary schools. They were a very strong and stabilising influence.

A few priests were also probably supported from the financial fringes. Their presence became known and important as we settled down; they certainly became an importunate group as far as I was concerned. While we were still working, non-stop, finding DPs and rehousing them, the priests were campaigning for good buildings for their churches. These would be invaluable in concentrating national sentiment and bringing the people together. Many DPs now desired to marry with the blessing of their church and to bury their dead with some dignity. The western Ukraines, Poles and Lithuanians were mostly Catholics looking to Rome for support and were welcome in the German churches. The Lithuanian group shared Sunday mornings in a Carmelite chapel, their service being taken by Dr Vaisnora, my secretary. The Russian Orthodox priests, Ukrainian or true Russian, had nowhere to go. At last, I obtained a small Turnhalle or sports hall and divided this into two, for it conveniently had doors at each end. This satisfied the Ukrainian and the Russian-speaking Orthodox congregations. Later, as the Ergolding camp in the country grew, we turned a well-lit hay loft into another church. We could give the priests some parachute covers; these were of silvered rubberised cloth which fell into satisfactory folds when used as copes or stuck fast to fretted plywood screens, in front of the altar, hiding the holy place where the Bible was kept. Before long, white paper roses had been made in profusion to decorate the screens, the choirs were in full voice and the much-revered Metropolitans arrived from Munich or Berlin to sanctify the new churches for the consecration of weddings, baptisms and funerals.

When I first went to the Orthodox services, they were held in a stone-floored building, not a church. Standing, I only stayed for an hour, but usually I was in time for the lovely, rising crescendos of the choir as the priest went behind the screen to bring in the Bible. This huge and heavy book was decorated with gilt and enormous glass 'jewels' twinkling in the candlelight, as the priest raised it above his head, to be seen by all. The old women remembered their youth and knelt with their foreheads on the cold floor, muttering little prayers of praise and sometimes weeping with relief that the old ways were returning. The cruelties of the war must have made Tsarist serfdom seem a lost piece of paradise.

They were planning to thank me properly, and after the consecrations, when my only involvement was finding a taxi for one of the Metropolitans, I was invited to attend the first wedding. I was not prepared to do more than watch but I was treated as an honoured guest. The sexes were separated and I stood with the women on the left; then I was rapidly installed on a chair near the bridal pair as a sort of parody of the inclusion of the owner of the estate. The bride was wearing white in Western style but with sprigs of green sewn on the dress and maidenhair fern on the veil. The groom too was in a Western suit with a beautifully embroidered Ukrainian shirt. They stood together with a pink-bowed bridesmaid behind each. An old woman placed a white cloth, with money resting at each end, in front of them and then they stood on it. Two young girls now held ikons, one of Mary and another of Joseph, framed by long, narrow linen towels on which the bride had embroidered cockerels in black and scarlet for her groom and St Joseph, and roses for herself and the Virgin. After receiving mass from the priest, splendid in a silver and gold cope, the pair each kissed a gold crown, brought from a side altar, one with a small image of Joseph for the groom and the other of Mary for the bride. The bridesmaids then raised the appropriate crowns over the nuptial pair and the ceremony proceeded; rings were given to bride and groom while the choir sang a lovely accompaniment. A short address followed and the couple's hands were joined with a white napkin and sealed by the placing of the priest's embroidered stole over the knot. The priest then led the couple, whose knees must have been trembling by now, to the altar where the girls with the ikons were stationed. The pair kissed both ikons, bowing to the altar, and then followed the priest around the other half of the church, finally bowing to me before repeating the whole circuit twice again. Jubilation broke from the choir as the couple reached the white towel and the napkin was untied. They had been married. The priest came to thank me and gently gave me the tiny cottage loaf used for the mass, stamped with the orthodox symbol. I still have it, with the little triangle of bread cut out for the mass; it has hardly deteriorated in fifty years.

The bride then came to ask me to the reception. I demurred, tears welled up, and I went. Dr Vaisnora was waiting by my place, which was next to the bride. She was shivering in her pretty dress so we sat close together for warmth. There were lumps like white chocolate on tiny saucers near each plate. Dr Vaisnora explained it was mutton fat and laughed at my disgust. He said I would be glad of it... and I was. The endless toasts warmed the bride, and the fat cubes seemed deliciously right. They were running short of suitable toasts after 'the Happy Couple'. The US and Mr Roosevelt were remembered... and I, as 'the Mrs Roosevelt of Landshut'. It was time to go home; a taxi was ready to take me. Before I could settle down at home, a messenger arrived with a small wedding cake wrapped in the lovely white bridal scarf embroidered with roses. I was so ashamed; I had nothing to give. I was warned it would be an affront to return the precious towel.

I found another forgotten corner of the Orthodox world. The Catholic DPs must have obtained their white wine for Holy Communion through the German church. I came across one of our gentler, older priests in a rural area. He was dishevelled and shy when I caught him gathering berries in the bushes near his village. He explained it was to make a red concoction that could be used for the service on Sunday. I wondered if his knowledge or his faith would make it safe to drink. Off I went to the US catering department and asked for a bottle or two of red wine, which, incidentally, we never received in our weekly allocation of alcohol. I was hounded out by an anti-Brit type accusing this Limey of being an alcoholic bent on getting more for herself. Feeling a bit upset, I bumped into a young US rabbi who laughed his head off and supplied the Orthodox needs very readily.

On Sundays, I trotted along to the Lithuanian service in the Carmelite chapel. It was a charming, well-lit building with a white gallery around two sides, hiding white latticed doors or windows. The vaulting was supported by rococo pillars like twisted barley sugar sticks, and the church housed monuments and relics in alcoves. One fascinated me; it was a greenish glass case, appearing at first like an oversize aquarium, but in fact the repository of a mummified saint, reclining uncomfortably and gruesomely at floor level. One particular Sunday I arrived to find that the church was packed. I wriggled in, as always in my uniform. I found the assembly was all German. Dr Vaisnora had not been aware that I was a regular attender and, when he agreed to transpose his service, had not informed me and I was too firmly wedged to be able to make an exit.

It was a service for the Carmelites; it was the betrothal of a bride to Christ, a noviciate joining the silent sisterhood. The girl was dressed in white but was far from central to the proceedings, dominated by a group of priests who had more ceremony with one another than with the girl. I could not see well, but assumed a mass was said. Then the girl was brought to the altar steps. The white grilles in the galleries opened and the nuns, divorced from the world, began to sing softly from a distance, moving slowly nearer with an ebb and flow of sacred music that to me sounded menacing, becoming all-embracing as it reached the church. A door opened by the altar and the girl was thrust through to the waiting Mother Superior. Despite knowing that the girl would have been long- and well-prepared for this day, I felt a shock at the relentless inevitability of the final disappearance. Her parents would have been comforted by their pride in their daughter.

My next experience of a church sacrament was a heartbreak. In our Bayreuth team there had been a delightful young Serbian waiting at table. She had apparently been invited out by a GI, but his dalliance in the jeep must have been unexpected after her quiet upbringing and she had jumped out, not able to measure the speed, and been killed. I represented the team at the funeral and the young soldier had the courage to come to meet the grieving family. It was very disconcerting. We were led into an ante-room with about six bodies lying on biers, probably hospital trolleys, and told to select our own deceased for the funeral. I recognised our lass, serene amongst the white paper roses. Led by a priest, we filed into the church taking her with us. We all were given thin, lighted candles and the corpse remained with us during the liturgy. Our prayers and grief for the lovely, wasted life were very real. Again, the lack of language meant only a brief though deeply felt expression of sympathy with the family.

Death is balanced with life. I attended the christening in a far-off village as the godmother of small Tamara. Her father had been selected as a camp secretary, our communications officer for small matters concerning national groups. He was a quiet, well-educated Serb, chosen from a tiny minority group which would not have the power to be manipulative. He recorded arrivals and departures, when any, looked after common services when faulty, and diffidently brought grievances to our notice. It was a rotten job. When his wife pressed me to be a godmother, despite my pointing out that I would be useless, I felt I owed him something for his patience. By the time the christening was arranged, Tamara was a sturdy three month old baby. The Orthodox priest had prepared a small room and I was sent in with the men of the family and their men friends. To my surprise, neither the mother nor the grandmother, or in fact any other women, were allowed in. It must have been a very old custom to enhance the male claim as chief creator. I was very glad of the male strength around me. Little Tamara slept quietly (doubtless tranquillised) on a feather pillow, itself an envelope, with three of its four triangular uppermost sections meeting centrally in a ribbon bow. The fourth section would have been under the baby's head. Tamara, pillow and all, was now placed on my outstretched arms. The priest prayed and chanted and then untied the little bows, which now turned out to be three, and anointed Tamara on her head, hands and feet. With all the fumbling with ribbons and lace, it took a long time. The little one behaved calmly and then the bows were carefully tied up again. I felt the strain, my face grew red, I sweated, my arms were trembling. The responsibility, in every way, grew heavier. Two stalwarts realised my imminent collapse and from each side supported my arms while the whole ceremony was repeated twice, other men now assisting in tying the dainty bows. I felt like Moses when Aaron and a friend held up his arms until the battle was won. No one could explain in English what the ceremony meant nor understand that as a Nonconformist I had had, myself, no experience of godmothering. I was not a wise choice. We got to know each other better at the party and they announced they had visas for the States. It was the last time I saw them. I knew no one over in the USA but they seemed very happy and secure. They had friends in high places. The news of progress, and even that Tamara's mother had graduated in law, indicated that they were coping very well... until I heard the parents were divorcing. Probably the father could not match the drive and ambition of his wife and mother-in-law. I had rather wistful pictures of Tamara visiting her father. At nineteen she married. As usual I did not have any acknowledgement of my present nor, for the first time, any new address. I had been of no spiritual or material help. In fact, I knew too little of America to understand their needs.

Christmas and Other Customs

The first post-war Christmas brought freedom to worship and make merry on very limited resources. But mirth had no spring, as the memory of relatives and friends lost, murdered or killed, as soldiers or as civilians, was ever present. I was invited to a Lithuanian party for children. Towards the end they formed a traditional circle around the Christmas tree and sang their own special Christmas song. As we got to the chorus, young voices were trembling and suddenly they dropped their held hands and used them to cover their tears. I went away, quietly.

The first harbinger of Christmas was a great surprise, eighteen days early. Dr Notel and I were desperately busy sorting out families into national and compatible groups to be housed in the available accommodation, when we were interrupted by a pair of white gauntlet gloves rapping the desk. It was an annoying intrusion but Dr Notel, loyal and perceptive, whispered quickly that this was St Nicholas bringing Christmas tidings and good wishes. I looked up to see the cultural leader of the Catholic Ukraines, heavily disguised as a shortish bishop, dignified in a white and gold mitre, holding a painted crosier. Once again, I regretted having promised my weekly cigarette ration to the welfare department; I had nothing to give her. It was a splendid turnout. Jaqui told me more. In Belgium, the 6th December was an All Fools day in honour of the worthy Saint Nicholas. One sent spoof presents and witty notes, anonymously, to get a few home truths off one's chest, on the understanding that no one would be offended... a true occasion of it being more blessed to give than to receive! The Saint was called Santa Claus in Western Europe and in Belgium he was accompanied by a Negro type called San'Mouffe. When we were all invited to the Polish Ukrainian Christmas party, a tall man was magnificent as St Nicholas, the bishop. He was accompanied by a small host of angel children, who were distributing presents as he directed, and also by a very smart Mephistopheles in scarlet jerkin and tights, sporting horns, a tail and neat whiskers. The Devil courteously but insistently presented each guest with a birch rod (twelve inches of gilded twigs) as they received their gifts. This was to remind us of our inadequacies and to encourage the children to bring home better school reports next time!

The Russian Christmas, shorn of religion for many years, made little sense. This, however, may have been the result of shortages. The large room was bare; a lot of tiny toys, made out of scraps, and only likely to last a few hours, were in a shallow heap on the floor, and being eyed with some curiosity by the many little children standing expectant and docile with their families. Father Christmas arrived, neither saint nor devil. He was unhampered by our custom of a red dressing gown. Instead, he cavorted about, exuberant with mischief, in a short foxy-red fur coat tightly belted. On his head was a fur boater with a red ribbon band and on his legs were trousers and high boots. Fox or wolf, his interest was in the young mothers who rollicked and laughed at his very welcome attentions. He carelessly kicked and squashed the poor little pile of toys which splintered into nothing. I pulled at a woman's sleeve, to prevent the damage, but the hilarity had made the adults indifferent and the children stood disappointed and on the edge of tears. UNRRA had not thought of toys; shelter had been the pressing objective.

The Yugoslav Christmas was related to the others as a nightmare is to a dream. The families had come only recently into camp, very poor and malnourished. The children were ill-dressed, still unsmiling from months of deprivation and quite devoid of joy. They huddled in a line against a wall and eventually sat on the floor, their small faces apprehensive. How right they were, to be fearful. St Nicholas seemed to be missing and we were back to San'Mouffe with a vengeance. A completely black Devil arrived with a red rubber tongue bulging in and out from a pocket control. His eyes rolled, he leered and he roared, and most of it was about the wickedness of the helpless toddlers and the need to put them into his big, black sack and cart them off to hell. As the little ones were propelled forward, he rattled some chains, repeated his threats and hardly mollified them by his flimsy gift. The mothers' merriment could not drown the desperate children's wailing. I represented an empty-handed UNRRA and was very sad to be there.

Our own Christmas was less of a celebration than Thanksgiving had been. It was not memorable except that Jaqui and I came to the conclusion that the men drew their satisfaction from their cigars. We chose one each; they were mercifully mild and we survived to finish them on a walk in the fresh, frosty air.

My happiest recollections are of the Russian Orthodox services which echoed the Catholic celebrations, according to calendar, twelve days later. The Russian Christmas service was held in a borrowed church. The chanting and choral singing engulfed one in ancient joys, the murmuring of reverend old women and the smoke of the swinging censers obliterated recent history and hatred, and the blending minor chords made me feel a deep affinity with the people. There was a surge of identification with the heritage of the past which visibly touched the young: it was rich and they could be proud.

On Easter Sunday, Dr Notel and I were in Regensburg. After a visit to HQ, my good companion determined to educate me in the town's history and I found myself amongst an excited German crowd looking at a mediaeval torture chamber. The Germans drooled over racks and pain-inflicting instruments. I was appalled and asked Dr Notel why the Germans had not been sated with the atrocities they had inflicted in Dachau, not so far away. He saw he had made a mistake and hurried me to the cathedral where High Mass was going to be held. He knew the nooks and crannies and I was pushed through a tiny door to find myself in a corner, in the front of the congregation. I was glad few people would notice my uniform in the dense crowd. On the way out, when the crowd had gone, I was shown the 'tomb' of the Devil's mother. It was a small stone carving at eye level; the crude mediaeval image was of a spitting cat.

The service astonished my chapel-educated soul. There was an irreverent use of the altar; men humped their bikes up the steps and propped them up behind the altar to prevent their being stolen during the service. Every one shoved his neighbour and the whole crowd pressed forward as we had done, to the bottom step. The bishop made an entrance on fur-lined cerise bedroom slippers; important, flushed and incredibly dressed in cerise velvet and lace. He and his supporting priests surged up the altar steps and he donned a mitre. Now he could turn, in its embroidered authority, to bring the people into the presence of God. I was unable to follow the service but was all the more riveted by the bishop making quick costume changes. In his mitre, he controlled the crowd, then in a show of humility he donned his little cerise skullcap, and communed with the Almighty who was confining His Presence to the altar.

There were further mitred discourses with the citizens interspersed with respectful reports from the skullcap to the altar. The bishop was now as cerise as his robes and his white hair was wild with hat changes. The ceremony was coming to the crisis when the bishop had to strip, in full view, out of the cerise mantle into a clean and lacy shirt, before being covered by more embroidered and lace-bedecked linen garments each being pulled over the tired head in an unceremonious rush. A beautiful stole and a cape and then a grander mitre were put on. The bishop was rightly anxious as to his new appearance and I was anxious about his health. Two muscular priests were called in and, with great effort, they mishandled a huge gold mirror of great value and antiquity, so that the bishop, with luck, could see his reflection in the polished flat side of the mirror, the other being heavily decorated in gold relief. By this time, at least six priests were bending and contorting themselves, trying to get the reflective surface at the right angle. The bishop's hoped-for serenity was stillborn. I think it must have been a shouting match in *sotto voce* but the organ played to full strength. Mass was being celebrated; the bishop was now in place. The bid for solemnity was lost as a woman decided she must partake in the service and proceeded up the steps. Perhaps she was well-known. Men tried to dissuade her while the final acts were hurried on it was finished; a fully-dressed bishop dismissed his congregation with a blessing and then, linking arms with the full priestly escort, he strode rapidly with the phalanx down the altar steps towards the congregation and main door. They swept the woman with them, lifting her and throwing her into the dense crowd. The priests went on and out, not a moment too soon for the bishop's blood pressure.

Other sacred days on the calendar perhaps owed more to ancient myth than to Christian custom. Peter and Paul were a joint holy day but, with two calendars, we celebrated it twice... a splendid way of spreading work and reducing unemployment while producing fun and feast. With all the saints of Europe, adopting each other's saints could be a solution for our problems.

To us, the most entertaining of these feast days was St John's on midsummer night. The Latvians had rented an open meadow, surrounded by woods. Near the gate was a very tall pole with a brazier on top, complete with a leaping fire. Below this, by a trestle table, stood our hosts. Father John, tall and simply dressed, important in a wreath of acorns and oak leaves, was accompanied by Mother John, also regal and wreathed. They were each the oldest of their sex in the Latvian groups and they were our hosts for the evening. We shook hands and were also invested with wreaths. They had overestimated my brain and skull, so my lovely wreath of roses rested around my neck, while I hoped no investigating earwigs would need to be arrested. We all now partook of fresh bread and a soft cheese containing caraway seeds. There was a home brew to wash it down. Before we could wonder what the night would bring, small choirs came singing through the woods and fields, bearing greenery to represent the traditional rushes. The girls had made simple national costumes, usually a long navy skirt banded with red, yellow and green ribbons near the hemline. The navy bodice was cut low to display Latvian embroidery on their white linen blouses, and particularly the three silver brooches, worn one above the other, the smallest at the top. These were fashioned as wide flat circles with engraved patterns on the silver; they were precious symbols and many would have been valuable heirlooms. The often-illustrated flattering headdresses were for brides and inappropriate for St John's night.

The assembled choirs were now harmoniously singing folk music, and dusk fell. Our handmade programmes told us it was the time to go into the woods to search for the mythical gold and silver flowers of the fern. A huge fire had been lit; it was low and perhaps three metres in length. The lads clasped their lasses and ran them so quickly through the flames as to make even a singed skirt impossible. Dzirkalis, a YMCA organiser on my staff, was gallant enough to rush me through the fire without helping me to comprehend any more of the midsummer madness. The custom of lighting need fires on May Day extends to the summer solstice in Russia and so also in Latvia. Frazer writes that these are for the health of humans as well as the cattle. The poetic interpretation seemed more to do with fertility rites. There may have been other saints' days with ancient customs obliterated from men's minds under the dictatorships.

There was one saint important to everyone. Most people had been christened in devout homes with the name of a saint. That saint's day had to be celebrated by the namesake instead of, or as well as, the baptised one's own birthday, preferential treatment being given to the saint. I was too busy to think of my birthday and I was not used to any fuss. Fortunately, I had no saint's day to revere. On a wet February day a phone call interrupted my breakfast. Dr Notel begged me to go in early as there were many people waiting to see me. I wondered what new catastrophe had arisen. I steamed off and was flabbergasted to find I was being congratulated on being a year older. Dr Notel was just as surprised that I had not thought about my birthday and would not have expected the staff to look up my records and broadcast the news. He was kind but quite unable to explain what it was all about. I recovered my equanimity; I conveyed my bemused appreciation as I received the dignified good wishes of group after group from half past eight until after three o'clock. I was most touched by individual callers, many unknown, who had waited for hours to wish me well. Some had embroidered a handkerchief, knitted a warm scarf or painted a greeting, all from scarce resources. I was devastated by those determined I should have some treasure they had managed to carry from their home – a small cup, a soft toy or even a goatskin from the best of the herd. I was ashamed at accepting and having nothing to return. Camp groups had used their cigarette ration to buy me jewellery and china, but the loveliest was a book, binding together the pages of carefully decorated good wishes from each camp. I knew I was unworthy, that the work in my office was performed by others. I then thought how difficult it was for these people of culture and education to be helplessly receiving the sort of assistance they would have been organising for others in different circumstances. I wondered if their gifts had helped them to hold their heads a little higher. I understood why I could not refuse the presents as a professional worker should do; we had become a family.

Education from Kindergarten to High School

The first priorities for the DPs had been food and shelter as far as the army and then the local military government could cope. When UNRRA, sooner than expected, was called in, the urgencies were better accommodation, cooking facilities, beds and blankets, toilet and laundry facilities and clothing. Medical cover was improvised and then improved. The Red Cross was linking the camps together and through this the families. Priests had appeared, anxious to establish churches in any spare but large building, but the people, of their own accord, were trying to cater for their children's pressing need for education. There were many teachers of all grades around and assistants were numerous and willing. Again, space was scarce and equipment from German stores meagre or missing. Tremendous enthusiasm bridged the gap.

Dr Hlushko was the Polish Ukrainian representative at our Monday meetings. In the summer, he asked me to be kind enough to supervise the standard of English at the final exams for his high school. I was to call at his home to discuss it. The visit was memorable. Dr Hlushko – tall, silver-haired, distinguished – presented me to his vivacious, auburn-haired wife who was still trying to look fashionable after losing most of her possessions but still retaining her black velvet hat. The Irish-wolfhound-on-a-smaller-scale rose to attention on my entry and ignored me. He, Rex, was then formally introduced to me and we shook paws gravely. Thereafter, he rose with a slight wag of the tail when I got up.

I was there for more important reasons and I agreed to attend the exams at the end of the week. There were six or seven girls in their late teens waiting politely, each furnished with a pencil and paper. About eight exam papers typed on flimsy pink paper were produced; every girl drew one from the pile. I found that each paper dealt with a different period of English literature. There were translations to be made to and from English taken from two set books with questions on other works by the same author, then quotations were to be explained and a short essay written on the background of the period in British and in European socio-political history. Having coped with all this, the girls had to read and to answer oral questions in English. I was asked to comment on their grasp of English and in particular on their accents. I could find no fault and had to compliment their fine teacher. Educational equipment was very sparse; night after night I had seen set books being written up on blackboards, as there would be only one book for teacher and pupils. The width and depth of the knowledge they had acquired to be able to cope with the luck of the draw was astonishing. One question dealt with the Arthurian legend and mentioned the Druids. I could not resist informing Dr Hlushko that the Welsh Eisteddfod included a company of Druids, in three ranks, that their altar was a huge stone within a symbolic stone circle and that there was a link with the Brythonic Celts in Brittany as shown by a symbol of one sword, split lengthways, half to each country, to be united (by a small catch) and carried on a cushion for each annual ceremony. We parted in a flurry of congratulations. I was very impressed and later decided we needed a team director of education to promote other nations' efforts. Posts were not advertised; Dr Hlushko accepted happily.

A year later, my fourth team in Bayreuth received a similar request from the director for education for all the DP camps in Bavaria. Our director, Baron von Zuylen, was so impressed that he invited the dignitary to lunch, a gesture unheard of in that regime, and asked me to cope. I tidied myself beyond recognition but at lunch the visitor, Dr Hlushko, greeted me warmly. I was thrilled that his earlier promotion had led to new honours. Their exam was of the same pattern as before. I was given the papers as a souvenir and on reading them found one to be based on Arthur and Welsh custom. Wales, a country not previously known to them, was on the map. I was sorry I could not sing to them; I was finding our music was alike. Whenever I played a Welsh hymn one of the house staff would rush in and hug me, shouting, 'Ukraina, Ukraina,' convinced that I was learning to play her country's music.

In Landshut, we had opened kindergartens for all the main groups, even though the equipment was inadequate. The mothers were happy to help the teachers and the little children benefited. One group was different. Late in the autumn a group of Yugoslavs filtered in and were housed in a village called Geisenhausen. Jaqui, the nurse, was deeply disturbed by the condition of children who were thin, hungry, under developed and perpetually sad. A villa, equipped as a health clinic, was available and Jaqui asked that it be given over to the children who would still be in daily touch with their parents. Good food and special medicines were provided and each afternoon the group slept blissfully on small beds and good blankets under carefully controlled sunlight lamps. Three months later Jaqui and von Genke asked me to visit the villa. They had every right to be proud of the laughing youngsters playing lively games and now physically fit to start school with their own teachers from among the parents in the village. The groups from the Baltic states had no difficulty in providing teachers. They seemed to handle the German economy as well as they worked with UNRRA and were quite well equipped. The Balts were almost entirely professional people and could produce a good range of educational subjects to interest the young. The larger numbers of Ukraines and Russians needed more help. National history and literature could be taught orally. This was just as well since books were unlikely to be found. The younger children, however, were learning each other's language, rudimentary German and some English. There was international harmony on the playground in the centre of the blocks of flats.

Only immense professional enthusiasm could overcome the difficulties in secondary education. Textbooks, if available as single copies, were written out on blackboards and copied by students into exercise books, one of the few things we could provide, though strictly rationed. Science could not be taught. National pride, flourishing in the new freedom, buoyed them up. They sat the statutory exams and at the end of the year several of our young people were admitted to the University of Munich.

The welfare office had early access to a printer who produced tickets for the Turnhalle concerts. This enterprise extended soon to camp news-sheets, of which I was officially the editor. The schools did not benefit – printing books would devour the small amount of paper available. The newspapers were popular and I relied on Dr Postoiev to omit articles defamatory to our ally, the USSR; the military governor would have banned further editions. After I left Landshut, Johnnie rang me up to warn me that there was a hue and cry from some DPs that our press was too muffled and I had been an anti-communist; simultaneously there were American complaints that I was a red-under-the-bed and should be dismissed – obviously the press was steering a centre line. It was, possibly, an attempt to ease me out of the Bayreuth team before the Landshut director caught up with me again, as he did. He had resented my influence with the DPs, built up under the four previous directorships. He was to take over a camp with a strongly developed welfare department for the second time.

The US Army always gave very generous help with outdoor sports. The hours spent on sport were a valuable antidote to the frustration of young people with little possibility of professional work or training or for repossessing a still occupied homeland and making a new beginning. Where the Germans had been driven back, the Russians had trudged in. And they were staying! The army gave us volleyball, useful in the Turnhalle and outside. There was plenty of healthy rivalry between national groups. The Balts had two YMCA organisers, Dzirkalis, a Lithuanian, and Netliv, a Latvian. They had got together, hired a large field sheltered by woodland, and, with helpful army provision of tents and a field kitchen, set up a camp which catered for the younger DPs all through the summer months. One happy day the whole team visited, joining in alfresco meals, washing-up and sports. Those who were of a more serious turn of mind attended the evening service at an outdoor altar taken by the ubiquitous Dr Vaisnora presiding, as the Balts were in residence. There were prayers for the independence of the three Baltic nations in which I could join. But no one envisioned that there had to be the break-up of the Soviet Empire before the Balts could be freed. The older folk had some glimmering of the ethnic damage that would ensue from the occupation. The history of the Baltic states and their neighbour, Poland, had long been one of changing boundaries and mixed peoples. It was surprising that they felt themselves to be entities at all but the groups appeared to be distinct.

Families Reunited, Fear in Repatriation

The confusion of nationalities and their unspeakable persecution by the invading dictators were epitomised in one family, Polish in heritage and culture, but Lithuanian by birth and domicile. Their story could have served as a basis for a Koestler book. Maria regarded Lithuania as her home. Hers was an average professional family, all living in one village. Early in the war when Russia was a German ally, the Soviets had arrested most of them. If the only objective had been cheap labour the long journey to Siberia for many sick and elderly people was ill-thought-out. It is more likely it was about genocide. In 1950, Dr Vaisnora wrote saying that it was reliably estimated that one hundred thousand Lithuanians had been deported to Siberia. Few came back. Maria said the boxcars had been drawn up at the station platform where her family was all assembled. A very old and ill aunt had been bundled along on a mattress and was left helpless and alone, to die, as the rest were herded into the train at pistol point. Maria's husband was also dying of TB, and Maria's whole energy was absorbed in staying with him. Her mother, as well as her uncles, was lost in the imprisoned crowd. Maria said there had been no water, no sanitation and her husband's need to half-sit or half-lie was an acute embarrassment as there was standing room only. Within a day or two of the slow, jerky journey he had passed from vomiting blood to quiet death. There could have been no alternative but to drop him on the railway line. Maria was thankful that she had been with him as long as he survived. That journey had gone on and on through Siberia to Vladivostock, a tale so tragic the lack of luggage and clothing was not mentioned. Maria was given factory work and, having survived, was worth keeping alive as a slave worker. Then the absurdity of politics gave her freedom. The Russians saw the need to confront the Germans before the latter mastered and controlled the strength of Europe. The Soviet Republic re-evaluated its partnership with Hitler and then declared itself on the side of the Allies and, therefore, of Poland. Logically the Polish prisoners had to be released, wherever they were but without assistance to return to their homes or find the scattered family. Maria and her surviving family were freed. I never knew how Maria got to Germany. She talked about walking and hitch-hiking, maybe she was in a group of refugees. She might in some places en route have earned her keep as a harvester. I did not press her. She was a very quiet person. Later she came to me; she had had news that her mother was alive. Her mother had been released too. She had been found in Georgia by British troops who were passing the refugees southwards out of the war zones. She ended up in a refugee camp in Tanganyika, as it then was. The warmth, fresh fruit and clean clothing had been welcome but TB was diagnosed and she was sent to the UK for treatment about the time I left UNRRA. By then Maria had acquired permission to join relatives in the States. They both spent a weekend with us when Maria got special permission to break her journey on the way to America. After a year or so, Maria, with a post as a librarian, had enough money to sponsor her mother's entry to the States. They lived together for many years. Latterly, Maria visited Poland and met her many relatives safely. In 1992 my Christmas card was returned with the news that Maria, then probably in her eighties, had been moved but there was no address.

The reunion of a few families out of the thousands milling aimlessly around was a tremendous achievement by the Red Cross, who were compiling a magnificently detailed survey of all DPs known to them. Each week, fresh lists of DPs and of their addresses in camps, hospitals etc. came to our offices and were passed to group leaders who scanned them on behalf of their people, who were anxiously searching for kith and kin. Early news of a lost family was of that of our one-time musical housekeeper. Her two little girls had been snatched from her home in Poland as Germans marched through. They were blond, aged eleven and nine and required by Hitler for his fantasy of an 'Aryan' Germany – blonds were to be captured from any country and to be kept in convents until such time as they would be honoured by the attentions of his beloved storm troopers, all chosen for 'Aryan' looks and strength. Indeed, we had some young women who had already produced babies and lost them to state institutions. Our Polish mother had traced her two daughters, on their enforced journey through Czechoslovakia, Hungary and Austria to Germany, where the trail had been lost. She was not a forceful woman but motherhood provided the immense determination and grit she needed. Suddenly she knew where they were! In Hamburg! The Cuban, Dr Roig, volunteered to take on my duty. He was a good friend. The weather was appalling for driving. It was a very long way and, if you were lost, it was not a safe country. In addition, there could be the usual hassle about taking DPs from one zone to another. Hamburg was in the industrial, heavily bombed British zone of Germany, very different from the less damaged and rural US Bavarian zone. Dr Roig, with a nurse, was a much better escort for the little girls. They were quietly reunited as a family. Their relief and happiness could only be slowly savoured as they regained strength and confidence. About six weeks later, I saw them in a Christmas pageant; the little one of nine looked more robust but the elder needed much love and peace to forget her anxieties for her small sister as well as for herself.

The problem of red tape between zones arose when our Lithuanian chauffeur, Joe Kepulis, discovered that his wife, Regina, was in Salzburg. He had received, by some devious route, a letter from her, showing great fear and distress. Apparently the Americans, in whose zone she was, had moved a group of women DPs, with no male protectors, to a wooden building outside Salzburg. This had been a well-known brothel and each night the women blockaded themselves in as best they could. Venturing out in daytime was dangerous but at night the number and determination of the men besieging the building was terrifying. Joe was distraught but no amount of telephoning could persuade the US army in the Austrian zone to let a DP go to the adjacent US German zone... even though this DP was the wife of a Lithuanian who was also a US citizen. Joe, Johnnie and I plotted. I was to drive with Joe as my chauffeur for an unauthorised spree in Salzburg shops. There was no trouble at the frontier and we went straight to the wooden hutment. Joe obtained all his wife's possessions and reassured her. Next we went shopping so that I could spend Regina's Austrian money on a lace tablecloth and give Joe my equivalent in British money which I had illegally. It was worth four times as much on the black market, but that was Joe's business. Next day, Johnnie and Joe went off, picked up Regina and the baby, and started for the frontier. The baby, safely asleep under a carelessly thrown mackintosh on the floor, knew nothing of the goings-on on the back seat of the car. Joe drove to the guard post, showed the papers for himself and Johnnie and indicated his contempt for the passionate embracing on the back seat. No GI worth his salt interrupted so much romance and the small family were reunited on Bavarian soil. I never enquired how Joe had met Regina or lost her or managed to keep in touch.

Those Red Cross lists produced a very delicate situation. We had a small block of two-roomed flats, six on the ground floor and six above them. One cold winter's night, forty-eight 'stateless persons' arrived. They were elderly, very tired and disheartened. Their expectations were zero. They were the refugees of the 1914–18 war, still not accepted by any country and once more homeless, whatever had been their status when the second war began. Jaqui and I had realised that this little block was just what they needed. It was at right angles to the bigger blocks, faced a thick, high hedge which gave quiet and privacy, however dull, and would just house all of them. Bedding, food and fuel were brought in immediately as the other DPs rallied round and they settled down with true relief. One flat sheltered a very strident Orthodox priest in one room and an important paediatrician, wife and daughter, in the other, the daughter also having a corner of the kitchen for her use. Dr Notel began to badger me to give another room to the doctor and I was irritated as any special favour would have meant endless pleas for more. They were all crowded but they had their own space and it was much better than anything they had come from. Then, one fine Sunday, I saw the family; the father, with grace and much dignity, had a lady on each arm and his daughter walked happily alongside. Dr Notel was with me and I asked him where the lady had come from. She was the first wife, lost in the 1914–18 war, and now reunited with him and his second wife via the Red Cross lists. Father Travin, the priest, readily consented to being moved to some other suitable room, and the second room was made available, as it would have been on the first request had there been a little less unnecessary discretion.

The first day I joined the Bayreuth team, the two Swedish welfare officers reported that a little Ukrainian girl of five was being held in a German farm. Apparently the Germans had placed the child in this isolated place so that she could grow up to look after the old couple, already in their mid-seventies. The Ukrainian committee had made representations to the military governor about her, and two days before my arrival he had sent a squad of GIs and a *tank* to bring her in to the UNRRA camp. It must have been a nightmare for the little one, having already been subjected to kidnapping tactics by the German army. Worse news was to follow. The UNRRA recruit who had travelled to Granville hugging a holdall of cosmetics had been senior welfare officer until my advent as area welfare officer. She was sympathetic to the Germans, having lived before the war at the German court. She was very sentimental about the frail old German couple. On a sudden inexcusable impulse she had returned the child to them the day after the US army had rescued the child and brought her into camp. The two Swedes were rightly apprehensive of our position after such a snub to the military. We immediately set out for the farm. It was a small cottage with a large barn, surrounded by fields and woods and far from a village or even neighbours. The child was not to be seen but we eventually found the farmer's wife and impressed on her that she must present herself and the little girl at our office at nine o'clock the following morning. She did. I had not realised how accustomed the Germans were to obeying orders. The crass use of force by the army had been, after all, totally unnecessary. I sent the couple into another room. Before I could start to reassure the child, a member of the Ukrainian committee arrived to claim her on behalf of her family in the States. They could (and did) procure a visa for her and, in the meantime, they spoke of her family. She seemed reassured by this and happier. We hoped she found loving relatives. We could only open a pathway and think a short prayer for her safety.

The DPs found their day-to-day provision acceptable but their urgent problems were their ultimate destinations. While the European DPs concentrated on writing to friends abroad, particularly in the States, for sponsorship, and the more gifted hoped for professional posts, the peoples from the west of the Yalta Line were still fearful of repatriation, and rightly so. Russia's stupendous war effort in Stalingrad and in driving the German armies back while the Western Allies prepared the 'second front' had won admiration and gratitude, but the Russian people knew the other side of the Stalin dictatorship with its sudden arrests and capricious cruelty through which the professional classes often suffered.

Once I drove to Ergolding, the Russian Ukrainian camp in the country. It was peopled by Russians from the east of the Yalta Line, of which we had heard in Reading and which Dr Postiev and I had decided would be one of the places where we would separate the vulnerable families from those other Polish Ukraines harking from the protected lands to the east. I found the hutments empty when I arrived except for the Lagerfuhrer. I asked him why the camp was deserted. He said that they had never seen me drive up in a truck before. The women had decided it was a roundup to transport them all back to the Soviet Union and they had grabbed the children and rushed into the nearby wood.

At that time, I had been deeply shocked by an event which underlined the danger for those who were considered to be Soviet citizens. I was passing by an army office, nearly level with the pavement, when a young GI ran out and begged me to go in and talk with him. He was extremely disturbed and badly needed to share his horror.

The town was Platling. He told me that two days earlier about twenty Russian DPs had been brought in to be put on a train for the USSR. The Americans knew the men were terrified and suspected that they would commit suicide. Precautions were taken; each man was housed overnight in a single cell, his shoelaces, ties, pocket knife and anything that could be used to end his misery being removed. The entire group was assembled next morning near the special train with its one boxcar and they were marshalled in. They must have been exhausted with deep fear, lack of sleep, and dreadful expectations. The train dallied for half an hour. The doors were locked and the soldiers could relax. As the engine was about to pull out, they gave the men one last inspection. They were all either dead or beyond rescue. Having no other means for suicide they had bitten each others veins open rather than face the torture and massacre which they expected on Russian soil. I sat with the young GI in silence. He had not finished. He had needed to talk because of his own connection with the atrocious events. He showed me the log of his hours of duty. He had been instructed to send a message to Army HQ which read 'Twenty Displaced Persons evacuated from Platling to—? without incident.'

Not long after this, we had a camp inspection by a three-star general. It was bitterly cold, and the ground everywhere was frozen to a sheet of ice. At 8.30 a.m., I was the first to reach the office where I saw, but ignored, a US army car with three stars on the bonnet and with steamed-up windows. I decided that the general had arrived and wondered whether our new director would be on time. I was trying to keep my balance on the ice, encumbered with a long, plastic skeleton, intended for a school, around my neck and shoulders, when the car door opened and the general shouted 'Jonesy'. I nearly fell and he was already by me, laughing and shaking my hand. He complained that he had been waiting a long time for us and I began to try to excuse the director. The general cut me short and asked who really ran the camp. I said I did. He said that suited him well. Off we went. It was a happy day. The American turned out to be really concerned and knowledgeable, and half-Welsh. He asked me if we were having trouble with the Russians after we had put in the all-mod cons. I agreed hygiene was a perpetual war and he suggested we had classes to train them to sit on the loos because, in Russia, it was all trench relief; apparently they tried to balance in a squatting position on the seats.

We skidded from camp to camp, General Roberts solving the tricky ice by dancing a sort of mazurka with me from car to door. We ended up at Ergolding where he asked point-blank whether their people feared to go back to the Soviet Union. His interpreter was good but I tried in DP Deutsch to stop the Lagerfuhrer, Miroschnitchenko, from answering, as we had been warned that the army would transport those who dishonoured our ally, the USSR. I was stopped and told to let everything be said. Roberts was aware that men were being returned to Russia for minor misdemeanours and faced capital punishment. We spoke of the two young men whom Langsam had sent back, despite the Russian official's advice. They had owned bicycles and so could have murdered a German living one hundred kilometres from their camp. The boys would have been executed on their return and were patently innocent. There was now another man marked down for deportation to Russia from our camp. He was ill but had no offence to answer. Roberts said it was high time that the Allies faced the USSR on these counts and refused to hand over personnel who were so obviously doomed for merely political reasons. He would start his campaign for justice with that day's report. And he did.

Before General Roberts could get his ideas accepted, the team was informed, as top secret, that, during the next two weeks, Russian Ukraines would be forcibly repatriated. Like Currey, the average GI did not believe in the oft-told tale of political murder and was fretting to get rid of the DP problem, its cost and its obstacle to his own return to the US. We had two camps which would be affected, one in the Landshut flats, the other Ergolding. The latter, with its willing, kindly farming people and my very loyal Lagerfuhrer, was, to me, an unthinkable tragedy waiting to happen and the most likely to be chosen. Leaking secrets was not then a cerebral possibility. I lost weight and my threatened friend asked me what enormity had so affected me. I could only say, 'I cannot tell you.' It was no way to allay the public fear. A fortnight later we were told at supper that the raid would take place that night. As we dispersed to bed, I walked over to our house with Herman Rademaker, the senior Dutch warehouse man. He was as distressed as I was. Then I said, 'We know there is nothing we can do to stop the bloodshed that will come but there is a last hope. We are the only two Protestants here who are taught and know the value of prayer. It says in the Bible, somewhere, that where two or three are gathered together, if they pray and believe, that prayer will be granted. I am too shy to suggest we kneel down together, but I will go to my room, if you will go to yours, and we will pray together for the lives of these people.' He was as distraught as I was and he agreed readily. It was about 10.30 p.m. No one in the team wanted to stay up. We would be on call by midnight. We slept and we came down to breakfast, on mental tiptoe. Nothing had happened. At lunchtime the news was through that the army had started down the road with a convoy of trucks, escorted by several tanks and armed soldiers. Some time after 11 p.m. the officer in charge had had his instructions cancelled and been ordered to return the unit back to barracks. Herman and I could pray with gratitude then. We had found another dimension, in faith, which enlists other powers when we ourselves know we can do no more on our own. It has to be practised before it is understood.

The unbelievable extent of the murder and torture of Russian citizens in the USSR is now being examined in documents recently made available. The criminal treatment of Soviet citizens was not confined to supposedly disloyal returnees; there had been a hidden and continual cruelty and slaughter for decades. Miroschnitchenko of Ergolding had been a kulak. He had owned two or three cows and this way had made some extra money in addition to his pay as an engineer. It was used to keep his extended family, including his parents. The father had wished to gain favour with the Communists and, as they were encouraged to do, denounced his son for his private and forbidden enterprise. The theory was that all belonged to the State and cattle should be in collective or cooperative farms. The dismal failure of those enterprises has been linked with the loss of individual ownership, and consequently care, of cattle which, like other domesticated animals, flourish on attention. Miroschnitchenko had been sent as a slave to a Tartar group, living in yurts, with their flocks of sheep on the high plateaux – where, I do not know. He was not allowed to join the families; even in the Mongolian winter, he was never allowed in the felt tents but had to sleep surrounded by the huddled sheep. He was used to living on very little food and was very fit. When he was released, he had taken on his father's responsibilities. There was no corrosive bitterness. He knew he was only one of thousands... but he had survived. He was caught up with the German retreat from Russia. His village in the Ukraine was captured en masse and driven as trench diggers, men and women, preparing the dugouts for the next fallback of troops. His best friend had been killed in the village and he decided to add the widow to his passport. She was a Russian; the marriage of convenience was unhappy but a daughter was born before the group went to Venezuela. I hope they succeeded.

Party Time, Hospitality and its Embarrassments

Of the three teams I worked with, Landshut alone had held parties to which DPs were invited. In Triers, we had invited a few of our GI protectors and neighbours to a quiet dinner. I stayed too short a time in Bamberg and in Bayreuth hospitality was very rarely offered. When I arrived there, the director introduced himself as Baron van Zylon and explained that since I was a commoner he would not rise as I entered the room! I said I thought we were all too busy for that sort of thing but, as I had not savoured the full import of his declaration, he informed me that there were five countesses to whom he would devote the courtesies of his directorship. Four of the five set no store by their rank; they had suffered for their people – one in Dachau concentration camp. The fifth was trying to maintain her importance. I greatly missed the opportunity to entertain DPs, for in Landshut the team had invited in office staff or those who had been working with them on some special task. US rations were still ample. I remember a Yugoslav doctor tasting tinned pineapple for the first time in his life. He explained that his country had not been able to use foreign currency for luxury goods. He took a tin back to his wife.

In Landshut, parties had started the week we arrived, with an invitation to meet the Polish Ukrainian community. After our own unappetising meal – we had not settled down – we arrived in a large room. Even DP Deutsch was not within our grasp, so all we could do was to hold up our small glass of schnapps and bow and smile at this one or that. Our misery was shortened by great platters of small, very varied and delicious open sandwiches. We forgot we had ever been fed and the platters were never-ending until I remembered a now unpractised Welsh custom of not allowing a guest to achieve an empty plate. When we stopped with a token of food left on each plate, the real meal arrived. We were stunned and greedily delighted. They must have used most of their cigarette ration to pay for the lavish feast. The next team invitation was from the Lithuanians. It was the night when Jaqui and I were welcoming the stateless people to their flats. When we had finished we decided we ought to go to the 'coffee party', but, as it was late, we made ourselves thick spam sandwiches and, on my advice, drank condensed milk in case we were offered vodka. Brushed up, we arrived to find our team and their camp officials around a long table, now empty. We were in time for a delicious cake called 'Napoleon' – thin discs of shortbread sandwiched with confectioners' very special custard. With this came the tiniest glasses of a yellow drink. Jaqui was dubious but Georg, the doctor's assistant, assured us that it was lemonade. It all seemed safe until we started home. Jaqui and I were sober, thanks to the condensed milk we had taken earlier.

I dallied behind so as to watch the director make his *adieux* as I wondered if he had drunk much and I was unsure whether he would say anything to hurt the hosts. Joe Kepulis came in to complain that he had got Dr Roig into his car, in the back seat, and Dr Roig was trying to find the pedals to drive from that position. Joe took him home. Meanwhile, time was oozing by, so slowly. I was on a stool screwing my tired face into what I hoped were appreciative smiles and making little bows to the tall, quiet, camp leader who was also waiting to be relieved of the duty of having to look after me. Half an hour had elapsed before Dr Vaisnora, the priest, whom I was now meeting for the second time, came out and said Mr Paxman was ready to go home. We said goodbye with relief. Weeks later I was told by Dr Vaisnora that Mr Paxman had spent that time on his knees in the loo, begging the priest to convert him. At home, Johnnie had been exhausting his friends. He had agreed to go in. Each time they reached his room, he dashed out to the roses in the garden, shouting, 'This bed, not the other one.' We agreed never to drink any yellow liquid again. Everyone had remained sober in every respect save for one obsession: but what fools these obsessions turned us into!

The second Lithuanian party was a summer farewell to all of us. We all remembered we should not drink 'lemonade'. It was very hot. By this time everyone wanted to be there and it was a big crowd. I had decided to have no more to drink when Dr Vaisnora said I had never honoured him by taking a glass with him. It was not fair. The drink was green. It was the end of the party and the younger people decided I should have three cheers in the Lithuanian style. It wasn't as gentle as it sounds. I was sat on a chair and the chair went up in the air, three times three. I was glad to be on my way home, still sober, I thought. The doctor's secretary, Esther, was with me, bless her. My linen dress was tight, my room looked awfully small and, like Johnnie, I kept rushing into the garden where I would have more room to wriggle out of the clothes. I must have fallen asleep, laughing. I have been told since that yellow or green chartreuse mixed with vodka is the devil's own cocktail.

Previously, on a very hot day in Triers, I had been sent to thank a Polish family for their help in a village where some DPs had been found. Their son was still helping us but I found the mother and two lovely fair-haired daugh-

ters under cool, shady trees, entertaining the inevitable GI
with wine and fresh plums. I was invited to join them. I had
not eaten for hours and I was very thirsty. After the first
courteous raising of glasses I took a second sip on my own
account. That was a breach of etiquette. Everyone hastily
raised their glass so that I should not have the indignity of
drinking alone. After that I waited and, sip by sip, emptied
my glass and was free to go. Small sips are more deadly than
a down-the-hatch method. I walked to my tiny, hot Opal
car; steadily, I trusted. The driving wheel had been
wreathed in red roses, thorns included. I signalled my
thanks for the charming gesture but I was lucky to be able
to steer my erratic little car out of the wide gate and home.

My next private party was a little disturbing. We were
winding up the team's work in Landshut, when Elizabeth,
the doctor's secretary, asked me to a small meeting of
Hungarians. They were not classified as DPs so I felt no
obligation to go and, indeed, was reluctant in case I were to
be under an obligation. I hesitated, her face was anxious and
I thought of all I owed Dr Notel; so I agreed. At four
o'clock I had spruced myself up, fortunately, and presented
myself at some flat. I was tired and was measuring the time
I had to spare before I was due elsewhere. To my surprise,
Elizabeth greeted me and introduced me to a dowager
Hungarian countess – small, neat and aloof – in her cocoon
of good breeding. My DP Deutsch was a loser to the High
German of the remnants of the Austro-Hungarian empire
so Elizabeth was a desperate interpreter of a very fragile
conversation. They had been to enormous trouble preparing varieties of thumbnail-size canapés, each elaborately
decorated. It was sad that manners excluded praise and
appreciation of, as well as indulgence in, the dainties. I felt
immersed in the artificialities conveyed by this mid-
European atmosphere of the nineteenth century. While I
was hoping that some other guests would arrive, my

hostess's son entered. The introduction and greeting were stiffly formal and I was now confronted with a handsome, arrogant and very bored young man, who, nevertheless, had been told to sit by me and make conversation, impossible as it was when we had no common language. I made some overtures to a monosyllabic wall and on consulting my timepiece decided I could make my exit, get on with important work and put the young man out of his agony. Consternation and dismay made my leave-taking embarrassing. Plans were all awry. I was relieved to breathe fresh air.

Next morning, to my very great surprise, Dr Notel produced a photograph of the Count's escutcheon, and pointed out that it had twenty-eight quarterings, taking the origins of his family back to Henry Plantagenet of England. Seeing my indifference, his discretion vanished and he told me that they, the Hungarians, had been very disappointed that I had not stayed to talk to the Count; it would have been an excellent match, especially with the twenty-eight quarterings. I thought that the quarterings would not provide for happy companionship. It was suddenly clear. I imagined how cruel it would be to subject my sensitive, gracious mother to that *passé* hauteur and how unrewarding our home would be to the mother and son. I gathered my thoughts while I was saying I would not marry anyone four years my junior, meaning I would not marry someone who would have no intention of being a faithful companion. Thinking of the problem of marriages of convenience, I conceived a version of British law which was that I would lose my nationality and the Hungarians would not gain mine! Dr Notel was astonished but it closed the subject.

Another aspect opened up; the idea of using me as a pawn had been disloyal. How were we all being manipulated? I thought of our offices and of how one national group, the Hungarians, beyond all others, knew exactly what was going on. If we left the camp to self-government, what guarantee would there be of fair play to the smaller groups? I spoke to other team members. I pointed out that in welfare, Dr Notel ran administration and Lazlo ran the cultural projects. As exceptions a Ukrainian and a Latvian supervised the workshops, a Lithuanian ran our household but Elizabeth, also an Hungarian, ran the medical administration. Something else had alerted me to the fact that the clerical staff of the military government was also partly Hungarian. The camp would return to the position in which we had found it. Anita had been in charge of a Hungarian network and the only nation to benefit from her organisation was a section of the Polish Ukraines who might also have been fighting, as some had been, with the Germans. No one agreed with me enough to alter their administration; so I asked Dr Notel to supervise work upstairs. It removed him from the hub of the work; he was very upset. I had been tired; perhaps I was unfair and over-suspicious. The team was soon to withdraw from the camp and the fledglings would be challenging each other as the nest broke up.

The Hungarian network seemed linked with yet another party which had introduced a tête-à-tête. Our director discovered that, when we departed, we would leave a considerable welfare fund in DP hands. That, with organised control, would have been sensible, but instead he decided to have a celebration and spread the spending over as many people as possible. I demurred but he went ahead with the organisation. It was dismal. The Turnhalle had been furnished with round tables and chairs. The team was aloof at one end waiting for guests from the military government. The guests never appeared; it was a deliberate snub. Unreasonably, the MG staff had expected invitations but we had restricted the party to our own camp. The MG staff had perhaps persuaded their chief, Major Melnik, that it was not for him either. In any case, the director had been humiliated without explanation. We ate, we drank and a band played. It was boring. I toured around all the tables to speak to the various groups, as by now we could understand each other. Many people danced but I was glad to be asked to take a pregnant wife home. When I drove back, the team had disappeared and German police had been sent in to restore order to a perfectly well-behaved party. A camp leader said all was under control and he advised me not to interfere. Someone had been making mischief.

A night or so later, Major Melnik rang up to say that he had arranged a party for his fellow Czech, the Countess Nikolska, who ran our ballet team. I knew the group quite well, so I was delighted that I would spend some time with her before I left. My own team mates begged me not to go. I would not miss it, brushed my uniform, grabbed some wine for the party and was ready when Melnik called for me. The house was quite a large modern villa, pleasant and quiet as the ballet team had not arrived. He took me upstairs to his room as only part of the house was heated. Fuel was a problem so he invited me to have a bath, a great treat to some of our own visitors, too. I declined, and while he went for coffee, pending the ballet team's arrival, I spent about half an hour trying to take an interest in his family photographs but I was happily primed with conversation when he reappeared with two glasses of wine. I wondered why a glass of wine took so long to make! I sat on the only chair while he stretched out on the bed. We drank and talked and then I said that as something must have stopped Nikolska coming, and I was very tired, I should be glad to be taken home. I was. It had wasted an evening.

Next day, I collected some documents from military government and was amazed that the Major's civilian secretary, a Hungarian whom I had often met, should have referred to the previous evening with such malicious amusement. The party that never was and the affair that never started had ended in a testimony to my unassailable good manners! I realised that little plots to discredit us were being hatched by staff to be carried out by a willing chief who enjoyed a joke, as a revenge for an unintentional slight. My previous respect for Melnik hit zero. Things became more sinister when the network deliberately spread the harmful gossip. Even the DP camps had all heard the wrong story. The regimental colonel's wife, a true daughter of the American revolution, had been given some version which caused her to ignore my usual cheerful greeting at the next concert. I was now sure that my disquiet about the Hungarian network had been justified. It might also have been a revenge for Dr Notel's loss of a key office, which was more important to them than the party.

I left Landshut after a splendid farewell party from the Lagerfuhrers and the clergy. It was cheerfully civilised until the younger team gave a demonstration of jive when the priests rose and left. Decorum returned. I still cherish their presentation letter of loving thanks. I do not remember how I left Landshut for Bamberg except that when every-thing was packed and bulging, Dr Vaisnora arrived as I climbed on to transport of some sort and gave me a delicate wooden cross. That, too, has survived.

Bamberg I remember as a poky office, scrupulously efficient under the management of a hard-working Czech. Our work was the repatriation of the Poles. He explained it carefully, the numbers, the boxcars, the rations and the Red Cross van. The US zone was organising the return of the Poles with a small bribe: enough flour, sugar and fat for a month. It really was enough to make many, longing for their home, take the chance of returning. They hoped the Russians had gone. There was no work for me to do. I was to be in charge and the good Czech would shoulder the work. I told the welfare organiser from HQ that the Czech and I should swop salaries. He told me I was frightened and had cold feet. I said, 'We shall never understand one another, our principles are not the same.' I was angry and had not thought that I was talking to a black American. I'd always got on with him. Now I think my words had been taken personally and had hurt. I was transferred to a hard post in Bayreuth but not before I had volunteered to take a train to Poland. I also had been affronted in that he had declared that I was actually finding the simple work beyond my scope.

Polish Repatriation Train

In November 1946, I took a train with one thousand DPs being repatriated to Poland. I was told I would be comfortable and safe. As I reached the platform at Lauf in the Bayreuth area, the train was moving out ahead of time. Its tentative lurches stopped. Everyone talked to me at once and I gathered that I was to share a boxcar, marked with white stripes and a Red Cross, with a young Czech nurse. The train was moving when two Red Cross food parcels were thrown in, then a tarpaulin and a cylindrical stove with wood for fuel. Someone shut the massive doors and the nurse and I smiled and exchanged names.

It was November and there was about sixteen inches of snow, soon to deepen to eight feet on the Sudeten ranges of the west. The tarpaulin was clearly useful and we spread it on the floor as far as it would go and then camped out on that. We had harnessed the shrill draught. The stove had been put together by kind invaders from the next car which was connected to us by a concertina passage, then in use on ordinary trains. It was erected in the corner in which we had established ourselves, and in the opposite corner was an enormous packing case as an uninvited guest. The self-invited ones from next door were cheerful and belied their looks of being wolves in sheep's clothing, literally; they wore long sheepskin coats with the wool on the inside. They brought in a 'squeeze box' and we danced to keep warm.

The long train chuntered to a halt at a wayside station. We were on the platform and the crowd of women kindly gave me first place at the only station loo. I hurried; it was not over-clean and many others were waiting. Then I met the sergeant in charge of the guard, elderly, slow-thinking and decent with six gun-happy GIs, marching with grinning enthusiasm on the lines, up and down the long train, firing into the air erratically. We had eighteen pregnant women on board; six, I was told, were within days of their delivery. I asked the sergeant to explain that sudden shooting was still a terror to the DPs and that we were ill-equipped for confinements. The nurse had told me this, adding that she would be leaving us halfway in Slovakia. I made it clear that I was not an obstetrician. The posse of GIs grew quieter and went in for dalliance instead. Then, at my elbow was Joe Sekula, the young Pole who had been the administrator-cum-interpreter for the Russian camp in Landshut. My amazement was followed by relief at my good luck as Joe assured me that he would see to it that I had no trouble. At this moment the train shuddered into movement and the wretched DPs squatting on the hedge surrounding a huge field screamed and started to run. I then understood the problem in Bamberg; however carefully the quota of DPs was filled, a good proportion never reached Poland. I told the sergeant to tear a strip off the engine driver and order him to wait for every Pole to board the train; Joe interpreted in forceful German. Polish mishaps were not to be a mirthful story in some German beer house. Eventually, ours was the largest contingent to reach the Polish terminal. We were two short of the thousand who started; one was the nurse who left us in Prague... perhaps there was another Czech.

The nurse and I held a powwow. As the DPs needing medical help had queued up she had hardly been able to get off the train because one old man with gangrene came at every stop, and mothers were bringing their children for remedies. We both needed to be on duty; we could not even afford to eat or drink since attending to the sick prevented our use of what can only be described as uncomfort stations. I had changed to trousers; I could not climb into the van in a tight uniform skirt. We slept as night fell and woke to find the packing case towering over us on our low camp beds. It was moving with the train. By the next night we were in a siding at Prague where bread was being distributed but we had to miss the queue. Instead, I took my canvas bucket, meant for water, and scrambled into the unguarded engines in the same siding, to steal as much wood as I could. I had discarded my moral sense in Normandy when I stole a bit of bread! We were hungry, thirsty and tired and we needed to keep that stove alight. The nurse was soon to find her home comforts at the next stop while I and the packing case carried on. That next stop at night brought a few men pounding at my door. They wanted the packing case which was addressed to UNRRA at our destination. I told them it wasn't theirs. That had no effect but, when I told them they could not come in because I had no clothes on, they went away. Complaints from an ally had to be avoided and I had guessed that the men were Soviet soldiers. In daytime, a young Czech with a red star on his cap was on station duty. I questioned him about the star. He was young and proud to be a communist and proud to show me that all the town buildings sported red stars on their gables. The Red Army seemed to be everywhere in Czechoslovakia and to be accepted – at least by the young men.

The following night, we drew up at a station at about 3 a.m. Several loud speakers blared slogans and jolly folk tunes and lights glared on every corner. Red Army patrols kept order over the silent train. We had crossed into Poland but the exhausting travel had stupefied the spirit. In the night we drew up at another platform and I had another tussle over my privacy and the packing case. Then they put a guard: not on me, on the packing case. The feet tramped rhythmically, back and forth, hour after hour, and I slept fitfully.

I dressed early but in time. There was a small, business-like group waving papers at the packing case and, seeing there were so many witnesses, I let them in just as a man arrived in UNRRA uniform. He said I'd done the right thing. Personally I thought I deserved a civic reception after my defence of whatever precious engine rode in that wooden case, but I got none. Johnny of UNRRA saw I was exhausted and took me to the restaurant. An omelette that cost one and a half shillings at home, cost thirty zlotis – about thirty shillings – there. Ashamed, I settled for a cup of tea at ten shillings. Johnny was a Mexican professional pearl diver with boxing ambitions, very proud of represent-ing his country in UNRRA. I was due to meet the Polish Red Cross organiser. Poor, tired man, he was in charge of the medical unit. He hoped that I had brought the often promised medical supplies. I gave him my own first aid kit, the aspirin and a few bandages left from our own poor supply plus my talcum powder. He was embarrassingly grateful. Joe Sekula came to say goodbye and I talked to an engine driver. He said wages covered the rent with a narrow margin for flour, fuel and fat. A garden patch was a necessity and repairing boots, if one could not do it oneself, was beyond hope. Johnny insisted on my reporting to UNRRA HQ where hot water, food and coffee restored my spirit. After lunch, I was to see the town. A Dutch boy who called me 'Sis' said he would come with me and Johnny to protect me. That team must have been very bored with their work.

The Americans had said that Poland was well-provi-sioned and on the way to recovery. Why did the Poles not go home? The answer came at the first stop – a clean coffee shop, its counter laden with luxury Swiss chocolates and bottles of coloured liqueurs, all reflected in brightly-lit mirrors and glass, just what a GI wanted. Very soon, a young Pole came up and said the last time he had seen me was in Tenby. I had visited that town once, fifteen years earlier. The two UNRRA men snorted with disgust, saying 'Spies everywhere!' and marched me out to a *thé dansant*. The dancers were glum, resenting our uniform. We left and window shopped. There was a big-windowed store. One window had three buckets, another had three rolls of the drabbest and poorest of cloth; both were lit up as if in celebration. It was dark. We went to a large restaurant on two floors. A band had just decided to go home but they saw us, sighed, and took the canvas covers off their instruments. An elderly waiter led us to the bottom of the empty room and produced a carafe of vodka and three glasses. They measure, by eye, the amount that is drunk at the end of the evening. The Dutchman had said he wanted a ham sandwich and disappeared. Poles started peering round the door and, on seeing our uniforms, came in in twos and threes to begin dancing. Johnny, with a quick boxer's footwork, had no sense of rhythm and, when the Poles 'cut in' to dance with me, he joined the band to croon into the microphone and was happy. My Polish partners were lugubrious and odd. Each pressed bits of paper into my hand for transmission to the UK. The messages were nonsense. Every man said to me, 'Last man no good; Soviet spy!' At midnight, somehow, we went home. The Dutchman had to be carried in. My bed was in the bathroom and I had to be sure that everyone had finished and that Johnny went on his way to his own bed. The director was disapproving next morning but I had been very grateful for food and cleanliness. At the station I climbed into my box car and lit the stove.

I read while it was daylight and then slept. Before we started, a young GI, whom I had not noticed, came in and said he represented the gang. They thought I would not wish to be alone and would like to know whom I would choose to spend the night with... but the one with the bright blue eyes had found a girlfriend; they were apologetic as they thought I would have liked him best. I kept my face still and thanked them for their kind thought, adding that I was tired and would be happy by myself. But they were right about my need for company, whatever their motives. Alone, I could not shut the heavy door, the snow was deep, and the stove burned its way through the thick plank floor and fell on to the railway line in a shower of sparks. In the middle of the night a man climbed in. I sat up on my bedroll and said all the words I could in Welsh as if they were a curse. He went through my luggage and found nothing because I was sitting on the cigarettes. He went and the train pulled on. Next day, I told the sergeant that I was claiming my quarters, and the GIs could move up. I wedged my army canvas bed between the two bench seats in a corridor compartment in the only railway carriage and bounced through a heavenly sleep. In the morning, I started to make a giant omelette for all of us. We were able to trade our rations for fresh eggs whenever there was a stop. I needed a tin of beans so I handed a tin and opener to a civilian who seemed to be travelling with us. He said his hands were too delicate. I said angrily that his hands had not been too fine to steal in the night and he opened the tin. We reached Lauf again. There I made a lifelong friend by giving my canvas bucket to an Australian who was taking the next train out, she still has it in Sydney.

The US army dentists looked at my swollen, putrid gums and said the gingivitis was too severe to be cured; my teeth with their exposed roots would just drop out. I had been starved of vitamins; earlier, vitamin C would have saved me. The journey to Poland with the necessity of starving myself had done more harm than all the rest of the time I spent in UNRRA where we were well treated by the US military government of our zone. As for dental treatment, when I got back to Blighty, I spent four weeks in Anglesey, most of the time wedged with my sleeping bag into some cliff crevice with a book and a bag of tomatoes, supervised by a very young and curious little seal. The teeth have lasted fifty years... most of them!

The Jews. Dachau. Preparing for Israel

When Arnold Foster prepared us for UNRRA in Reading, the shocking pictures of the liberation of the concentration camps had not yet been published. We knew that the Jews had been victims of degradation and mass transportation; the reality of extermination had still to be seen.

The Allied armies had liberated the concentration camps and opened the military hospitals to bring the dying back to life. Of the living, the great numbers taken for slave labour from Western Europe had been repatriated as speedily as trains could be sent out of Germany, but millions of homeless people had been the problem UNRRA should solve. The displaced persons and the return of looted treasures to the West were a distraction for the military and the human problem was the most urgent. The armies urged that UNRRA be sent into Germany instantly, without waiting for peace as was planned. This accounted for the early haphazard scatter of small teams and the uncoordinated approaches to problems.

In Triers, the transit camp was submerged by the urgency of the daily intakes waiting to be repatriated. Our later camp had the duty to assemble Polish groups into the caserne prior to the organisation of trains in midsummer by Poland and Russia who both hoped to repatriate all their nationals. As those trains left, we imagined we had completed the task and would be discharged. Then it was that

UNRRA found the great numbers of DPs who were political refugees. The British had been alive to the overrule of the USSR in Poland, the Baltic and other states of Europe; the Americans had discounted this detail, despite their obsession with the Russian menace. They did not allow the small European nations the luxury of fearing the same very real terror at their doors. To the United States, the mid-European countries were useful as a barrier to contain the spillage of the Red Pollution threatening to cross Europe and then the Atlantic.

The international status of UNRRA brought the Jews within our scope. Ravensbruck and Dachau were names we had heard; but we were not involved. The armies did what they could as they liberated the camps. Doing a magnificent job, they provided food, requisitioned clothes and blankets from the local towns and opened the military hospitals to the pitifully loaded ambulances. The soldiers tell, if they can talk about it at all, of the horror of near-skeletons attracting attention from the piles of living dead. We saw great piles of photographs of these ghastly scenes but we could not bring ourselves to buy such evidence from the men touting for sales. The men, in fair health, were dressed in the concentration camp uniform of blue and white pyjamas but looked less like victims than collaborators or even German guards. We should have bought the photographic evidence of the holocaust for the unbelievers of today. When we reached Landshut, military governments had already requisitioned housing and furniture for those Jewish survivors recovering in the towns and countryside. No Jews appeared to need our help although we were not far from Dachau and its dreadful crimes.

The army forbade us to go to Dachau. Later we learned it was because the trials of the SS were being held in the caserne that the SS had once proudly occupied. Some were now prisoners of war cleaning up concentration camps.

The director thought we should see the camp, despite the embargo and he took four of us. We motored along a flattish landscape towards Munich, and from there into slightly hilly farmland to a small village, outside of which was an enormous, new caserne built around a large drill square for the training of the SS troops. The storm troopers would have been immaculate in grey, with their black badge embroidered with a white edelweiss flower. Behind the barracks were blocks of well-kept wooden huts around a small parade ground contained within concrete posts and barbed-wire fences between the huts. We reached this through double gates in a high hoarding which excluded curiosity. A mile away we had smelled glue; in the camp, where human bones had burned, the smell was strong. Around the corner, at the back of the huts, was a tumble-down shed with a corrugated iron roof, an unkempt, corner in this tidy yard but adequate enough, in Dachau terms, for the few wretched Jews who had lived there. They had been forced to service the three adjacent ovens, now rusted and defunct, which had burned their kith and kin until the ovens themselves burnt out. We had then been conducted round by a healthy ex-inmate (so he said) in the pyjama-like camp uniform of blue and white stripes. He took us to a new building of which he was surprisingly proud. The first section, furthest from the camp, had four partitions. Each was a small gas chamber, not for gassing Jews but for sterilising clothes and shoes shed by the crowd due for annihilation. Everything was recycled in the name of efficiency. Adjacent was an office. The imagination balks at the importance and cynicism of the officer in charge of the obscenities and at the 'loyal' congratulations he would receive for a job well executed.

Then there was a room about twenty by twelve feet. It was white-tiled and scrupulously clean; no graffiti had yet been added by tourists; this was the gas chamber. In the ceiling, with no attachments to pipes or anything else, there were large sprinkler heads, as if for a shower. The gas had welled up from two vents near ground level. The victims had been made to strip for their 'shower' and, in one last humiliation, herded in regardless of sex and age. Two thick glass windows enabled the guards to watch their dying. Our escort pointed out that the next section in particular was conveniently planned. The new gas ovens, made necessary by the tremendous increase in work during the war, had been placed next to the gas chamber, so that the thin bodies could easily be fed to the ovens, again by Jewish labour. At first, each body had had its own asbestos disc and after the 'cremation' the disc and the ashes was packed off in a metal container to those relatives who had requested such a service. Next we saw an open room where another 'inmate' was coping with the barrels of powder and charred bones from the ovens. The cremations had been speeded up as the Allied troops drew nearer. The man used terracotta jars, made like old-fashioned milk coolers, filling them with a trowelful of grit and cindered bones from a huge bin. He then threw in a disc for the relatives and sealed it. It seemed likely that this was a demonstration of the former efficiency of the camp to gratify tourists, the majority German.

This efficiency was confirmed in the Bayreuth team by the Dutch countess who had listened to the illicit BBC radio each night and helped to produce and distribute a clandestine news-sheet in Holland. The Gestapo had discovered her and arrested her for transportation. She recounted to us her experiences in Dachau. She emphasised the correctness of the camp; food was served at tables covered with clean chequered cloths, on clean plates in exact rations, but the helping was always less than the minimum needed. Slow starvation had been the goal. She said that the horror of the camp had not impinged on her awareness because hunger was such that one could not stop thinking of food. Despite this confession, I believe she must have carried deep-buried memories of the atrocities. For instance there were steel bars above those new ovens where men had been strapped and threatened with death by slow burning, until they told the guards their secrets. We were smilingly assured that they were never used. Neither were Jews actually killed. They admitted there was a pit where men were slaughtered to fall on the sand at the bottom, blood-soaked sand for which the farmers competed; it had produced a much valued fertiliser mixed with burnt bones from the ovens. Another torture, described by our guides, was the custom of standing ninety people on the edge of this infamous ditch if there were any uproar. The ninety were held as hostages until docility was restored when the troublemakers would be shot instead.

The full evil of this order was later underlined on my visit to our UNRRA HQ at Regensberg, before I went to Bayreuth. They had found meticulous camp records for Dachau. They showed me a stack of foolscap size 'flimsies' – the very thin paper used to make carbon copies of typed material. The stack was a little deeper than the length of the foolscap itself and it had been close-packed for months or even years. Each sheet was typed in single spacing and had two parallel columns of names – names of dead children. The sheet was headed with dates, the ages of the children, the disease with which they had been infected, the diet they had been fed and against their names, the time it had taken them to die. This is obscene but it must be told; it was the record of the ultimate limit in experimentation in the cause of producing a master race. The blonds would go free but the rest could be useful on their way to extermination.

Shortly after this, we visited a comfortable UNRRA team consisting entirely of men. They were in charge of the orphaned babies found in Dachau. I was nonplussed; I should have admitted my anger and asked someone to investigate, but our communication channels had not yet been established. A coward, I did nothing. The babies were in good cots, isolated from all contamination, and looking as wizened and tiny as newborn infants. Women were brought in to bath and feed them. Contamination or no, I held my hand down to some of them and they grasped my fingers fiercely in their little hands. They needed cuddling and love more than food. The worst deprivation is that of mothering and these babies were between four and twenty-four months old. They may have been infected with TB or other diseases and been considered too much of a risk to nurse; or there might have been a difficulty in selecting DPs or Germans for the nursing jobs. A team of UNRRA women with experience in nursing would have been a much better idea.

In Bayreuth there was a further link with Dachau. It was there I met large groups of Jews for the first time. When Elizabeth handed over her work to me she was glad I had 'inherited the tiresome Jews'. As she said, she hated the Welsh more than the Jews and she possibly felt they had met their match! They were eager to find out if the change was for the better and they presented themselves as a small committee. It turned out that they occupied seventeen farms used for training their young people in agriculture before they went to the kibbutzim in their 'new homeland' of Israel. The weather happened to be atrocious and I could readily appreciate their plea for heavy boots and waterproof clothes. It was simple to solve since the camp was receiving a very good consignment of angora jerseys and pretty dresses from requisitioned German factories. I said we would give them rubber boots and army surplus coats, if they persuaded their women folk to forego their share of the attractive clothing. This arrangement would be widely known and above board. I would be issuing ration books as soon as I could get a quota of paper. It was a successful transaction except that we had an American PR man who was busy using up our paper quota on totally unnecessary cardboard exhortations to work, written in largely unknown English. I fought hard, got the ration books, and ended the under-the-counter distribution of the best clothing to favourites.

There was an extra useful Jewish presence in the camp. We had three women from the voluntary Jewish agencies of Australia. We cooperated well and through them and a Jewish RAF officer all went quite smoothly with the Jewish group. The Jews coming to the camp were interested in an 'underground' route going south. Later, there were fresh waves of Jewish refugees, alarmed at possible pogroms starting in Poland, coming into Hof during the early months of 1947. I was told that up to eight hundred persons were coming, each night through the Czech mountain passes. It happened that we had a subsidiary team stationed in this area at Hof. The Jews had come west hurriedly and with few belongings. Their welcome was poor despite goodwill and hard work by the Jewish Agencies. There were no available casernes with vacant troop accommodation. The army gave us tents, blankets and food. The Jewish refugees had to live in rows of dark tents in the deep snow.

In the small Landshut camp, I would have been responsible for the situation; but here there were more than twenty thousand DPs and an ever-expanding team. As other camp centres became self-governing, the UNRRA personnel was shunted about depending on decisions as to which camps would remain open. Work was divided out and, though I organised the rationing of clothes, I never saw a warehouse. Once I took the Jewish trucks to Nuremberg to get their kosher meat supply. The butchers and the meat all needed to be consecrated by sprinkling with holy water. The yard of the huge slaughterhouse was crammed with Jews from many camps, several hundred. The meat could only be distributed after the consecration. Daylight was fading, it was about fifteen degrees below zero and the rabbis were unsure how to begin. One made a decision which was accepted in a very good spirit. He got the thick hose used for washing down the yards and began to sprinkle both meat and the shivering mob of butchers with his thumb, unsuccessfully squeezing the mouth of the tube. With their Sabbath meal, most of them went home in very wet coats.

A doctor and her young daughter joined the Bayreuth team late in 1946. They were the first former Auschwitz prisoners I had met. Considering how much is known of the camp now, it is surprising that we knew so little, but we had no newspapers or radio. Television was unknown. Our new doctor told me that as the war was ending and the American front got nearer, the Germans decided to evacuate the Auschwitz camp as the German soldiers retreated. All who could walk formed a huge queue four deep, interspersed with German guards who had orders to shoot escapers and stragglers and those too ill to struggle any further. As the night grew dark, the mother and daughter saw that they were walking alongside a deep ditch and they agreed to drop and roll into it as if they, too, were dying. They dropped quickly into the snow and the shots missed them. She relived the tense moments as she talked and I did not question her further. I had no other opportunity before I left.

Mike England was the British Jew who had served in the Royal Air Force. He told me that I ought to see the Jewish orphanage for which we were responsible. Though important it had not previously been mentioned to me. We drove to a recently built stonewalled castle of mediaeval appearance. It had four round towers to a height of three floors. Living quarters at first floor level with no ground floor connected the four towers completing a square and acting as a bridge. Only one tower had a door opening on to the courtyard. It was good for defence and useful for keeping persons under supervision but certainly a bad fire hazard. We received an exuberant welcome from Jewish Agency staff proffering white bread and cottage cheese in the traditional manner. The place was alive with enthusiastic children learning Hebrew and the geography, history and politics of the Holy Land. Like the young farmers, they were also learning to live the hard way. The place was spotless. Boys and girls had separate, clean and airy dormitories but the beds were too close together for hygiene. The camp leader appeared. He was nineteen years old. He knew exactly what he was doing but I did not. The youngsters obeyed and respected him. I tried to fathom what it was all about. He said that most of the children had been in Dachau; their numbers were tattooed on their arms. Some belonged to religious sects and some to political groups. They were all ardent Zionists. I remonstrated with him on the subjects of overcrowding and fire risks. He smiled indulgently and said, 'Come again next week; seventy of the hundred and twenty who are here will have gone.' Where, he would not say. Their training and living conditions were excellent but I was deeply disturbed by a talk on the way home.

Mike said that the castle collected children and every two weeks sent a contingent, for instance the seventy already mentioned, on the underground route through Rumania. This would have entailed travelling through Austria and Hungary down the Danube basin to the Black Sea where they would board small ships and sail to Israel. I was shattered by this. I had read Koestler's *Thieves in the Night* and latterly reports in *The Guardian*, which I received from home, to the effect that Britain was not allowing the Jews into Palestine ahead of the agreed date when part of

Palestine would become a permanent homeland for the Jews in a multi-ethnic state. The British army was preventing the frail boatloads of children from landing, though some escaped their vigilance and got ashore. Those who did not set sail for Greece, but many drowned. I tackled the US director as to the prevention of the probable death of these young Jews but he said the US supported the underground exodus; the British were wrong. The children were political pawns. The 'orphanage' was a reception camp for children orphaned in the concentration camps and also from families with strong Zionist motivation. They were splendid youngsters.

One boy, David, had a visa for the United States where he would join his relatives. I was to take him to a point of departure. Bavaria sparkled with snow as I drove with this vital, intelligent fifteen year old. He asked me if I was a Christian.

I said, 'Yes.'

David said, 'I was in Dachau with my parents and they prayed night and day for deliverance. I saw the way the people were lined up at the camp desk and the fit ones went to the right for work and the old and ill to the left and then to the gas chamber. They came to line up our group. I told my parents it was time to stop praying and I ran for it, through the Alsatian dogs – one bit me – over the barbed wire into hiding. My parents prayed and are dead; I am alive! "Aide-toi, et Dieu t'aidera."'

Help yourself and God will help you. He said 'Goodbye' and was on his way full of confidence in himself and his future; he could expect success in the States.

Faith is not a road to magic; it is more a steadying influence. Miracles do occur, though the sceptical would hasten to call them coincidences. The SOS of urgent, unspoken prayer at times of stress may be a communication with a power outside ourselves when we believe we have run out of our own resources. We receive push-button adrenaline and more inward calm, clearer thought and a sudden perception of possibilities. The success can feel like a miracle unless we dismiss it as common sense.

Instead of exploring the positive power in faith, many find it simpler to say 'there is no God!' Some disbelievers keep an amulet they call 'God' in their back pocket so that they can blame Him for all our ills, excused from thanking him for the infinite diversities and joys of the natural world. For them superstition suffices... and it is easier.

Man has been trying on the crown of Lord of the Universe, plundering fossilised energy and precious materials. He interferes with the natural rhythms of the world, clearing forests, spraying chemicals and over-working, over-fishing, over-producing as he craters the surface and abuses the soil in pursuit of industry and agriculture. Each new success awaits its side effects. We have not weighed the needs of the Third World against our extravagances or even used our new knowledge to curb the demands on the land. Increasing deserts, famine, floods and diseases convince us that God does not care... or is it us?

Christ's life on earth has provided us with a simple blueprint for an understanding of divine love. If our intellectual pride prevents our using this, we could at least acknowledge the sanity and psychological wisdom in his teaching.

Part Seven

The Conclusion that Faith was the Necessary Ingredient

Suddenly I was redundant and away without even the means and time to find Mike and apologise for missing the Sabbath meal I had been invited to share. I wondered if my journey to the UK would be as fraught as the home leave I had experienced after eighteen months' work. On that leave I had been dropped at Munich Railway station with no pass or money. I produced two packets of cigarettes when I asked for a first-class fare to London. The grave German flushed red and said no one now dealt in cigarettes. I was aware that two packets were still very valuable and I said angrily that I did not know what he expected when we were given no German currency and only funny money for the US PX canteen. He said nothing but passed me the tickets. I spent an interesting hour or so with a Belgian diamond engineer from the Congo and, when he had gone, I ate my apple and slept. I awoke to see two men on the opposite seat. I apologised for being stretched out full length on my side but the younger, though heftier, man swung himself on to the long luggage rack and slept there. I was exhausted and probably snored but they tickled my toes only when it was about 8 a.m. They announced they were going to breakfast and would I come too. Penniless, I refused, and they understood. They convinced me that we could have coffee without paying for it as they had packets of coffee and condensed milk in tubes... all from Switzerland which had been developing these wonders while we went to war. They tipped the waiter, unseen by me, and he brought the cups and hot water. I was really very grateful. In return, they explained themselves as a boxer and his trainer and entertained themselves by trying to make me blush with mildly suggestive stories all the way to Paris.

The crossing was rough and I went leeward of the smell of oil and let the sea spray freshen my face. In the customs queue, I asked an UNRRA girl next to me, 'Why have you got a blue passport? Mine is green!'

'You silly,' she said, 'that's a PX (US NAAFI) card, not a passport!'

My tired brain cleared, I must have picked the wrong one from my drawer. I hung back in the queue and I was the last to go through. 'You won't believe me. I'm afraid I've brought my PX NAAFI card instead of my passport.'

The customs officer replied 'It's stupid enough to be true. But you'll have to prove you are a British citizen. Have you got any papers to prove it?'

'No. But I can speak a little Welsh.'

He said, 'Well, I agree with you that ought to be enough. It's not. Look in your pockets.'

I was desperately tired and wet. My coaxing laughter dried up as I went through my side pockets and then the breast pocket. He was patient and encouraging, quite useless I thought, but I made a show of being thorough. And there in the bottom seam, as if left where the cleaning fluid could not destroy it, in the thickness, was an half-inch deep strip saying that I was a British citizen having the rank of a lieutenant. I remembered the document we had been told to carry with us and thought how wonderful that that bit had survived. The officer waved me through and hoped I would arrive home safely. In the summer of 1996 I found the original document intact.

I went to the UNRRA hostel for a night's sleep and next morning to the British and Foreign Bible Society, then in Victoria Street. I went past the rows of bombed-out offices, razed down to the empty cellars. They stood in a cheeky row of stone boxes, each with its safe still all in one piece.

The makers had not lost an opportunity, each stone-walled space had its noticeboard: 'Safe by Chubb.' It cheered me. The Society was very kind. I pulled out the only stop and introduced myself as a great-great-granddaughter of the founder of the society, Charles of Bala. In the modern set-up he was irrelevant but they listened to my plea for Bibles in the Central European languages, gave me a cuppa and showed me their museum exhibits; I was to pick up what they could give me on my return to London in five days.

Home leave went quickly. It was the bitterly cold winter of 1947, so I kept my beret and greatcoat on in the house. A room had been on fire; buying furniture and restoring the house and my mother's morale soaked up the short holiday until I reached London again. I dashed for the Bibles and there were two sacks full, thoughtfully portable. I arrived at Victoria station at 9.50 p.m. to catch the 9.40 p.m. because I was still tired and could not work out the time at 21.40 as it was now known. The porter saw my dismay and said, 'Jump on this train, it's slower but by the time it gets there, the last passengers will be going through customs.' He was right.

I went into the gloomy shed and said, 'I have left my passport in Germany.'

A voice from a corner by a warm stove said, 'I've seen her before. Let her go. What's in those sacks?'

'Bibles,' I said.

'Ha! And I can quite believe it.'

I must have dozed on the Newhaven packet-boat, sitting with my luggage. A sailor came up and said, 'Shall I mark your luggage for the officers' passport control? Then you won't have to take it through; it will be on the Dieppe station platform.' That deserved five shillings and we were mutually pleased. I saw the stack of luggage in the distance. I knew I had no hope of getting the French to let me through, so I started a very casual walk, sauntering to the end of the platform where the ramp went down to the rails. I did not look round; I drifted across the lines and up the opposite platform ramp and on to the luggage. Of course, I was one of the first to settle down in a compartment, sacks and all. To savour the relief of having got into France without a passport, I opened the window and blinked in the morning sunshine. Then there was a noise and coming up the platform, with a gendarme on each side, was the girl who had told me my passport was a PX card. She was shouting hysterically, 'There she is!' while she waved in my direction.

'Shut up, you idiot,' I said as she got to my window. I was wondering if they still put people in the Bastille.

'You've left your luggage in the customs office,' she said. My heart returned to normal. I said sweetly, 'No. It's all on the rack.'

That night, trying to get a taxi for the Warsaw Express, I had an altercation in the UNRRA hotel. I used what few swear words I knew and a short man by my side joined in with enthusiasm. When we had beaten the arrogant receptionist into submission and providing transport we discovered we came from the same town. Such coincidences and miracles assured my return to Landshut.

The Bibles were distributed. Some men hoped to dull my satisfaction by saying the paper was being used for rolling cigarettes. The Jews probably did not want the New Testament and the Roman Catholics were nervous of the unexpurgated text. The miracles en route convinced me that Bibles, even in pieces could, as texts, fall into hands which needed encouragement.

A year later, the day I left UNRRA, I was eating in the transit canteen in Munich when a quiet woman introduced herself. 'I am a White Russian,' she said. 'Until now, our sad history has made us afraid to reveal our nationality and we have called ourselves Polish, Ukrainian or Lithuanian.

Now there is a sign that men and women are coming forward to admit their true nationality. Have you come across this?' I said that during the early spring one or two had said they were Byelo-Russ. She was delighted at this. She explained that a group of patriots were hoping to draw their people together, to make themselves a nation again and achieve a homeland. One thing they hoped would overcome the decades of terror would be the availability of their own Bible. She said that as a staff member at HQ she had known about my taking Bibles in many languages to Landshut. Could I possibly get the sources in Britain to trace their Bible and print it? There were only two copies left; one was in Finland and one in Switzerland, but she had no idea who had them. This talk had not lasted many minutes but someone was already impatiently asking me to join the transport. I said I would do all I could and I even forgot to get her name.

Once in Britain, I contacted the British and Foreign Bible Society again. They replied kindly and positively. In about three months they wrote to say that they had traced the Swiss copy of the Byelo-Russ Bible. In about six months they sent me a jubilant letter. The Metropolitan of the Byelo-Russ church had arrived in their office to ask for help in finding the Bible and their mutual joy was immense when the society told him his country's Bible was already on the printing press.

We redundant ones were repatriated in boxcars like DPs; we, however, had linoleum on the floor and could sit on that. As we were a mixed bunch of Europeans, the GI in charge did not bother with courtesies. To be fair, I doubt whether he would have shown much concern over American soldiers or officers. GIs are lax and proud of it. We were disgorged into a corridor train, either six or eight to each section. We sat there glumly, missing friends and the sense of purpose which had kept us alert. Our tickets were checked by another disgruntled GI. Perhaps the spell of duty had messed up his 'dates'. We passed into the British zone and were rechecked. The door slid open and a smart, alert Brit said, 'Good morning, may I see your tickets please? Thank you, sir. Thank you, madam.' The door slid quietly to. I was trying to control my own feelings when I saw tears on a Polish face, and some glistening in British eyes while others bit their lips. We had been refusing to admit our feelings of humiliation at being discarded rubbish after the two years of hard slog. There was also relief to be out of a laissez-faire atmosphere as we changed zones. Our countries had a different sense of values – then.

We boarded the train for Dieppe. The shorter journey was enlivened by armed police hunting a smuggler up and down the train corridor; he was thought to be carrying gold dust. When we got to the British customs, they picked on me! I had to open my fat bedroll on the platform. It had blankets, uniforms and my DP souvenirs – mostly Ukrainian embroideries. A disappointed customs officer brightened up when he saw the wooden desk set, especially the rocking wooden block to hold blotting paper, and also a pair of heavy wooden platform shoes decorated with Estonian paint and pokerwork. We all sat on our luggage in a circle around him as he tried to penetrate the depths of the solid wood. Our fatigue reduced us to helpless laughter as he got progressively frustrated with the unyielding pine. Each time he looked at me he got fresh impetus. He gave up and we went to the UNRRA hostel accommodation. I spent a good day shopping and a glorious hour trying on every sort of hat, encouraged by the empathetic assistants of Dickens and Jones. I met the Australian, to whom I had lent a canvas bucket on her way to Poland, we exchanged addresses and she has spent two holidays with me in Wales. Some of the Reading friends turned up and we exchanged news over a Chinese meal. An abortive attempt was made to form an UNRRA club before we dispersed.

At home, I found my mother exhausted by war and post-war privation. She needed support as reliable 'help' was no longer available. I took on the house and garden, learning the hard way. Meanwhile I tried to keep in touch with the few DPs who could write in English or French but all my previous communication had been in 'DP Deutsch', often supplemented by mime and body language. Dimitri Poliwianyi, the camp leader of Regeirungsgebaude, the Russian camp, came to Wales. He stayed a few days with us but his hopes of finding a post as an engineer in a fur factory could not be realised. He got work in a creamery, instead. He tried to tell my parents how much the DPs thought of me. In seconds, my embarrassment and two Russian words stopped the flow... and the astonishment.

I did not know how to help other DPs. I had been able in Landshut to encourage the camp. It was only possible because I was supported by the UNRRA framework. Inside that framework, the DP leaders, chosen by their people or appointed by us, developed the work with their abilities. Alone, in Britain, I was useless, submerged in housework and my mother's terminal illness. I had no drive or know-how to organise work, accommodation and permits for DPs. Iadwiga, a brilliant Polish captain, who had worked in the Warsaw underground, literally in the sewers, preferred France but found it unfriendly with no licence to work. She obtained a visa and reached the US. Here she found scientific work and a happy marriage. Her wonderful daughter visited me thirty years later. I spent a delightful day in Greece with her, her air-pilot husband and small Christoff. Tragically, she developed cancer and Iadwiga, already in poor health, went to Greece. My letters have been unanswered.

A group of twenty-six went to Venezuela. I had a close working friendship with their leader but our embryonic knowledge of each other's written language made follow-up impossible, although I had a smattering of news through Poliwianyi in Lancashire. Dr Vaisnora wrote to me but by this time my mother was desperately ill and I lost both his letter and one from Robbie Berkes, our Hungarian chauffeur who had returned to Budapest where I hope he had found his Liberal roots in journalism. I am very sorry that all these people have gone out of my life but I was soon to be engulfed in an even harder post, which left no surplus energy for private living. I still draw great comfort from the camaraderie and trust I had experienced from so many single-hearted DPs and from UNRRA, working for the common good.

Certainly over the two years I had achieved much more than I expected of myself. From the instant I was offered work in Germany, I was sure that in taking the opportunity, I had no need to measure myself against the task before me. I had no fear when danger emerged; all I had to do was to forget about myself and to be certain that the Almighty, who had backed up my longing to be part of post-war rescue, would not let me down. I prayed as problems loomed, and the all-covering précis of need in the Lord's Prayer was sufficient for sound sleep, sense and sure-footed action. Somehow, I made the right decisions and said the right things. I knew that my strength was more than my own effort could produce. As David from Dachau had said – 'Aide-toi, et Dieu t'aidera.'

I visited my university tutor in Liverpool. She said, 'You have changed! What has happened to you?' I thought she would expect a love affair but my happiness lay elsewhere.

'I have become a Christian,' I replied. She was surprised and asked if I knew she was a Communist. I smiled at the irrelevance.

'Well, what has Christianity done for you?' she asked.

I replied, 'I shall never be alone again.'

She said slowly and quietly, 'You are very fortunate; few can say that.'

Determination had brought me the 'one pearl of great price'.